Perspectives in English Urban History

Each volume in this series is designed to make available to students important new work on key historical problems and periods that they encounter in their courses. Every volume is devoted to a central topic or theme, and the most important aspects of this are dealt with by specially commissioned essays from specialists in the relevant field. The editorial Introduction reviews the problem or period as a whole, and each essay provides an assessment of the particular aspect, pointing out the areas of development and controversy and indicating where conclusions can be drawn or where further work is necessary. An annotated bibliography serves as an up-to-date guide to further reading.

PROBLEMS IN FOCUS SERIES

Perspectives in English Urban History

EDITED BY

ALAN EVERITT

Macmillan

First published 1973 by
THE MACMILLAN PRESS LTD
London and Basingstoke
Associated companies in New York Dublin
Melbourne Johannesburg and Madras

SBN 333 08556 6

Printed in Great Britain by
HAZELL WATSON & VINEY LTD
Aylesbury, Bucks

Contents

List of Illustrations

Note on Transcription

THE spelling, punctuation and capitalisation of quotations from contemporary sources have in general been modernised, except where authors have considered it necessary to retain the original orthography.

Acknowledgements

THE editor thanks Her Majesty's Stationery Office for permission to reproduce details from the Ordnance Surveys of Croydon of 1954 and 1961; and the Principal and Fellows of Brasenose College, Oxford, for permission to reproduce the 1898 plan of Taylor's shop in the High Street, Burford, in the college library.

A. E.

Introduction

ALAN EVERITT

I

THE study of urban history has made great strides in these islands over the past fifteen or twenty years. There are those who tell us that the future of history, as a field of study, is doomed; that in our educational system it is bound to go the way of classics; that in many schools it has already virtually disappeared from the curriculum; and that in others it survives only by masquerading under another name. Fortunately this is not the place to dispute these disagreeable forebodings; neither is the present writer competent to do so, so far as the situation in schools is concerned. It must be admitted that it will be a sad day for the human race when it ceases to be interested in the past, for then it will cease to be interested in civilisation.

But what are the facts? In the fields of historical interest with which the editor of this volume is acquainted we certainly do not seem to be witnessing a time of stagnation but one of unprecedented expansion. Certainly there is no sign of a decline of interest in history in the universities, amongst either dons, graduates, or undergraduates, though there are signs (on the whole welcome ones, too) of a shift of interest from purely political and diplomatic history to the more social, economic and local aspects of the subject. Among intelligent amateurs, moreover, it is hard to detect any decline of interest, if we may judge from the demand for extra-mural classes in subjects like English local history, and the foundation of new history societies over the past generation. The establishment of county record offices in nearly every shire of England and many in Wales since the war is yet another proof of a major expansion in matters historical. The wealth of local manuscript material these repositories have brought together, and the growing number of students utilising them, are among the more important factors in the silent revolution that has taken place – and still is taking place – in the study of history in these islands over the last generation.

In few fields has this revolution in historical studies been more

evident than in that of urban history. As everyone interested in the
subject knows, the *Urban History Newsletter*, founded by Professor
H. J. Dyos at Leicester University in 1963 and produced by him twice
a year since then, has become the guide to all that is happening in this
field. In December 1965 the *Newsletter* included a list of 'British
University Theses on the Urban History of Great Britain since 1911'.
Analysis of this list is revealing. Of the total of about 220 theses, only
64 were produced before 1950, or an average of no more than one or
two a year. During the 1950s 85 were produced, or an average of eight
or nine a year. Between 1960 and 1964 a further 70 were produced,
or an average of fourteen a year. Since then the study of urban history
has continued to expand. The *Newsletter* also provides an annual register of research in progress. This is not confined to students reading for
higher degrees, and its coverage has no doubt become more complete
since the first number appeared in 1963. Nevertheless, when all allowance
is made, the expansion is impressive. In the first issue the register comprised the names of 143 historians engaged on urban topics; in 1965 the
number rose to 220, in 1967 to 417, in 1969 to 510, and in 1970 to
657: a four- or fivefold increase in a period of only seven years. It is
easy to become bemused by statistics, and it would be foolish to pretend
that there are not also causes for misgiving in some of this expansion.
Urban history has tended to develop in the happy-go-lucky way characteristic of English movements, and not all this research has been either
well conceived or well ordered. But the facts themselves are indisputable
and in this case the prophets of doom have been proved wrong.

In all this growth what is the place and purpose of the present volume?
It is not to provide a theory of urban history or to chart a path for the
beginner among the confusing thickets of a prolific field of study.
Neither does it set out to provide a schema to which subsequent research
should conform, or define exactly what an urban community is. In most
cases we can recognise a town when we see one, just as we can recognise
a human being without resorting to elaborate definitions. There will
always be the exceptional places, of course: at what point in the nineteenth century, for instance, did the settlement of Coalville in Leicestershire cease to be a dismal mining village and become a still more dismal
mining town?[1] But for the most practical purposes, so far as this volume
is concerned, the question of definition need not trouble us.

The intention of the present volume is a more modest one. It may be
described as an attempt to take soundings in the subject, by selecting
a number of widely scattered towns as case studies, and in each case

examining in some detail one particular theme in one particular place over a limited period of time. The essays purposely vary widely in time-span, as well as in place and in topic. They range in date from the thirteenth century to the end of the nineteenth, in place from York at one end of the country to Margate at the other, and in topic from the development of a medieval town council to the clearance of a Victorian slum. In the present state of urban studies such variety is a sign of the times: it reflects the fact that here, as in other fields of historical endeavour, we are breaking out of the old limits and exploring in new directions. There is much to be said for having a clearly defined conception of one's subject before one commences research. But in a rapidly expanding field, where new tools and new methods are being tried out, there is also something to be said for *ad hoc* experiment. In most branches of urban history we need many more local monographs before we can arrive at theories of urban development – if in any case we really need to theorise.

The present volume utilises some of these new tools and indicates some of these new methods, but it does not set out to provide a survey of the field of urban history or of all its more important branches. Such a survey would extend far beyond the limits of a small book, and inevitably therefore many subjects have been omitted. Nothing is said here (except in the case of Margate) of the origins of urban communities, that intriguing subject, although one of the more important historical works to appear in recent years, Maurice Beresford's *New Towns of the Middle Ages* (1967), ought to be mentioned as a pioneer study in this field. Nor do the essays deal specifically with the demographic or industrial history of English towns, or (except incidentally) with their topographical development, all of which subjects would require a volume of this size to themselves.

The aim, then, has not been to provide a handbook on *How to Write Urban History*, or a systematic catalogue of historical problems requiring to be studied. It has rather been to bring together a varied collection of essays in which some of the more pressing of these problems are examined by a group of people interested in diverse aspects of the subject. Six of the essays deal with particular towns – Stamford, Burford, York, Margate, Coventry and Croydon – while two, though primarily based on the evidence of two particular boroughs (Northampton and Leicester) are of a more general nature. The authors hope that by this means some at least of their readers will not only be informed but also encouraged to pursue studies of a similar kind in other parts of the country. Many advances in historical science are made by the time-honoured expedient of picking other people's brains, in the sense of imitating their methods and following up their sources. Those of us who have written this volume have, so to speak, tried to take the shop-shutters down and invite a little daylight robbery of this kind. Each essay includes a brief discussion, either in the text or in a bibliographical note, of the principal types of source utilised for the study and more or less likely to be available for other towns. It also contains references (in bibliography or notes) to background literature and (where it exists) comparable work on other towns.

In recent years the growing enthusiasm for research in local history among educated amateurs, and the habit of putting students at universities and in colleges of education on project work, have stimulated a search for new topics of study. This expanding audience has been very much in mind in the compilation of the present volume. One sometimes hears the complaint that before long there will not be enough subjects to go round. To the student of urban history such a suggestion can only be greeted with incredulity. It is no exaggeration to say that there are thousands of topics in urban history that have scarcely begun to tackled as they ought to be. There are well over 700 towns in England and Wales (there were more than 800 in the seventeenth century) and it is safe to say that for few of them have the topics broached in the following essays, selective though these are, been adequately examined. It is hoped, therefore, that this book will suggest (by example rather than precept) a few of the topics that still await examination.

Obviously not all the subjects studied here will be suitable for research projects of a restricted nature, such as are required for undergraduate dissertations, for which time is necessarily limited. The essays have therefore also been designed to cater for different levels of research. Some, such as Mr Laithwaite's on 'The Buildings of Burford', suggest lines of enquiry making heavy demands on time and requiring considerable technical expertise. Others, such as the last in the volume on the country carriers of Victorian Leicestershire, may be studied at quite an elementary level of research from easily accessible trade directories. (It is also only fair to add, however, that a whole book could be written on the country carriers of a single county during the late eighteenth, nineteenth and early twentieth centuries.) Others again, such as Dr Stephens's on the provision of education in Victorian Coventry, might well be studied at varied levels of research in different towns. All the essays, however, have been devoted to subjects by no means peculiar to the towns in question but more or less echoed (though never precisely repeated) in other urban communities. Although, for example, there is only one English town called Margate, some of the themes illustrated in Mr Whyman's study of this Hanoverian watering-place will be repeated, in varying guises and degrees, in other seaside resorts such as Brighton, Ramsgate, Scarborough or Blackpool.

II

Are there any distinctive themes running through this volume, re-appearing in the work of various contributors? The essays were not selected to prove a particular thesis, but taken together they underline a number of recurrent themes in urban history. All of them, except Mr Whyman's study of Margate, relate to ancient market towns and illustrate old societies adapting themselves to the challenge – mercantile, social, educational, dynastic or the like – of a new generation. Margate was essentially a new town in the eighteenth century, though not so new as one might suppose: it had in fact already become a small market centre by the 1630s (by what authority seems dubious), and it was one of an interesting group of towns granted new market charters by the crown in the early years of George III's reign. The remaining towns were all markets of greater or less importance from the early medieval period if not before. In the cases of Leicester and York the marketing functions of the towns may be traced back as far as the Roman period.

No excuse need be offered in defence of this emphasis on market towns. The majority of English towns have originated in this way, great industrial cities like Birmingham, Manchester, Leeds and Wolverhampton as much as picturesque survivals like Burford and Barnard Castle. The marketing and shopping functions of these towns – comprising all that varied network of activities denoted by the word 'trade' – have in fact always been among their principal features. They remain so today in the case of towns like York, Leicester and Northampton, which are still the principal shopping centres for a wide stretch of country. Yet until comparatively recent years the retail functions of provincial towns have been largely neglected by economic historians. The principal reason is probably not far to seek. With some exceptions economic history has been written largely by men; and to the ordinary unimaginative male the importance of shopping is rarely apparent because he doesn't usually have to bother with it himself.

Dr Palliser's study of York shows one of the most important provincial towns of the sixteenth century becoming increasingly involved in this ever-expanding network of inland market trade. (The same theme is implicit in other essays relating to subsequent periods, such as the editor's contribution on urban inns.) The development of this network is one of the more striking features in the English economy of the Tudor era, gradually linking together as it did, by means of wayfaring traders, every part of the kingdom. Evidently the city of York was affected by it exceptionally early in the century and before many towns further south – a fact that makes one question whether the relative backwardness of the north at this time has not perhaps been exaggerated. By the seventeenth century, certainly, the network of wayfaring traders extended all over England and Wales. Their activities, moreover, were not limited to trade alone but also facilitated the broadcasting of news, fashions, ideas and beliefs, thus practically uniting the country in a way that perhaps few European countries at this period were united.

Two of the factors in the nation-wide character of this trading network were obviously the insular position of England and the remarkable revival in its national trade fairs. The importance of these wholesale trade fairs to English towns from the late sixteenth to the early nineteenth centuries would be difficult to exaggerate; but we know remarkably little about them. Every fact, therefore, such as those Dr Palliser has unearthed for York, is almost worth its weight in gold. For most provincial people these fairs were probably more important than that other great clearing-house of trade, luxury, news and ideas – the metropolitan market. Every year the principal fairs were personally visited by thousands of quite ordinary unrecorded individuals, many of them returning to the same fair season after season. When Northampton was destroyed by fire in September 1675, one of the reasons for the extent of the damage was the fact that its tradesmen had recently returned from Stourbridge fair near Cambridge, laden with a year's supply of goods for the following winter and summer. The wagons streaming homewards from Stourbridge fair to every town in the Midlands, as well as to London and many north-country places, were among the great autumnal sights of Stuart England. Stourbridge was the greatest fair for commodities such as hops, cloth and household goods. But Stourbridge itself was overshadowed where other goods were concerned: in the case of sheep, for example, by the enormous fair at Weyhill in Hampshire; in the case of horses by the fairs at Northampton, Leicester, Penkridge and other towns; and for cattle by the great Falkirk tryst in Scotland and by Tan Hill fair on its desolate windswept ridge in the Yorkshire Pennines.

The other growth-point in the network of urban trade, and the accompanying commerce in ideas, was the provincial inn. The fourth essay attempts to touch on this problem particularly with reference to Northampton, and it is a theme that reappears, explicitly or implicitly, in other essays such as Mr Laithwaite's in the case of Burford and Dr Palliser's on York. It is one that might profitably be explored in almost any 'thoroughfare town' between the late sixteenth and mid-nineteenth centuries. The development of the inn was one of the most obvious ways in which old towns adapted themselves, often with remarkable versatility, to the new requirements of the time. Inns multiplied and innkeepers prospered not only because of the increase of travel – by stage-coach, by private coach, by carrier's wagon, by post-horse, by pack-horse – but because they became the meeting-places of travelling merchants, of justices on county business, and of the leisured classes in search of amusement, culture, news, gossip and political discussion. In a sense the Hanoverian inn was a kind of epitome of Hanoverian society: a society in which the leisured classes particularly were more numerous, more cultivated and more wealthy than ever before.

The development of an essentially urban stratum among the leisured classes in the seventeenth and eighteenth centuries is another theme reflected in more than one of these essays. It was an element in urban society that was scarcely dreamed of (except in London) before the seventeenth century. We may conveniently call this element the 'urban gentry' or 'pseudo-gentry', or adopt the common contemporary phrase in towns like Northampton, the 'town gentry' in apposition to the 'county gentry' of the countryside around. What were the distinguishing marks of this new social order? It was characterised by living in the style of country gentry, possessing independent sources of income, but lacking the support of a landed estate to root it in the countryside, and hence as a rule preferring to take up residence in a provincial town on grounds of convenience, economy and sociability.

The emergence of this new social group is certainly one of the outstanding developments in urban society during this period. Visually its impact is still apparent in every English town with a legacy of late seventeenth- and eighteenth-century buildings. Next to the parish church, the town houses of the pseudo-gentry are in many places the principal architectural evidences of the past. They are perhaps especially numerous in some of the southern counties like Kent, which enjoyed exceptional prosperity at this time, but they are by no means a regional peculiarity. Many of the finest examples are to be found in counties like Shropshire, Yorkshire and Lincolnshire: for example at Louth, where a whole street of eighteenth- and early nineteenth-century town houses survives almost unaltered. They are particularly numerous in the county capitals and cathedral cities; but once again they are by no means confined to these major social centres. The little market town of West Malling in Kent, for example, with barely a thousand inhabitants at the first census in 1801, has a particularly good series of town houses, the earliest dating from the end of the seventeenth century and the last from the early decades of Queen Victoria's reign.

Who lived in these houses? What were their social origins? How did they come by their independence? How did they expend their energies? In spite of all that has been written about 'the rise of the gentry', there has been virtually no systematic study of this interesting and influential class. If it is thought of at all, it is usually described vaguely as 'the middle class': a phrase in which it is difficult nowadays to discern any useful meaning since it has come to be applied to every social stratum between viscounts and villeins. Yet there is a wealth of evidence about the urban gentry in monuments, wills and inventories alone. Though it is not always easy to connect a particular family with a particular house, or to elucidate its social and economic origins, it is an important task for the urban historian to attempt. To take a single place and to study all its 'town gentry', as a complete society, between the Restoration and the second Reform Bill would provide a very rewarding subject for research.

If the present writer's experience is any guide, some of these families will be found to be younger sons of country squires, with a modest competence of their own (often inherited from their mother), but insufficient to support a house and estate in the countryside. Several will certainly be moneyed spinsters of similar origin and status, often living together in twos and threes. Others will be found to have naval or military connections, particularly after periods of warfare like the Seven Years' War and the Napoleonic Wars. Others again, a growing number, may have colonial connections of some kind, having originated with some minor nabob, who himself was perhaps the junior scion of a local gentry family. Yet others (also a growing class) will probably be descendants of second-rank London merchants or of the wealthier trading dynasties of provincial cities, particularly of the ports.

Possibly the most numerous and certainly one of the most interesting sources of this 'town gentry' class will be the new professional men: especially the wealthier lawyers and doctors but also occasionally school-masters and clerics, and later in the eighteenth century bankers, apothe-caries, an architect or two, and an occasional surveyor or engineer. In the little Kentish market centre of Charing, for example, the two grand-est houses in the High Street were both built by doctors in the early decades of the eighteenth century. These medical men had married two sisters, daughters of a minor armigerous family of the neighbour-hood, through whom no doubt they inherited some of their prosperity and social standing. This kind of phenomenon is so usual that the historian is apt to ignore its significance. But to anyone coming to the eighteenth century from the sixteenth its novelty is at once apparent. The professional classes were in fact largely a creation of the seven-teenth to nineteenth centuries. Along with the other 'town gentry' they became inevitably the leaders and originators of most of the social and cultural life of the time in provincial towns. In most places this cultural life has been little explored, but much of it can be recovered from contemporary newspapers and memoirs, and it is often exceedingly interesting.

The rise of the 'town gentry' must necessarily, therefore, form an important theme in any urban history of the period. The spas and watering-places of Britain, such as Bath and Tunbridge Wells, or Mr Whyman's Hanoverian Margate, owed much of their meteoric rise to the expanding fortunes of the town gentry and professions. The com-parative smallness of this class in Coventry is one of the factors adduced by Dr Stephens for the feeble state of early Victorian education in that city. For a remarkable contemporary picture of the kind of cultural life that the 'town gentry' might support the reader cannot do better than turn to a book like William Gardiner's *Music and Friends* (3 vols, 1838–53). Gardiner was writing principally about the musical life of his native Leicester from the 1770s onwards, but his work sheds a good deal of incidental light on that of other places that he visited. By his day the 'town gentry' of Leicester had come to be considerably aug-mented in wealth and numbers by a newer social group, that of the well-off but sometimes highly cultured hosiery manufacturers, to whose ranks Gardiner's own family belonged. With the rise of the 'manufac-turer', however, we may be said to touch on a new era, an era in which the old order of the town gentry, though by no means disappearing was to some extent eclipsed in terms of opportunity, wealth and power.

Another theme that becomes apparent in several of these essays is the importance of dynastic connection in the development of urban communities. It is often said that English cities did not give rise to long-lasting dynasties like European city-states. Certainly the medieval and Tudor town houses of English merchants do not compare, as symbols of solid and enduring wealth, with the mercantile palaces of a city like Venice. The Englishman, we are told, has normally preferred to set up as a country gentleman when he has made his pile and, after two or three generations of city life, cut himself off from his vulgar origins. There is a lot of truth in these views, if only because the way to social influence in England has long been by way of a landed estate and your Englishman has always been something of a snob. Yet as generalisations such remarks require qualification and raise a number of questions to which some attention ought to be paid.

In the nature of things only a small percentage of provincial merchants could become country squires: what happened to the rest of them? In most cases we do not know, but it is safe to say that many of them must have founded urban families of some kind or other, unless they succumbed to the cruelly high urban death rate. For how many towns have we in fact a systematic reconstruction of these groups of local trading dynasties between, say, the sixteenth century and the nineteenth? The answer must be that for most towns we have not even a rudimentary study of this kind.[2] How far was the migration of merchants to the countryside a phenomenon characteristic of all kinds of urban community, and how far was it a peculiarity of particular types of town? Once again information is scanty; but there is reason to think that it was often more characteristic of seaports than of inland towns, at any rate before the Industrial Revolution. Unless an inland town was dominated by a great staple industry, such as the cutlery trade in Sheffield, its wealth was normally built up more slowly than in seaports and on a less flamboyant scale.

The fact that wealth was amassed more gradually in inland towns was sometimes remarked upon by contemporaries. When Northampton was destroyed by fire in 1675 an observer commented that the townsmen's loss was all the greater when it was considered how slowly a business could be built up in an inland town that was on no navigable river and possessed no staple industry. Where family fortunes were concerned, it was said, it might take twenty years to repair the ravages of a few hours. This is not to say there were no well-off people in towns like Northampton: there were certainly plenty of them, but their riches had not been amassed so much by brilliant speculation as by solid toil. In places of this kind there may have been a more powerful tendency, therefore, for wealth to remain in the town instead of migrating to the countryside, so that long-established urban dynasties developed quite naturally. Certainly at the centre of society in Hanoverian Northampton there was a whole nexus of solidly urban families, such as the Coxes, Lyons, Peaches, Mulliners, Jefferys, Jeyeses and Jeffcutts. As a rule families of this kind were closely related to one another, quite as closely as the country gentry of the surrounding shire. Their origins reached back at least to the sixteenth or seventeenth centuries, and they often continued in Northampton until the nineteenth century and in several cases until today. It must not be suggested that all families in the town conformed to this pattern, or that the group itself remained unchanging. But through every change a powerful nucleus of inter-related families remained at the centre of Northampton society, forming a distinct and virtually indestructible establishment to which individual newcomers were driven to assimilate themselves if they wished to succeed.

There was nothing peculiar to Northampton in this kind of social and economic structure. It may have been more pronounced there than in some places, but there are distinct signs of it in medieval Stamford as described by Dr Rogers in this volume, and it was also characteristic of a nineteenth-century town like Leicester, dominated as it was for so long by its caucus of predominantly Unitarian hosiery manufacturers. There is reason indeed to think that this kind of social set-up had long been a familiar phenomenon in provincial towns. It may be that in the case of mercantile families, as with the country gentry, historians have tended to be too much impressed by the startling and exceptional success stories – the tales of plutocratic merchants who *were* able to set themselves up as county gentry – and have paid too little attention to the much more numerous class of moderately successful tradesmen who remained to found dynasties of a distinctly urban character. It is for this reason that the present writer would stress the desirability of studying these urban dynasties in any particular town *as a group*, a complete society in themselves, instead of as isolated instances. Individually none of the Northampton families mentioned above would have been considered especially striking, even in their own day. Beyond the town they would hardly have been recognised except among their trading contacts in London and other towns. Their power – and in their own community it was a very real power – consisted in their position and cohesion *as a group*.

The development and influence of these dynastic connections reflect the pronounced introversion of the urban organism at this period. Until the nineteenth century most provincial towns were still sufficiently small and in certain respects sufficiently isolated* for such family groups to form a distinct social focus in the community, a kind of magnetic centre to which new and alien elements necessarily gravitated, drawn into orbit around it or in some cases becoming wholly assimilated to it. This introversion of the urban community needs, of course, to be viewed in perspective. Trading contacts with the world beyond the borough were continually on the increase during the seventeenth and eighteenth centuries, and at all times town populations were to a large extent recruited from outside, particularly from the immediate hinterland within five or ten miles of the town.

Yet there are signs that, in one important respect, places like Northampton were becoming more self-centred during these centuries and that the influx of outsiders was declining. The Northampton Apprenticeship Registers show a continuous inflow of 'foreigners' to the town between Queen Elizabeth's reign and George III's, but the *percentage* of alien apprentices declines quite dramatically over this period. The decline was not due to a fall in the annual intake of apprentices, which in fact more than trebled in numbers between 1560 and 1760 at a time when the population no more than doubled. It was due rather to a much larger intake of apprentices from the families of the townsmen themselves. In the late sixteenth century nearly 70 per cent of all Northampton apprentices came from outside the town, including more than 10 per cent from quite remote areas, chiefly in the northern shires. Under the early Stuarts the alien proportion dropped to 63 per cent; during the later seventeenth and early eighteenth centuries to 54 per cent; and under George II and George III to a mere 34 per cent. By the mid-eighteenth century nine-tenths of all Northampton apprentices came from the town itself or from the adjacent countryside, while long-distance migration, from the northern counties, had almost completely died out. The increase of purely local recruitment, moreover, was an absolute as well as a relative one. In Queen Elizabeth's reign only 39 boys apprenticed in each decade were the sons of townsmen;

---

* Mr Whyman points out (pp. 152–3 below) that as late as 1804 the journey to Margate from London took thirteen hours by road, and by the Margate hoys eight or ten hours if you were lucky, or two or three days if the winds or tides were unfavourable. For the journey to Broadstairs, about 80 miles from London, you normally had to spend a night in Margate on the way.

by the middle of the eighteenth century this number had risen to nearly 170. In other words the number of local boys apprenticed in the town annually had more than quadrupled during a period when the population had only doubled itself. Like other towns of its kind, Northampton came to be noted as a craft-training centre and it possessed an ever-expanding pool of specialist skills. It was from this kind of pool that the inventive originality of the Industrial Revolution often took its rise.

These developments powerfully reinforced the tendency of the older Northampton families to remain in the town and to extend their local dynastic connections, while their businesses were continued by their sons and grandsons. It is possible that Northampton was untypical in these respects, but there seems no real reason to think so. The probability is that it was rather more subject to alien immigration than some towns because of its relatively liberal apprenticeship regulations and its central position at the junction of important coaching and trading routes from the south, the north and the north-west. If it was more or less typical, there were clearly deep-seated demographic reasons for the growth of dynastic connections in provincial towns between the late sixteenth and early nineteenth centuries.

If in these respects the urban organism was becoming in a sense more self-centred, it was also becoming subject to intense social, economic and topographical pressures from within. Some of these new pressures in old towns of the nineteenth century are discussed by Dr Stephens and Dr Cox in their essays on Coventry and Croydon. The problems they raise were not local peculiarities of these two towns, however. Though in both places they seem to have been of unusual intensity, in themselves they were of widespread occurrence and call for urgent examination in other towns. The total inadequacy of the traditional means of education in Coventry to meet the elementary needs of a vastly increased population may come as a shock to some readers, but it was in fact far from unusual. In a town of nearly 30,000 people the old Free Grammar School educated in 1827 no more than ten pupils, and in 1833 precisely one. This situation was repeated not far away at Leicester where, in a town of 40,000 people, the number of boys in the Grammar School about this time actually sank to *nil*. More alarming than scandals of this kind was simply the overwhelming problem of how the new masses should receive any education. However efficient the grammar schools might have been made, they could not educate the swarming thousands of urban children. One might as well have tried to plough a field with a coal-scoop. The truth was that the people of towns like Coventry were faced with a situation to which their past experience offered no kind of parallel.

The problem of an old market town like Croydon, the decay of its ancient town centre into slums of the most squalid description, also raises more general issues. The problem was not simply due to a legacy of old buildings and a rapidly rising population. These obviously played their part, but in most places there was after all a lot more land available for building than there is today. In many towns the problem was rather due to a combination of population growth with other factors of a different kind. One of these other factors was the development of a rapidly growing class of migrant labourers (and other workers) in search of temporary lodging-house accommodation. Dr Cox has indicated the origins and consequences of this development in the case of Croydon with an unusual wealth of detail. Local scrutiny would reveal a similar warren of noisome lodging-houses in the old market quarter of many towns at this period. They certainly existed, for example, in the Nottinghamshire town of Newark.[3]

Another factor in this kind of urban decay was connected with industrial development. Nowadays, when we speak of the Industrial Revolution, we think instinctively of northern cities like Leeds and Manchester and of those in the Midlands like Birmingham and Wolverhampton. But in fact until long after the mid-nineteenth century there was a good deal of industrial development in the smaller market towns of England. In most cases this has now died out and has been forgotten. As a rule it was on a 'workshop' scale, moreover, so that its evidences are less obvious than among the factory chimneys of Lancashire and the Black Country. Yet in the aggregate it was probably of far greater importance than is generally realised. There is a lot of evidence for it waiting to be pieced together in contemporary directories, in the census returns, and on the ground.

One of the characteristic places for much of this kind of industry was in the long narrow yards and courts running back from the market places and high streets of small provincial towns. These courts were not peculiar to any one region, but were to be found in all parts of the country. Mr Laithwaite provides evidence for them in the case of Burford in Oxfordshire, and they also existed in towns as unlike and as far apart as Faversham in Kent, Market Harborough in Leicestershire, Yarm in Yorkshire, Kendal in Westmorland, Louth in Lincolnshire and Newark in Nottinghamshire. In many cases they were of medieval origin, in the sense that they developed along the lines of ancient burgage plots and were often accessible only by a small alley or opening, a few feet wide and a single storey high, between two burgage tenements. So far as the present writer's observation goes, these courts were often not filled up with cottages, workshops, warehouses and in some cases small factories much before the mid-eighteenth century. There are cases, however, where they were built upon at an earlier period than this, and there are also others where their use for industrial purposes did not take place until the nineteenth century.

The mingling of cheaply constructed tenements with industrial premises is highly characteristic of these market courts. It was the principal reason why in the early censuses they figured among the most densely populated areas and why so many of them became slums. During the past ten years many of these courts have in fact been destroyed in the name of slum clearance. There is urgent need that those that remain should be recorded and photographed before they too have disappeared. They provide, after all, visual evidence of one of the most interesting periods in the history of our market towns.

These were a few of the pressure points within the older urban communities of the nineteenth century. If the problems were acute in market towns as modest in scale as Faversham and Louth, neither of which had as many as 7,000 inhabitants in 1831, they were of course far more so in industrial towns like Coventry and Wolverhampton with four or five times their population, not to mention the great industrial cities like Manchester and Birmingham. Yet if there was much in the Victorian city that was new, harsh, horrible and fantastic, there was also something that was still medieval, almost immutable; and this was the continuing function of hundreds of ancient towns and cities as markets and shopping centres. Every Wednesday and Saturday the people of Leicester and Leicestershire swarmed into the county town in their thousands, along the whole network of main roads converging on the market place, just as their ancestors had been doing, on the same days of the week, for more than seven hundred years. The old and the new were strangely mingled together in the Victorian town, even in an industrial city like Leicester. It is this country trading, essential and indestructible, that forms the theme of the last essay in this volume.

1. Late Medieval Stamford: A Study of the Town Council 1465-1492[1]

ALAN ROGERS

I. INTRODUCTION

THE study of town government is an immensely significant one especially for the Middle Ages. Throughout the centuries which succeeded the Danish invasions, townsmen sought anxiously for the powers to govern themselves. One by one they acquired by charter from king or private lord the various privileges they believed to be essential to their well-being. The highest of these, granted to very few towns before the fifteenth century, was the right of incorporation, whereby the burgesses of a town formed themselves into an undying institution, able to own property, to sue and to be sued. Here was finally achieved the complete exclusion (at least in theory) of all other authorities, especially that of the royal sheriff. This growth of self-government, however, must not be seen as an 'opting out' of the government of the realm. Rather it was an 'opting in', for the king and his administration now dealt directly with the town itself instead of going through some external official. The central government retained all its powers; it was the local community which increased its powers and with them its duties.

In these circumstances it is clearly of importance to see who actually was in charge of towns at the time of their incorporation. Did the charters of incorporation really result in full self-government by the communities which acquired them? And if so, who were the first councillors? What sort of people governed the town? For if the charter of incorporation was really effective, then the burgesses were now important cogs in an administrative machine. The aim of this essay is to look for the answers to these questions in respect of one town, the borough of Stamford at the end of the fifteenth century.

Stamford is today well known as one of the most pleasing historic towns of England. Situated on what was formerly the main route from London to the north of England, it has attracted a great deal of favourable comment. Its small size and relatively unchanged appearance have made it a charming place to explore, and its wider setting, at a point where the wide-open skies of the fenlands meet the undulating uplands of England's main limestone belt, has added to its attractions.

But if the town of Stamford is now small, overshadowed by its neighbour Leicester and the more modern giants of iron and steel at Peterborough and Corby, it is a relic of a great past. For during the Middle Ages, Stamford was one of the most important towns in England, in the front rank of national urban centres. Its significance then was not based, as later, on its strategic position on the Great North Road. Rather it was a military and ecclesiastical centre, with a royal castle and a multitude of religious houses of all varieties. But most important, it was a great trading and perhaps industrial centre: its international fair had a reputation abroad that spread as far as Italy and Spain. The town was a national centre; and although the castle has now vanished, the evidence of this past is still to be seen in its town walls, its churches and monastic remains built in local stone, in the merchant almshouse Browne's Hospital, and in the wide market areas scattered throughout the borough.

It is therefore of some significance to discover how this important medieval town was governed. For a town is not just a place, a collection of buildings. Rather it is a group of people, a community, and the historical process must be to use all forms of evidence to get behind the visual appearance of any locality to the people who lived there. And few things reveal a community so profoundly as a study of those who are called, or who take it upon themselves, to manage the affairs of the people as a whole.

For all its importance, Stamford was not a royal borough. It was one of that class of towns known as 'seigneurial'; for most of the Middle Ages it belonged to some great lay magnate until in 1461 its 'seigneur', the duke of York, became king in the person of Edward IV. Even after that date it was treated seigneurially. There were thus in the town stronger outside interests than in those truly national boroughs like Lincoln, Exeter or York. Such royal centres have been explored in some depth in recent studies; seigneurial towns are still largely unknown.

II. THE BOROUGH COUNCIL: THE FIRST AND SECOND TWELVES

Stamford achieved its 'great charter' from Edward IV in 1462, less than a year after his accession to the throne. It was the climax to a long series of grants, stretching back to at least the end of the thirteenth century and probably much earlier. By its terms, the governance of this newly incorporated royal borough was placed in the hands of a council comprising an alderman (as the chief officer was to be known), chosen annually, and twelve comburgesses who were to be elected for life by the whole community. As a contemporary English summary of the charter put it: 'Item, that the said commonalty by these presents have power at a day of election to choose an alderman so he be one of the first xij, and the first xij to continue during their natural lives, unless reasonable excuse be laid to the contrary.'

This being so, it is a matter of some surprise to find when the records of the borough begin in 1465 that there were in fact two councils in Stamford, a First Twelve of comburgesses under the alderman, and a Second Twelve. The two were clearly distinguished. The First Twelve had a close relationship with the alderman – indeed the Hall Book suggests that they were chosen 'for' the alderman – while the Second Twelve were chosen by 'the commons'; 'all the fore-named, both the First Twelve for the alderman and the Second Twelve for the community, were sworn'. It is probable that this is a continuation of what had been the practice before 1462, but the silence of the charter on the Second Twelve is puzzling.

The government of Stamford thus lay, at least nominally, in the hands of twenty-five men who, once elected, held their office for life or until they retired. There was in fact no re-election, just the filling of vacancies. During the years 1465–92[2] one or two possible cases occur of a councillor being reappointed to the First Twelve after resigning, and one similarly on the Second Twelve,[3] but only one of these is certain. Resignation is on the whole uncommon and seems to have been recorded in the Hall Books. No one in this period was removed from office, although the charter made provision for this to occur if necessary.

As a result some of the councillors had long careers in the local government of Stamford. Two persons, John Gregory and Robert Hans (or Haus), served on the First Twelve throughout the whole of the period, while John Wykes served on the Second Twelve from 1466 to 1490. Some, it is true, served for only four or five years, perhaps a sign that they were elected late in life or that the high mortality rate of the late Middle Ages made for short working lives; but a career of over twenty years as councillor is known for at least half the members of the First Twelve during this period, and one member had a combined service on the council of more than thirty-two years.

In all, twenty-eight persons served on the First Twelve during the years 1465–92, an average of one appointment each year. The average for the Second Twelve was nearly double this, forty-eight persons in all. Part of the reason for this is that a number of persons served first on the Second Twelve and then passed to the First Twelve; but this does not fully account for the difference. For one thing, only eighteen of the forty-eight members of the Second Twelve were promoted in this way; and second, such a promotion does not account for the shorter period of service on the Second Twelve of those not promoted. No councillor on the Second Twelve lasted throughout the whole period 1465–92; of the forty-eight appointed to the Second Twelve during these years, only eight served twenty years or more in office. This shorter average of service is difficult to explain. It may be that the prestige of the Second Twelve was sufficiently lower than that of the First Twelve to encourage more members to retire from the office, but the figures on this are not conclusive.[4]

It is quite clear that the First Twelve enjoyed a greater prestige than the Second Twelve; for instance, a double fine was to be paid for an assault against a member of the First Twelve. Indeed the First Twelve at Stamford at this time was undergoing an interesting transitional stage similar to that which had taken place in many other English boroughs then or earlier; it was well on the way to becoming a closed 'livery'. Elsewhere it was growing more and more common for those who had served in the office of mayor or alderman to form an élite group in the town's government, with privileges of wearing their gown or 'livery' and precedence over those councillors who had not served in that capacity. In Stamford a trend towards this position can be seen. In 1481 one of the borough's constitutions equated the First Twelve with those who had been alderman of the borough, when it ordered that on the one hand 'each person who had been in the office of alderman shall have two men arrayed' and on the other hand 'each of the Second Twelve shall find one man similarly arrayed' to attend on the alderman at the great Lenten fair feast. But at the beginning of the period such an identification of the First Twelve and past-aldermen was by no means clear; of the thirteen comburgesses in 1465, only six had already been alderman of Stamford, and three of the others died having never held the office. Gradually, however, the feeling grew, as more and more of the First Twelve held the office and thus wore the livery of past-alderman, that the First Twelve was composed of this group of persons. Thus of the fourteen promotions to the First Twelve, twelve held the office of alderman, most of them during their first three years as members of the upper council. Indeed at least two of them were elected straight from the Second Twelve to the office of alderman before taking their seats on the First Twelve, a procedure which the 1462 charter might seem to have ruled out. Of the members of the First Twelve in 1492, only four had not already been alderman, a much lower figure than in 1465, and only one person of the upper council never served in that office at all.

The differences between the First Twelve and the Second Twelve, however, were largely of status rather than of function. The picture of Stamford borough council in the last years of the fifteenth century would seem to be one of a body of twenty-five councillors, with one of them an annually elected alderman, and the rest distributed between a body almost entirely composed of past aldermen, and a council which was considered in general a necessary preliminary for membership of the First Twelve. The principles of promotion are obscure, for although there are clear signs of a hierarchy in each of the Twelves, it was not always the top members of the Second Twelve who got promoted. Indeed the leader of the Second Twelve (a quite clear post held by four persons during the years 1465–92) was only once promoted to the First Twelve; normally he stayed in office on the Second Twelve until he died or retired.[5]

It would thus seem that there was at Stamford one large body of twenty-five councillors, rather than the thirteen comburgesses which Edward's charter prescribed. Only in one important respect was there any significant difference between the First Twelve and the Second Twelve. The charter provided that the thirteen comburgesses, together with one 'learned in the law', were to be the justices of the peace for the borough under the chairmanship of the alderman. But apart from this, the council of Stamford seems to have been treated as a whole. The sessions apart, there are no signs of the First Twelve transacting business without the Second Twelve. In November 1466, for example, the alderman and the twenty-four passed regulations concerning public health in the town. That this should be the case despite the charter of 1462 is puzzling. A later charter in 1481 made no change in the system, and confirmations in 1483 and 1504 merely repeated the provisions of the 1462 charter. It would seem that the 'great charter' of incorporation made little difference to the traditional method of governing Stamford which had grown up in the fourteenth and early fifteenth centuries.[6]

III. THE REALITY OF POWER

How far did this council of two parts, the First and Second Twelves, in fact enjoy power? Was the government of the town in reality in their hands? Pressure and rival authority might be exercised by a number of interests. Other persons had rights of jurisdiction over parts of the town or over a number of persons within the borough boundaries, thus withdrawing those areas or inhabitants from the control of the council. At the same time the authority of the council might well be challenged by other groups, either burgesses of the town or sectional interests.

(a) The Yorkist lordship

The most important interest was of course the 'lord' of the town. Stamford was still a seigneurial town after 1461, although its lord had become king. Earlier in his reign the king settled the borough on his mother, Cecily duchess of York, and she held the manor and lordship of Stamford; and it was perhaps as much in his capacity as the town's seigneur as king of the realm that Edward IV granted the charter of incorporation to Stamford in 1462. Up to that time the town was administered on behalf of its lords by bailiffs who were subject to the steward who supervised the duke of York's estates. Not a great deal is known of this administration, but it is quite clear that the duke of York's main interest in Stamford was financial. To him and his servants the value of the town was its yield in terms of revenues. Some measure of self-government ment was not of course incompatible with such an aim. In 1450–2, for instance, the town was 'farmed' to the alderman of the borough, who paid what seems to have been a fixed rent for the borough. Thus prior to the 1462 charter some of the powers of the duke's officers seem to have passed into the hands of the alderman, and the bailiffs were already in some respects his servants to exact the customary dues. Nevertheless the steward apparently continued to hold his court in the town and before the end of Henry VI's reign a new rental was drawn up and the estate had reverted to a policy of direct administration; a later account shows detailed exactions by the lord's bailiffs under the supervision of Humphrey Bourghchier, Lord Cromwell, the steward of Stamford.[7]

The charter of 1462 created a situation even more advantageous to the inhabitants than that enjoyed in 1450–2. A fixed farm for the town was established, and the bailiffs passed entirely into the hands of the council. The remaining rights of the dukes of York were granted by the king to Cecily his mother, and in 1466 she was represented in the town by her steward, the ambitious lawyer William Hussey. Under Cecily the borough council seems to have suffered little interference, although her officials still maintained a separate bailiff resident in the town. The interests of the duchess in Stamford were once again primarily financial and the disputes which arose between her officers and the community were over matters like the control of the pinfold rather than more important matters of urban control.

This relationship did not last, however. From early in the reign of Henry VII there are signs of increasing interference in the affairs of the borough. Perhaps this is to be associated with the settlement in 1492 of the town, in reversion after the death of Cecily, on Elizabeth, Henry VII's queen. More likely it is part of the same royal policy which led eventually to the grant of the stewardship of the town jointly to Sir Reginald Bray and John Hussey, esquire, in 1496. In fact, however, it antedates these grants by some years. In 1488 the king's Council was writing to the borough and in November Christopher Browne, the most prominent of the town's merchants, was summoned to London to attend a meeting of the Council. In October 1489 there are signs of an audit of the borough accounts by the royal Exchequer. But much more important was the pressure brought to bear on the office of alderman. Prior to 1495 the alderman took his oath of office in the common hall in the presence of the comburgesses and the commons, usually immediately after his election on the feast of St Jerome (30 September); but in that year the Hall Book records that the alderman, together with the congregation, adjourned to the castle and took his oath 'according to ancient custom' before John Walcote, lawyer, who was acting as deputy for the steward. Thereafter this became common practice, and on occasion the oath before the steward or his deputy was delayed for some weeks. In 1500 the 'presentation of the alderman' was as late as 1 November; the date seems to have depended upon the holding of the steward's court, the view of frank-pledge, in the town. Until the alderman had taken his oath, the previous alderman continued to preside at the sessions.

The change may not have been sudden; there are perhaps signs of it as early as 1484 when the oath was administered in the hall, not on the day of the election (30 September) but somewhat later – on this occasion 30 November. The same happened in 1485 and 1487. In 1490 the previous alderman, Thomas Philippe, held sessions of the peace on 5 October, after the election of his successor William Gaywode; while in 1491 it would seem that there was a double election, one on 30 September as usual and the second on 3 November, although the records do not indicate whether this second election was held in the castle or elsewhere. But these incidents may have been caused by the absence of the mayor-elect from the meeting at which he was chosen, or by some process of pre-election which clearly occurred at least once, in 1475.[8]

Nevertheless there is clear evidence that at the end of the period 1465–92 increasing pressure was being put on the council and officers of the borough by the servants of the town's seigneur. On at least two occasions the borough's recorder was the deputy steward, and the connections became strongest under Henry Lacy, the deputy steward who served on the First Twelve and even became alderman in the reign of Henry VIII. This was not so much a new demand as a revival of earlier custom, for one of the town's earliest charters, granted in the early fourteenth century by William Earl Warenne, had insisted that the alderman be presented to the earl's steward for approval after his election.

Unfortunately the court rolls do not survive to indicate how far the affairs of the borough were managed in the steward's court; but it is most probable that the officials were still more interested in the financial returns from the town than in detailed administration. Certainly the borough council itself regulated the crafts, the trading habits of the burgesses, the town amenities, the moral welfare of all the inhabitants and even the common field agriculture of the town's lands. In 1466, for example, it ordered a fallow field to be left each year in three-year rotation and regulated the dates of admission of sheep to the open fields and their withdrawal. The council administered the market in the town on behalf of the duchess of York, even before they secured their own (Monday) market in 1481. The various customary assizes, such as bread and ale, were in the hands of the hall, and they were also responsible for the taxation of the borough for the king's subsidy or for the maintenance of the town's walls and bridges. There is little reason to doubt that when the alderman of Stamford made a declaration 'on the king's behalf and on my lady's' concerning searching the market, he was acting on the authority of his own council rather than on instructions received from other officers. Perhaps later, as there was greater control over the office of the alderman, so there was greater interest on the part of the lord's officers in the affairs of the town. Certainly 'constitutions' passed by the hall declined in number, while agricultural regulations ceased; and the few orders which were passed were entirely concerned with urban security and amenities. The contrast between the earlier and later periods is most marked.

(b) Other lordships

Apart from the duchess of York, there were of course a number of other interests within the town, each with their own privileges and exempt from other jurisdictions. Thorney Abbey, for instance, had extensive rights for its own tenants in the borough, but by the later fifteenth century, the abbey's property was occupied by one man, Thomas Kesteven, a wealthy draper.[9] Pembroke fee, an earlier lordship, was by now absorbed into the York holding, but two other holdings were of considerable influence.

The most important was the Peterborough Abbey fee, which with the lands of its daughter house, the nunnery of St Michael beside Stamford, covered a large area of the town. Almost the whole of the ward of the town which lay in Northamptonshire south of the river Welland was in the possession of the abbot, together with some property within the town walls on the north side of the river. The relation of Stamford Without (Stamford St Martin, or Stamford Baron as it was usually called) to Stamford Within is difficult. It was not just a problem of landlordship. The abbots claimed extensive privileges within their territories and appointed reeves (sometimes hereditary) to administer the area. For long the abbots strove to make their lands in Stamford, or at least the southern ward, distinct from the rest of the town and eventually they were successful. Although tenants of the nuns at least were admitted as freemen of the borough on occasion, the area of Stamford Without did not share in the privileges of trade nor in the responsibilities of taxation which the rest of the town enjoyed. Stamford St Martin was used as a distinguishing mark attached to personal names; and on at least one occasion (in 1490) restrictive by-laws were passed by the council: 'no inhabitant shall buy victuals or merchandise in St Martin's of any dweller in that parish, or leave their money there; and no inhabitant of the borough shall employ any dweller of St Martin's . . . without any such person be sworn before the alderman'. The case in 1496, when the justices of the peace in the town of Stamford entertained a plea from 'Robert Wright of St Martin's parish within the liberty of the borough', suggests that those dwellers in Stamford St Martin's who were not tenants of the abbot were regarded as being within the borough limits; and in 1469 the council appointed taxers for 'Stamford Baron beyond the bridge'. But somewhat later (1542) a decision was sought on this matter and it was shown by a search of earlier records that the inhabitants of Stamford St Martin's were taxed, not with the borough nor indeed in Northamptonshire, but in the rural wapentake of Ness in Kesteven. The authority of the borough council did not run throughout the whole of Stamford Baron.[10]

If the role of the nunnery of St Michael beside Stamford was solely that of an impecunious purchaser of local goods and a ready home for the daughters of prominent Stamford tradesmen, St Leonard's Priory, a cell of Durham Priory and centre of St Cuthbert's fee in Stamford, had little higher status. St Cuthbert's fee comprised the tenants of the prior of Durham and claimed its distinctive privileges. The fee was entirely a financial entity, and to sue defaulting tenants of the prior for debt, its court had little significance in terms of government. It was on occasion used by parties and it enforced the assizes of bread and ale on the prior's tenants. The chamberlains of Stamford paid a regular fine to the prior for diverting the channel of the Welland for Hudd's Mill which the council owned. But these were profitable rights rather than administrative conveniences, and the court was certainly no challenge to the authority of the borough council. In 1478 the prior claimed against the council for the goods of an outlaw 'under St Cuthbert's law', but the council refused to allow the claim. Several of the more prominent councillors were tenants of the fee, but those under the jurisdiction of the prior of Durham formed no separate entity within the town.[11]

(c) Borough officers

There are thus no signs of any real challenge to the power of the borough council from any of the alternative jurisdictions within the town. Nor was there any challenge from the borough officials. There were few permanent officials, perhaps only a town clerk,[12] always an obscure office, and the serjeants. The lawyer who was always to be associated with the thirteen borough J.P.s was at first apparently nominated, probably by the borough's seigneur rather than by the Chancery, for in 1472–3 it was Sir William Hussey, steward of the duchess of York's estate in the town and father of John Hussey, the later steward. But in 1481 the new charter granted to the borough the power of nominating the legal adviser, and from 1490, when the name of the 'one learned in the law' was regularly noted, the office was shared by John Walcote and William Elmes. Little enough is known of either man: Walcote was probably a local man and acted as deputy steward for John Hussey in 1496; William Elmes, esquire, was the grandson of William Browne of Stamford, although his father, a Calais stapler, came from Henley-on-Thames, where he retained many interests. He held many local government commissions, especially gaol delivery and sewers, was J.P. in no fewer than seven counties and served as M.P. for Stamford in 1495 and as supervisor of the subsidy in Rutland and Kesteven in 1504. When the office of recorder of Stamford was formally established in September 1502, it was granted for life to Elmes at an annual salary of £1 6s. 8d. secured from town lands in Stamford.[13]

The division of the office of recorder between two men, perhaps reflecting the two major interests in the borough, seems to be unusual, but whether it reduced any impetus towards the establishment of rival authorities within the town is not clear. All the other officers were only temporary and their duties were usually exercised in turn by members of the council. There were, it is true, still survivals of the ancient group of lawmen (mentioned as early as Domesday Book) in Stamford in the late fifteenth century, but it is clear that their functions were obsolete and their title was derived from their tenements rather than their duties. The king's coroner was regularly elected from the First Twelve, as the 1462 charter prescribed.[14] The two chamberlains were more frequently chosen from the Second Twelve than the First Twelve and at first held office for three years, but later for one year only. In 1485, for the first time, men who were not councillors were appointed as chamberlains, and in 1486 and 1489 one of the two chamberlains was not a councillor; but in every case except one (when one of the constables was also chamberlain) this appointment heralded election to the council. No one person held the office at all unduly often, but the responsibilities were shared widely among the members of the council. The constables, bailiffs and serjeants were minor officials, under the control of the council. Three constables were chosen annually, often from the Second Twelve and never from the First Twelve, but in many cases from persons not on the council at all; while the two serjeants (one for the alderman and the other for the liberty of the town) were reappointed annually and held their paid office for many years.

(d) The Community

If there was then little challenge to the real authority of the council from its officials, what about those who elected the councillors? In 1469 oaths in English were taken at the common hall: the First Twelve swore to maintain the alderman, the Second Twelve to attend the

common hall, while the 'commoners' swore not to take livery or maintenance from others without the consent of the alderman. Was the sole
interest of the 'commoners' to obey?

Clearly the 'commons', that is, the rest of the burgess population of
Stamford, played a larger part in the government of the borough than
just to listen and obey. In 1465 it was reported that 'the whole commons
of the said town and borough . . . have elected and chosen [the alder-
man] and the xj [sic] for the alderman's council and brethren', while
they chose 'for them[selves]' the Second Twelve and also the two
serjeants. In 1475 'the community' of the burgesses chose the alderman
from a short-list of three, selected by the First Twelve from among
themselves; and after every election 'all the commons gathered in the
common hall, by raising their hands, swore to maintain the alderman'.[15]
It was 'the commons' who appointed John Murdoke to the First Twelve
and gave him a promise not to burden him with the office of alderman
without his consent; and in 1488, when Henry Cok died in the office
of alderman, the rest of the comburgesses and the commons met in the
common hall, and the commons elected a new alderman. Further, they
attended meetings of the council, not just by their representatives, the
Second Twelve, but in a group; for the statement that 'it was ordained
and premised by the alderman, comburgesses and all the commons in
the hall . . .' amplify the more normal phrase, 'provided by the alderman
and the community'.[16]

Nevertheless there was apparently some attempt to formalise the
part played by the commoner burgesses in the government of the
borough. At the special audit of the accounts of borough officers in
1489 there were present the alderman, 'all the substance of the First
Twelve', the Second Twelve and '12 men chosen in the names of the
commons'. Little is heard of this third twelve; it made only occasional
appearances for special purposes. In 1496 a list of twelve names is given,
with the statement that 'all these were elected by common election that
they should be continually ready at the order of the alderman to enter
into such negotiations with the First Twelve and the Second Twelve
for the welfare of the borough of Stamford as often as shall seem necessary'; and again in 1503 there was a third twelve as a 'council for the
aforesaid Second Twelve chosen by the community of the town'. But
it is clear that this third twelve had no official standing. Thus it was
'ordained: that the First Twelve shall have commons for 60 sheep, the
Second Twelve for 40 sheep; that every "iconomy" or husbandman
with a large farm to have 40 sheep commons, and every commoner to

have 20 and no more'. The borough council of Stamford had no permanent place for a third twelve.

(e) The 'greater citizens'

If the council resisted pressure from below, what about from above? For it is clear that there was a level of merchant and gentleman in Stamford above that of councillor. These men had wider spheres of interest than just the borough. They were active in the government of the neighbouring shires, like John Chevercourt, the former clerk of the peace in Kesteven, or William Spencer, the notary who bought an estate at Casewick in Kesteven. For some, like David Phillip, fishmonger, John Parker, merchant, or John Tyssyngton, gentleman, it was their business concerns which gave them interests far afield, especially in London. Others were royal servants who came into the town to collect the fruits of their service; indeed a long range of royal officials looked to Stamford for rewards in property, annuities or offices from the steward of the town downwards.[17] It was this class of resident rather than the councillors who supplied the M.P.s for the borough; of the ten persons who represented Stamford in Parliament during this period, at least two were never councillors. And this number is misleading, for several of the others were harnessed temporarily to the council, occasionally straight on to the First Twelve without prior service on the Second Twelve. John Trunke may be one such person, a saddler whose Yorkist interests got him into trouble in 1452; in 1465, as yeoman of the new king's chamber, he received a grant in Stamford and served as bailiff for the royal estate in the town. He served on the First Twelve for a few years (1465–8), and was M.P. for the town in 1467 – a useful choice of a king's man of local origins. Richard Forster and John Murdoke are even clearer examples. Forster seems to have established a lien on one of Stamford's seats; he represented the town in seven consecutive Parliaments from 1467 to 1484. But his sole interest in the town was as a royal servant (yeoman of the buttery) who received a forfeit within Stamford in 1465, at first with Trunke, but from 1476 alone; and in 1482, for one year alone, he was appointed to the First Twelve. Murdoke is similar. In 1456 he received a royal grant in the borough, at first on his own but from 1464 with Sir William Hussey. He was on the First Twelve until 1468 and again in 1472 temporarily (at the same time as he was M.P.). Nine years later he was perhaps again pressed into service as coroner and member of the First Twelve, although he was excused from being alderman; and in 1483–4 he was again both M.P. and member of the First Twelve. Murdoke was at least a Stamford man, but Forster's links with the borough were minimal.

There were other examples of Stamford citizens who were only loosely tied to the council, wealthy and influential as they were. William Monke, gentleman, whose interests lay in London and Northamptonshire, and who seems to have served as recorder of King's Lynn, was M.P. in 1478. John Thurlby, who was alternatively described as husbandman and yeoman, had left the town for Empingham before he became M.P. in 1485. David Malpas, a Cheshire esquire and yeoman of the crown who made an advantageous marriage, had lands and other interests in Rutland, where he was J.P. and sheriff three times, and served on almost every county commission from 1475 to 1488. In 1483 he was admitted (as esquire) to the freedom of Stamford and was immediately appointed to the First Twelve; he became alderman in 1484 and M.P. in 1485. Nevertheless his main interests lay outside Stamford.

There was of course some overlap between this class and those Stamford councillors of somewhat narrower connections. From 1482 onwards a number of gentry like Malpas appear on the council. Christopher Browne, esquire, the nephew and heir of William Browne, may be included in this group. He, like Malpas, was appointed straight to the First Twelve, and it is clear that most of his interests lay outside the town. A Calais stapler,[18] and an Adventurer trading with Scandinavia, he was made free of the town in 1481; the next year he was alderman, and from then until his death in 1519 he was a member of the First Twelve. But he was purely a nominal member whose links with the government made him valuable; in 1488 he was to go to London to meet the king's Council and in 1500 he accompanied the king to Flanders for the meeting with Archduke Philip. When in 1502 he was made alderman of the town for the third time, it was pointed out that as he was a member of Lady Margaret Beaufort's council, he should be allowed to appoint a deputy; and the next year the council urged him to find a house in Stamford so that he could remain on the First Twelve. For by then he had settled down in the country nearby. From 1492 he served as J.P. and sheriff in Rutland, Northamptonshire and Lincolnshire, as well as acting as mayor of the staple at Boston, and his three marriages each brought him considerable property. John Freebarne from London, yeoman, was made free in 1486, served on the Second Twelve for only four months before he was promoted to the First

Twelve, and in 1488 was made alderman; after that he seems to have headed the First Twelve and in 1494 was auditor for the town. Richard Cavell (or Canell), a Calais stapler with interests in Louth, was admitted a freeman and appointed to the First Twelve in 1495, and in 1497, after he had served as M.P., he was made alderman. David Cecil, the Herefordshire esquire and lawyer, is a similar example. He was not a native, but he married the heiress of a wealthy Stamford glover to lay the foundations of his family's fortunes, and indeed he served on the Second Twelve for a short time before he was promoted to the First Twelve. But his royal service (he too was serving Lady Margaret Beaufort in Essendine and Collyweston and later was yeoman of the king's chamber) called him further afield, into Rutland, Lincolnshire and Northamptonshire, although he still remained active within the town of Stamford.

Christopher Browne and David Cecil were both servants of Lady Margaret Beaufort. It would seem that although Elizabeth of York, Henry VII's queen, was still alive when Cecily duchess of York died in 1495, the manor and town of Stamford came into the possession of Margaret Beaufort and remained her property until her death in 1509. But before 1495 there are few signs of her direct influence on the borough. The effects on the town of the presence of a nucleus of men in attendance upon Henry VII's mother cannot now be assessed. The fact that she lived close to Stamford (at Collyweston in Rutland) does not mean that during this period she exercised any direct influence upon the town, any more than the influence of other great neighbours like the Trollopes of Uffington can be traced. Clearly she and her like had to be considered in any decisions to be taken relating to the town's external affairs, but she does not seem to have had any residence or indeed much property in the town. Few magnates of the realm in fact owned estates in the town and there are no signs of any 'inns' of the greater lords. The most considerable absentee landlords in Stamford in the later Middle Ages were religious houses, especially monasteries ranging from Durham in the north to Huntingdon in the south.

There were therefore few burgesses of Stamford like Christopher Browne and Cecil who owed allegiance to some great lord outside the town. The borough councillors of Stamford came largely from that class of trader which was primarily interested in the town itself. Many of the wealthy merchants of Stamford, apart from the Calais staplers, had of course trading interests outside the town, in Boston, London or even further afield;[19] but there are few signs of their acting as country gentlemen with all the duties that that status implied. Perhaps John Wykes (Second Twelve) came from the gentry family of Little Burley, Northamptonshire, but there are no signs that he himself was active outside the borough. William Radclyffe, gentleman, another servant of Lady Margaret Beaufort, originating from Yorkshire, settled in the town and made it his main field of interest; he was admitted a freeman and promoted immediately to the Second Twelve, and two years later he joined the First Twelve, becoming alderman in 1495. William Browne himself invested a large part of his enormous wealth in estates in Lincolnshire, Northamptonshire, Rutland and elsewhere; but he never seems to have resided on these estates and he never sued out arms as a gentleman should. Stamford councillors (apart from those named) did not on the whole serve as taxers, J.P.s or sheriffs of the neighbouring counties. Thus, for example, in 1486, out of sixteen commissioners of sewers dealing with the Welland through Stamford, only one councillor (David Malpas) appeared. William Browne and Malpas served as taxers in Rutland in 1488, a county in which both served as J.P.s. But few others followed suit. The 1462 charter of course exempted the burgesses from county service against their will, but the burgesses of Stamford on the whole did not choose to buy lands in the counties and serve there. They were townsmen first and foremost. Clearly the fact that there were very few long-lived family dynasties helps to explain this. Few of the councillors left sons who were admitted to the burgess roll of Stamford free of the entry fine due from non-natives; fewer still left sons who followed them on the council. The creation of a landed estate by urban merchants was a process which normally took three generations.

There was, then, a class of Stamford burgess, wealthy and influential, who were not members of the town council. But such a class provided no threat to the council; rather its special privileges were there to be drawn upon by the council at need. These men were interested in the town, whenever such an interest did not conflict with their wider responsibilities. They were prepared to help, if time allowed. But it cannot be said that they wielded real power in the town. It was the councillors who were the town's rulers, its J.P.s and its taxers, its officials who raised and spent the town's money. In 1467 there survives one list of those who elected the town's Members of Parliament;[20] of the thirty three electors, twenty-three were on the council at the time, six more became councillors later, and only four are not known to have served the town in any capacity. When in 1478 the central government appointed a commission of gaol delivery in the town, the only nominated commission for Stamford in this period which survives, it was filled with councillors and reinforced with two lawyers, Sir William Hussey and Reginald Gayton. The conclusion must be that in Stamford, apart from the powerful royal interests which grew stronger and more interfering under Henry VII, it was the borough council who ruled the town and no other body.

IV. INFLUENCE WITHIN THE COUNCIL

There is, however, one further aspect to this study of Stamford's government at the end of the Middle Ages that needs exploration. If the council could maintain itself, at least until the 1490s, from outside pressures, could it also avoid internal divisions? Are they any discernible groups of interests within the council itself? It may be doubted if there are enough records to arrive at any completely satisfactory conclusions on this matter. Some lines of enquiry are, however, productive.

(a) Occupations

First, and perhaps most obvious, is an occupational grouping. Of the eighteen aldermen elected in the period 1465–92, seven were mercers or drapers; of the twenty-eight members of the First Twelve, nine were from the same group.[21] Six of these were on the council in 1465 but the other three did not join the First Twelve until towards the end of the period. Other textile workers and members of the victualling trades were comparatively rare (three each), and the smiths were represented solely by a pewterer. The only other significant body was the leatherworkers, glovers, saddlers and the like (three). Among the forty-eight on the Second Twelve there was more divergence; seven mercers and drapers (one of whom served for twelve years before being promoted to the First Twelve, where he served for more than twenty years, and four of whom did not proceed to the First Twelve) and five other textile workers; four victuallers, five leatherworkers and three metalworkers were also included. But there are few signs of any trade warfare in Stamford. There were no craft gilds: one of the first things the borough council did after the charter was to group trades together into eleven 'pageants', of which, somewhat surprisingly, one comprised drapers, hosiers and tailors, and a second mercers, grocers and haberdashers.

There is no evidence at all that any of the aldermen abused his term of office by admitting more burgesses of his own trade to the freedom of the borough, or indeed by excluding them.[22] Nor did any of the councillors act as entry pledge solely for others of his own trade. The leatherworkers were certainly closely knit, and John Molle, a saddler on the Second Twelve, is found acting as a surety for the shoemaker and entry pledge for a saddler. But William Gaywode, glover, is more typical. A member of the Second Twelve from 1469 to 1485, he was promoted to the First Twelve in that year and acted as constable, chamberlain, alderman and searcher of the market in succession. He acted as entry pledge for two glovers, a mason, two husbandmen, a fisher, a labourer, an ironmonger, a fuller, a weaver, a draper, two mercers and a fletcher during his lifetime.

(b) Gilds

While there were no craft gilds in Stamford in the late Middle Ages, there were of course a number of socio-religious gilds. Exactly how many is not certain, and indeed for some of those that did exist, such as the gild of St Nicholas, little more is known than the name. Almost every church had its own gild: 'All Hallows gyld' in All Saints' church, St Martin's gild in St Martin's church, the gild of St John and St Julian in the church of St John the Baptist, and so on. St Clement's church housed a chantry and gild of St Clement, and the united parish of Holy Trinity and St Stephen's maintained its own gild. The links between these gilds and the borough council are not always clear, although of course councillors on occasion played a large part in gild administration. Robert Crane, for instance, a mercer who served on both the Second Twelve and the First Twelve, was steward of the Trinity gild.[23]

But in two cases the links are seen to be much closer than such occasional references would imply. The gild which met in the church of St Mary at the Bridge was the united gild of the Virgin and Corpus Christi. It may have provided the town with its Corpus Christi plays, which were performed by the various pageants and recognised and regulated by the borough council. In 1486 the common hall of the Stamford council fell into disrepair and the council adjourned to the gildhall, a place where it met on other occasions, especially for the audit of the chamberlains' accounts. The gild was a very wealthy one, with a lot of property in the town, and an elaborate chapel in St Mary's church built or refurbished in 1467 by William Hykeham (First Twelve), a wealthy baker, councillor and alderman, partly as a chantry chapel for himself and his wife Alice. In view of these links, it is not surprising to find William Browne alderman of the gild in 1484, but its other officers and members are unknown.[24]

Perhaps just as important, however, and certainly better documented was the gild of St Katherine, which met in the chapel over the church door of St Paul's church.[25] The gild was re-established in 1480, when twenty-eight new members were added to the existing fifty-one. It was clearly an important gild, although not very wealthy. William Browne was its alderman from at least 1480 until his death in 1489 when he was succeeded by his nephew, Christopher Browne, until 1495; for the rest of the period for which records survive (up to 1534), this office was held by Thomas Philippe, another mercer. But St Katherine's gild was not a stronghold of the drapers; its steward from 1480 to 1498 was John Hikson (or Yetson), a butcher who was also a member of the Second Twelve. Of the seventy-nine members in 1480, no fewer than eighteen members of the council belonged to the gild. It attracted to its rank a few of the neighbouring gentry, nobility and clergy, like Sir Richard Sapcote of Rutland, the abbots of Crowland, Bourne and Spalding, Lady Margaret Beaufort and Cecily Lady Welles, the daughter of Edward IV, although its membership was in no way so illustrious nor so widespread as the great Corpus Christi gild at Boston.[26] Nevertheless here was an important social group to which most councillors eventually belonged.

(c) The Browne family

For most of the period under review the gild seems to have centred around the Browne family. Here was by far the most important social adhesive in the town. And yet even here analysis cannot detect any distinct grouping created by relationship or personal ties which would seem to have dominated the borough council. This may of course be merely the result of the non-survival of records, for in many cases even the names of the wives of prominent Stamford merchants are not known, let alone the families from which they came. Nevertheless a brief account of the Browne family ties will show how little the body of councillors featured in it.

This family of drapers was known in Stamford in the middle of the fourteenth century and their service in office began in 1374. In Edward IV's reign the family was represented by two members, John and William, both sons of an earlier John Browne, draper and thrice alderman of Stamford who died in 1442. John Browne, probably the elder of the two brothers, died some time after 1480, leaving his son Chris-

topher to carry on the family business. Like his father John and his
brother William he was a mercer and draper, a member of the company
of Calais staplers and alderman of the town three times between 1448
and 1462. But it was his brother William who was most prominent, 'a
marchaunt of a verie wonderfulle bigness', as Leland described him.
His fortune was made largely from wool, and he was clearly one of the
wealthiest of the Calais staplers. But he also benefited from the Wars
of the Roses and although, unlike his brother, he managed to avoid the
widespread accusations of helping the Yorkists in 1452, he nevertheless
profited from the accession of Edward IV in 1461. Thirdly, his marriage to Margaret, daughter and heiress of John Stokes of Warmington
and Lilford, Northamptonshire, brought additional advantages in land
and perhaps connections, for her brother was Thomas Stokes, canon of
York. Browne bought extensive estates in the neighbouring countryside,
but although he acted as sheriff of Rutland on four occasions and perhaps
once as sheriff of Lincolnshire, it is quite clear that he resided and
worked almost entirely in Stamford. His interests were far-flung: in
1481 he was not only alderman of the gild of St Katherine in Stamford
but also of the great Corpus Christi gild in Boston.

But such a prominent figure did not build up for himself a party in
Stamford. His wife brought her brother into the town, where he became
vicar of All Saints', not one of the wealthy livings of the town. His
sister Alice married a person of the name of Bradmeydew who is otherwise unknown. His daughter and heiress Elizabeth married a stapler
from Henley-on-Thames, a member of the Oxfordshire firm run by
the Stonor family, and one of their sons, William Elmes the lawyer,
came to Stamford to work with his grandfather.[27] William Browne left
the bulk of his estates to finance his great hospital in Stamford, a foundation which still survives, and his business was taken over by his
nephew Christopher. At least two of Christopher Browne's three wives
came from outside Stamford.

There is nothing here to suggest that William Browne ran anything
like a party on the borough council. Nor does any other evidence point
this way. An analysis of the trusteeships set up by councillors reveals no
close-knit group: the feoffees, as often as not, were not councillors.
Browne's own trustees on occasion included his brother John and
John Murdoke, but more often they were Thomas Stokes, clerk, or
Henry Wykes, a member of the Burley family who became later vicar
of All Saints', and William Halle, chaplain. Even less revealing of
close-knit personal groupings are the lists of witnesses to the many

deeds executed by councillors; nor did councillors create groups by acting as pledges or by admitting as apprentices the sons or other relations of other councillors.

(d) Political groupings on the council

There were of course groups of the more prominent councillors. The common seal of the borough was kept in a chest under the care of six of the councillors, all of them on the First Twelve; and in 1485 three of these six and the acting alderman (John Stede) sealed the indenture returning the notice of the election of the town's M.P.s. Four of this groups were mercers, it is true, but other than ocupation there are no signs of permanent links between John Gybbes, John Gregory, John Stede and William Browne. In 1481 the alderman was empowered to appoint a committee to administer the town lands set aside for the repair of the walls, but this does not seem to have been done, for the chamberlains regularly accounted for these revenues.

Perhaps the clearest evidence of inner groups comes from the years 1482–5, when the country at large was in its most disturbed state. In March 1482 a number of locally born men, including Christopher Brown, were made free, the largest number of 'natives' in one year for the whole period. Some of them were appointed directly to the First Twelve, without having served on the Second Twelve beforehand, the only occasion during this period on which this happened. The details are informative. Two men of the Second Twelve resigned or died and were replaced by a farmer from outside the town, Bernard Richman of Pilsgate and Tallington, and by the steward of St Katherine's gild. Regulations against councillors taking the livery of any person without the alderman's consent were passed. Despite this, when John Nele, barber, and Robert Nevour, furbisher, resigned from the First Twelve during the year, Christopher Browne and a royal servant, Richard Forster, were immediately appointed to the First Twelve, both without prior service on the Second Twelve, while John Murdoke was re-appointed to the First Twelve with a promise of exemption from the office of alderman. Christopher Browne became alderman at the end of the year, but Forster soon resigned and David Malpas, esquire, a yeoman of the crown, took his place, after having first been admitted a freeman without fine or pledge. Malpas then (1484–5) followed Browne as alderman; and at the end of that year four more councillors were replaced, two on the First Twelve (one being John Murdoke) and two on the Second Twelve, while Thomas Philippe, mercer, was pro-

moted straight from the Second Twelve to the office of alderman.
Despite Browne's later connections with Lady Margaret Beaufort, it is
unlikely that these moves represent involvement of Stamford councillors in the momentous events in the country at large, but they do suggest
some manoeuvring by groups within the council. Browne admitted as
a freeman Nicholas Byllesdon, dyer, who was to act as his deputy in
1502, and a little later acted as pledge for John Freebarn, yeoman, a
London draper who was made free in Stamford and in four months
passed from the Second Twelve to the First Twelve. It may be that
Browne was building up for himself a party in Stamford, but if so his
interests were soon diverted elsewhere, outside the town.

(e) The rewards of councillorship

In general, however, such political or personal groupings are hard to
discern. There are few signs of them when one reviews the rewards of
government. These were not great in Stamford. The offices were not
always confined to councillors, but to elect someone else into some offices
may of course have been one of the fruits of serving as councillor. Thus
those who assessed and collected the taxes in the town parishes were
rarely councillors, but from 1474 'helpers' were appointed, two from
the First Twelve and two from the Second Twelve, and on occasion
the councillors taxed themselves to save a general levy. Lists of leases
of the town's lands in 1469 and 1486, now among the borough records,
show that most of the tenants were councillors or officers, but the
tenancies were small and the rents per acre standard. Members of the
council (and no one else) secured licence to knock postern gates through
the town walls at the bottom of their gardens. But these few rewards
were evenly distributed throughout the council.

Why then did twenty-five members of the middle stratum of Stamford society serve as councillors? It was no doubt the influence and prestige of being a councillor, a large fish in a smallish pond, which made
the job worth while. Perhaps there were some fruits for one's relatives.
The alderman was patron of the gild of St Clement, and at least three
of the chaplains appointed bore the same surnames as members of the
council. But the alderman did not always act in this on his own; William
Hykeham twice appointed 'with the consent of his comburgesses'. Again,
one of Browne's feoffees was a Thomas Hykeham, clerk, who later
became vicar of St Peter's church.

There is no reason to think that the borough councillors of Stamford
in the later Middle Ages were very different in their general social or

economic standing from their counterparts at almost any other period, either before or after. They were worthy men, by no means unimportant among their own circle, but not so great as not to relish the added dignity of councillor. And it was the sense of power and influence which drew them to the work rather than its immediate rewards. It would certainly seem that they enjoyed the power, even if, in the later years of Henry VII's reign, there was a growing threat of interference from the town's lord. Otherwise their work was more or less unhampered, either by the permanent officials, by pressure from the commons, or by powerful, organised, vested interests in the town. These men were interested primarily in the welfare of the town, affecting as it did the welfare of their own businesses; and in acting for the promotion of this welfare they harnessed gentry and others with specialised interests to their ranks. But the power lay with them, not elsewhere, nor indeed with just a few of them. In 1467 William Browne, having just vacated the office of alderman, 'gave to the commonalty of the town certain instruments and other necessary things for the town's prison and gaol, namely four iron collars, with chains and staples fastened to one piece of timber, a hammer, chisel, four pairs of braces for legs, two great locks, one pair of chains of 15 links', and so on. But William Browne did not bind the town council to his own interests by such a gift. Rather his interests and the town's interests followed the same lines, and therefore he was willing to serve the community which helped to create his great wealth.

2. York under the Tudors: The Trading Life of the Northern Capital

D. M. PALLISER

THE editor, in a recent survey of the sources available for a study of inland trade in early modern England, has reminded us of the neglect of the subject. In this essay I shall try to remedy the deficiency for one small corner of the field, showing (I hope) how much we can learn from the scrappy records available, even of one city over a single century. The emphasis will be on inland traffic rather than the better-documented overseas trade, and this alteration of the usual balance is deliberate. Professor Everitt suggests that overseas trade between 1570 and 1770 was perhaps only a fifth of the volume of inland trade, and yet it has all but monopolised attention in most studies of the Tudor economy.

I. YORK AND ITS RECORDS

York, the most important town in northern England since its foundation by the Romans, was a natural centre of communication and therefore of trade. It was built where a glacial moraine crossed the Yorkshire Ouse, still then tidal above the city, and so was on or near the main east–west and north–south routes of Yorkshire. The Ouse and its tributaries gave access upstream to much of the North and West Ridings, and downstream either to the Humber and the sea, or (by turning up the Trent) to much of the Midlands. In addition the Great North Road from London to Scotland passed only a few miles west of York. The city was also a natural meeting-point for different local economies. It was in the centre of the fertile vale of York, a mixed area of arable and pastoral farming, but with the dwindling Galtres, a scrubby area of forest economy, just to the north of York, and some way south of it a rich area of marshland round the lower Ouse which merged, further south again, into fens. To west and east the vale was hemmed in by the sheep-rearing uplands of Pennines, Moors and Wolds, the last a lush chalk region producing particularly fine wool.

In Tudor times York was about the sixth largest city outside London, with a population of some 8,000 around 1550, rising by half as much again to 11,500 at the end of the century.[1] Like Beverley and Lincoln it had enjoyed a flourishing textile industry, but this was declining in the face of West Riding competition. Henceforth, utilising its natural advantages of position, it was mainly a distributive and mercantile centre, with no very important industry except leather. Judging from the registers of freemen (the independent masters with their own shops or businesses) the two largest trades were the merchants or mercers, and the tailors and drapers, each accounting for nearly 10 per cent of all freemen. The former were occupied in general trade, especially lead, and the latter in cloth and clothes; both the lead and most of the cloth came from other parts of Yorkshire. It is a remarkable contrast to the pattern in other large provincial towns, whose largest trades tended to be manufacturing ones – the cappers of Coventry, for instance, or the worsted weavers of Norwich.

The merchants and the tailors were not only the largest but also, it seems, the wealthiest and most important of the city's trades, and it is symbolically fitting that theirs are the only medieval trade gildhalls to survive in York. The mercers or merchants were particularly dominant, and provided half the city's mayors in the sixteenth century. Given a certain independence of the corporation in 1430, when they were formed into the gild of mercers by royal charter, they acquired even more when a second charter of 1581 (almost always mistakenly dated 1580 in York histories) reconstituted them as the Company of Merchants Adventurers of the City of York, and granted them a monopoly of the sale of all goods imported from overseas except fish and salt. The leading York merchants were also members of the national companies with overseas trading monopolies. Sir Richard York (d. 1498) was the last of several Yorkers who were mayors of the staple at Calais, while a number of merchants (seven in 1560) belonged to the Merchants Adventurers of England. Of the new companies formed in the sixteenth century, at least two (the Muscovy and the Eastland) also received York recruits.

York's economy has been well summarised by Miss B. M. Wilson as standing 'on five main bases: it was an ecclesiastical and an administrative centre, a river port from which goods, principally cloth and lead, were exported overseas, a distributive centre for goods brought from London or from abroad, and a market town for the local trade of a large agricultural region'.[2] Said of the period from 1580 to 1660, this classification can also be applied to the whole Tudor age, and it will be roughly followed here. For each of the city's functions I shall indicate something of the sources available as well as of the evidence which they can be made to yield, and it is hoped that the essay may serve as an example of what can be done for other inland towns. But since no two towns will have exactly the same array of materials, a word is first needed on what the main sources are for York.

Overseas and coastal trade are the most systematically documented, thanks to the customs accounts and port books at the Public Record Office, but with an inland town even these present problems. Because of navigation difficulties on the Ouse, and the increasing size of ships, York was no longer a main port, but effectively a 'member' or dependency of the port of Hull (even though in legal theory the relationship was the other way round). York merchants traded coastwise or overseas from Hull, and a shuttle service of smaller boats operated between Hull and York, for transhipment of goods. When port books were instituted in 1565, York (along with Hull's other members) was issued with its own, but the only surviving York book is significantly blank, and separate York books soon ceased to be issued. So the city's seagoing trade must be looked for in Hull's books, and even there we cannot obtain a really statistical picture of the trade. The few overseas books (most surviving Hull ones are coastal only) do not normally specify the cargoes at all,[3] though the coastal ones fortunately do. Moreover the homes of those trading through Hull are not given, and York merchants have to be identified from their names, with all the risks of ambiguity that that involves.

For inland trade systematic records are even scarcer. Much of the trade at York's fairs and markets must have been documented for purposes of toll (we have occasional references to such records being kept), but all the toll books have vanished except for a solitary survivor of 1771–3. Records of river traffic have fared little better: there survive only some scrappy notes at York of cargoes going upstream in the 1520s and 1530s, and two records of goods going downstream in the 1560s. And some of the other likely sources yield little on York. Much of the richest material in the editor's study of Tudor marketing comes from the records of the central government's equity courts. But these contain very few York cases after about 1540, largely, I believe, because the Council in the North (re-established near York in 1537) would have handled such cases from the northern counties, and its records are, alas, lost.

Yet the following pages will demonstrate that a good deal can be learned of an inland town's trade even when specialised sources are scarce. Some of the most useful facts come from scattered governmental records, both manuscript and printed. Much more is drawn from miscellaneous York sources, especially the many citizens' wills, the city merchants' archives and the corporation minutes. Most of our knowledge of fairs and markets attended by Yorkers, for instance, comes from corporation orders forbidding such visits because of the danger of spreading epidemics. Just as useful, where they have been printed, are the archives of other towns and institutions having contact with York. The difficulty of studying the trade of a single town is that it has to be seen largely through its own records and those of the central government; time forbids an extensive search of the unpublished archives of all the towns with which it traded. The examples quoted here from the records of Durham Priory and of the corporations of Chester and Beverley serve to remind us how many valuable records of regional trade must be still inaccessible in manuscript.

II. A RIVER PORT

Long-distance trade to and from York was mainly carried on along the Ouse, then navigable as far as Boroughbridge. There was also road traffic, of course; the bequests of city merchants in their wills for the upkeep of highways testify to that. Goods were brought overland by the London carriers, and even the journey to Hull was often made on horseback by the city merchants, presumably for the sake of speed. But the normal form of transport was by river, especially that ferrying of goods to and from the point of transhipment at Hull already mentioned. A freight agreement of 1555 shows that goods transported between Hull and York, and vice versa, included iron, flax, ashes, tar, herring, stockfish, coal, wainscot, salt, grain, eels, lead and cloth.

Goods sent from or through York were weighed, and paid toll, at the city crane on the right bank of the Ouse. On the opposite bank was the main quay for unloading goods, the King's Staith just south of Ouse Bridge. (After the Dissolution it was extended to include the adjacent quay of the Franciscan Priory.) From the staith a small army of sledmen, porters and labourers took goods to merchants' warehouses, at charges fixed in relation to the distance. The tributary river Foss, which joins the Ouse at York, was also used commercially, and the merchants' hall stood on its bank. Both rivers were lined by warehouses, all now vanished, though a solitary early Stuart brick warehouse, with a Dutch-style gable, survived in Skeldergate until its shameful demolition in 1970.

The growing size of boats would probably have killed York as a major port anyway, but decline was hastened by difficulties of navigation, especially silting, and obstruction by fishgarths, large fishing weirs which had been making river journeys difficult and even lethal since the fourteenth century. From 1462 the mayor and corporation enjoyed statutory power to remove garths from the Ouse and its tributaries, but the problem remained a serious one until the mid-sixteenth century, largely because there were powerful vested interests involved. Silting remained more intractable. There were attempts at deepening and dredging the river from at least 1538, all apparently unsuccessful. By 1603 the corporation was instead considering making a cut to shorten the winding course of the Ouse, but although this project was entertained for many years it came to nothing, in contrast to the similar canal scheme at Exeter. (The dates here given are a little earlier than those in B. F. Duckham, *The Yorkshire Ouse* (1967). A narrowing of the river was carried out *c.* 1538–40. The first record I have found of the canal scheme is dated 8 July 1603, but it had clearly been considered before.)

As a result York was throughout the Tudor period a port at one remove. It was engaged in trade on a large scale, but mostly through Hull, to the benefit of both towns. Hull and York tended to trade to the same areas and in the same commodities, with York men the more important. As late as 1609 the largest trader through the port of Hull was a Yorker, and not until the later seventeenth century could Hull's trade be carried on mostly by and for her own townsmen.

The Ouse carried other trade besides that between York and Hull, and much traffic passed through York to and from river ports further upstream. Most important was the lead shipped downstream from Boroughbridge, best considered in conjunction with York's own lead trade. There must have been a good deal besides, such as the malt or beer which passed between the Percy mansions at Wressle and Topcliffe, on either side of York. And for several years in the period 1520–35 we are fortunate in having surviving lists of some of the cargoes passing under Ouse Bridge and paying 'free passage' for the privilege. They consisted chiefly of linen, grain and beans, shipped upriver to various places (especially Bedale, Ripon and Boroughbridge), but also cargoes of linen to Cockermouth and Penrith in distant Cumberland.[4] Goods

actually shipped to or from York paid cranage and lastage. But all
these financial controls could provoke evasions. In 1541 it was reported
that many goods had been delivered at nearby Acaster Malbis and
other 'foreign' places to avoid the payment of cranage, lastage and
passage at York.

III. EXPORTS AND IMPORTS

The chief commodities sent through or from York downstream, to other
parts of England as well as overseas, seem to have been lead and cloth.
It was cloth made in York, from East Riding and perhaps also Pennine
wool, which had helped to create the city's record prosperity in the
century after the Black Death: it had been exported as far afield as
Prussia. As late as 1468–75, if the aulnage figures can be believed,
York was easily the largest cloth-producing town in Yorkshire.[5] But
slowly it lost its primacy in the face of West Riding competition,
especially from Halifax, Leeds and Wakefield, and this in spite of the
fact that York was nearer the fine Wolds wool. This geographical shift
is often assigned to the restrictive nature of civic craft regulations and
to the need for water power for fulling. This, however, is not the whole
story, or why should the drift to the country, begun during the 'Industrial Revolution of the thirteenth century', have been reversed in the
century 1350–1450? The reasons given by the lord mayor in 1561
for the renewed decline of York's clothmaking were that in Halifax,
Leeds and Wakefield 'not only the commodity of the water mills is
there nigh hand, but also the poor folk as spinners, carders and other
necessary work folks . . . may there . . . have kine, fire and other relief
good and cheap which is in this city very dear and wanting'.[6]

Already in 1485 a York draper was stocking West Riding cloths,
and special provision was made for them in the new markets granted
in 1502. By 1561, the mayor said, only ten woollen and linen weavers
remained in the city. But the decline, real though it was, can be exaggerated, and the 1561 count was made just after York's worst epidemic
of the century, when numbers may have been unusually low. In the
same year a woman of Leeds (of all places) bequeathed a gown cloth
she had recently bought at York. Cloth certainly continued to be
shipped overseas from the city, even if little was made there, and in the
early seventeenth century it vied with lead as the chief overseas export.

Worsted weaving weathered the crisis better than woollens or linen.
It was in the hands of the 'tapiters', who made coverlets, bed-covers and

wall-hangings, and who formed one of the larger city crafts, ranking third after the merchants and tailors in the second quarter of the sixteenth century. An Act of Parliament in 1543 gave York a monopoly of coverlet-making throughout Yorkshire, forbidding rural competition. Its preamble asserted that the city had hitherto been maintained 'most principally by making and weaving of coverlets and covering for beds, and thereby a great number of the inhabitants and poor people . . . have been daily set on work in spinning, carding, dyeing, weaving . . .'.[7] The use of 'principally' may have been more than just rhetoric. The tapiters' third place in the ranking of crafts is based on freemen's admissions, but weaving was just the kind of activity to employ many non-freemen, and particularly to use much female labour. The 1543 monopoly was apparently effective for at least the rest of the century, and the city's coverlets and carpets sold widely in Yorkshire and Nottinghamshire. Whether they also travelled much to southern England or overseas is not known, though a Kentish squire owned one in 1489.

While clothmaking at York declined, cloth exporting continued to be important, as we have seen. But lead, rather than cloth, seems to have been the city's most important overseas export. Here there was no question of an urban industry, but only of Yorkers buying to sell again. The lead passing through York (usually after being embarked at Boroughbridge) came from the Richmondshire and Craven fields, though York merchants seem also to have trafficked in lead from the Peak. 'The city sought to make itself something of a staple for Richmondshire lead', never with complete success. 'It tried to insist that lead should be discharged at York, weighed at charges which were sharply increased in 1499, and sold only to citizens.'[8] Certainly York merchants had a large share in the trade, aided by the city's custom of 'foreign bought and sold'. This denied the right of a non-freeman to bring lead (or any other goods) to York to sell directly to another 'foreigner'; a freeman had always to act as middleman. True, a determined merchant might win the right to trade freely in lead at York by appealing to Star Chamber, but such actions were rare except by Londoners, who had special privileges overriding the York custom, and these exceptions were bitterly resented. During one such suit, in 1521, the York corporation reminded their recorder that 'cloth making in manner is laid apart, whereby our said city was maintained in times past', and that 'lead is the greatest commodity that we have for the supportation of our poor city'.[9]

For one short period only, the primacy of lead was dislodged. In 1523, through Wolsey's intervention, the city was granted the right to ship to Hull, and thence overseas, the wool and fells of the greater part of Yorkshire, much of it coarse wool but including also the finer product of the Wolds. Hitherto only Newcastle had enjoyed such a licence, all other wool exports being monopolised by the staplers at Calais, who naturally resented the new privilege. And if we may believe the corporation, it was a mixed blessing even to York. They told Wolsey in 1526 that it had greatly enriched the citizens, but that they had taken it up so eagerly that they had allowed Londoners to supplant them in the lead entrepôt trade. The grant did not in any case endure long. In 1529 Parliament repealed it on the grounds that it was not profitable to the city, but only to three or four persons there, and that it was keeping the country clothiers from their supplies of wool. Probably the lament of 1526 was exaggerated, and the lead trade was not altogether lost; or if it was, it later recovered. In 1552 [10] York merchants had ships ready to sail to Antwerp, Bordeaux and Danzig, carrying 401 fothers of lead (about 2,500 lb. each), valued at the huge sum of £3,809 10s. In the final third of the century less is heard of the lead trade, but in the early seventeenth century, although it had declined, it was still York's most profitable overseas export after cloth.

The only systematic account of York's overseas trade in Elizabeth's reign confirms its concentration on the two staple exports. Between Michaelmas 1602 and Easter 1603 the recorded goods sent overseas by York merchants consisted entirely of lead (to Bordeaux) and northern shortcloths and short kerseys (to Bordeaux, La Rochelle, Middleburg and Elbing). Imports in the same half-year were more varied, including white rye from Danzig, flax and iron from Elbing, hops from Enkhuizen, wine from La Rochelle and Bordeaux, Seville oil from La Rochelle and Flushing, and very mixed cargoes from Flushing also (honey, paper, figs, frying pans, soap, Spanish sack, etc.).

Other Elizabethan port books do not give systematic information about cargoes, but they do show Yorkers trading with a large number of ports all along the European coastline from Narva to Spain, as well as with Scotland (two cargoes arrived from Kirkcaldy and Kinghorn in 1578–9, probably of Fifeshire coal). The main areas of trade seem to have been the Netherlands, south-west France (for wine) and the Baltic. The Baltic trade flourished, especially with Danzig and Elbing, and also, in spite of the Muscovy Company's monopoly, with Narva and Russian Lapland. In the late 1570s sixty-six York merchants were trading through the Sound, and by the early seventeenth century Hull and York shared a third of England's Baltic trade.

The situation in 1602–3 seems not to have been untypical. Many scattered references throughout the Tudor period present the same general picture: nearly all York shipments overseas were either of lead or of cloths, whereas imports were much more varied. Fish came from the Netherlands, north Germany, Scotland and (at least until the late fifteenth century) Iceland also; iron from France, Spain and Danzig; window-glass from Normandy and Burgundy; wine from Spain, Germany and above all Gascony; furniture from Flanders; gunpowder from Hamburg; and a variety of foodstuffs and raw materials from the Baltic, especially rye, flax, pitch, oil, wax, tallow and hides; and almost certainly the wainscot which was becoming fashionable as panelling in the wealthier York households. In 1579 the York merchants said they served all northern England with Baltic goods, especially flax.

IV. INTERNAL TRADE

But what of York's trade with the rest of England, almost certainly much more important than this overseas trade? Leaving apart the city's immediate hinterland for the moment, we find that York-made goods were distributed over wide areas of the county and of the whole north. A trading rather than a manufacturing city York certainly was, but its manufactures were not confined to coverlets. Its misleadingly named goldsmiths, for instance, made silver plate for churches all over Yorkshire and even beyond (e.g. Northamptonshire), and they also had secular patrons, like the corporation of Beverley who commissioned a mace and plate. The goldsmiths also traded regularly at the great national fair at Stourbridge, near Cambridge, but of their clients there we are ignorant. The pewterers, who in the early sixteenth century had a national reputation second only to London's, must also have served a wide market. So must York's book trade, which involved not only the sale of London and continental books but also, in the early Tudor period at least, others printed and published in the city. A lawsuit has preserved the isolated fact that about 1510 a stationer and a goldsmith imported 1,221 French service-books, and they will not all have been intended for local sale, even in over-churched York. In 1510–11 pricksong copies were bought at York for the churchwardens of Louth, and in

1616 a city stationer is known to have been owed money by many of the Yorkshire gentry.

One other industry, maltmaking, may have provided an important export. It was certainly practised on a large scale, but has largely escaped notice in York histories, probably because it was a profitable side-line rather than a full-time occupation. In 1540 Layton complained that there were perhaps, 40, 60 or 100 malt kilns at York; every merchant had one, and they scoured Lincolnshire for barley. This led to an abortive government bill against the York malt merchants, who were said to have used up all the woods within twenty miles of the city. Certainly there were 117 kilns there in 1598, when the corporation commanded half to be closed. A maltster might be such an unexpected figure as the registrar to the York Ecclesiastical Commission who in the 1580s was regularly buying much Lincolnshire barley for the kiln at his York house. When we consider that there was a city malt market held on three days in the week, and that dealers came from at least as far as Skipton to buy there, we can accept that malt trading was a major activity.

Building and furnishing provide another case of the city's links with a large part of England, in this case the provision of services as well as manufactures. Before the Reformation York was an important centre for the making of bells, glass, images, alabaster retables and other church fittings. Information is tantalisingly scarce, but it points to a very wide market. A glazier did much work at Furness Abbey, and the carver Thomas Drawswerde designed the surviving rood-screen at Newark, and submitted an estimate for image-work in Henry VII's chapel at Westminster. Professor Lawrence Stone has suggested attributing to York a major school of carvers who, between 1489 and 1527, designed screens and stalls over a wide area from Manchester to Bridlington. Again, the city was probably the chief bell-foundry for all northern England. This church patronage dwindled at the Reformation, and we find, for instance, no carvers admitted to the freedom of York after 1543–4. But in compensation an increasing demand for domestic comfort provided new outlets. The glaziers increased in numbers again after a temporary fall, probably because of the growing use of domestic window-glass. Even stained glass did not altogether vanish, and in 1585 a York glazier made much heraldic glass for Gilling Castle in the North Riding. A school of plasterers of more than local fame was rising at this period, and it was they who installed ornamental plaster ceilings at Edinburgh Castle in 1615–17.

So far we have looked at goods produced in, or services based on, York. With some other commodities it is hard to draw a clear line between exports and imports, and it is best to consider them together. A trading centre was constantly importing goods and redistributing them over a wide area, and this is particularly true of foodstuffs.

About a quarter of Yorkshire's markets specialised in corn at this period, York being one of the most important. To a great extent Hull and York acted as focal points where grain, peas and beans were gathered from the rich arable lands of Holderness, Lincolnshire and East Anglia and sent on further inland, especially to the growing West Riding towns. Already in 1460 grain was being brought to York from 'outward' areas of England. By 1503 Lincolnshire and Norfolk victuallers were regularly coming there, probably with grain, and in 1506-7 one Lincolnshire man was licensed to sell 40 quarters of barley there. The next stage came when Yorkers went out to those areas to buy on the spot. In 1535 three leading traders were buying Lincolnshire and Holderness grain, one of them to the value of £100, and from the 1540s at least, Yorkers were also buying corn at Lynn. A famine would cause the net to be spread very wide. In 1596-7 York collectors were scouring Nottinghamshire and Leicestershire for corn as well as importing from overseas, and when one of the city's licensed purveyors of corn and grain was stopped from taking Leicestershire beans to York, the corporation wrote to the Privy Council to ask that he should trade unhindered. The stoppage, they said, had been harmful 'not only for the provision of ourselves but of her Majesty's subjects of the west country [West Riding] and other places 30 or 40 miles distant from the city, who have yearly used to make their provision of corn here and to carry the same from hence on horseback, having no rivers for any boat or carriage by water to convey the same to them otherwise'.[11]

The corporation may well have been sincere in wishing to serve the region in this way; but there is another side to York's entrepôt role in grain, the attempts of at least some individual merchants to forestall and regrate – that is, to intercept grain before it reached the market, buy it as cheaply as possible, and sell dearly, profiting even in a time of scarcity. The three merchants of 1535 were said to have regrated so much Lincolnshire and Holderness corn that prices at York had risen. The complaint produced a speedy response, the corporation investigating and listing all the corn buyers, presumably with a view to better supervision. In the famine year of 1596 the corporation was trying to stop all shipments of corn and beans downriver, and ordering that the poor be first served in the corn markets, and at reasonable prices. Vigilance was certainly needed, for according to the East Riding J.P.s that year, much corn was being bought there by York men pretending to be licensed to serve York, but actually hoarding and engrossing the corn to sell wherever they could get a high price. This may well be why two York merchants were selling rye in 1597 as far afield as Chester, at a time when the York area was still suffering from severe dearth.

A very ugly story is told of an earlier famine year (1587), though it comes from the pen of a hostile witness, a Harewood man trying to find everything bad to say of York. He told Burghley there was a common rumour in his area that for two years Hull and York merchants had been stopping the import of corn into the county so as to sell their own at higher prices, 'yet it is well known that divers in these parts have perished this year by famine'. Recently, when corn was cheap at Selby, and all 'these west parts' were going there for supplies, Lawrence Robinson (a York city councillor) had gone there on purpose to raise the price. He was nearly murdered by a 'western' man, who said: 'Better I die for killing thee than so many people should perish for food by thy means.' [12]

Fish was another foodstuff for which York acted as a redistributing centre. It was traded over wider areas than meat, since it was required everywhere but was not everywhere available. (Even after the Reformation fish was the obligatory diet for a third of the year.) It came regularly to the York seafish market, in the fifteenth and sixteenth centuries, from the Yorkshire and Durham coasts. Some was brought there by the coastal fishermen, especially those of Scarborough, Whitby and Hartlepool, but other supplies were bought by the York fishermen on the spot. One of their regulations, drawn up in 1593, was that if any of them bought fish on the coast between Bridlington and Redcar he was to allow any other members who were there with him to share in the purchase as partners. Supplies also came to York over greater distances. Instances are known of men from the smaller Suffolk ports trading there, probably in fish. Certainly this was the case in 1535 and 1538, when herringmen of Walberswick and Dunwich rented shops in the city during Lent, and in 1555 when a Yarmouth man brought herrings to sell. Fish came too from overseas, though this import trade is obscure after the end of the Icelandic traffic in the late fifteenth century. In 1585 the Council in the North were told that until 1581 the merchants of York, Hull, Newcastle, Lynn, Boston and other ports had been importing 'staple fish', ling, cod and salted herring from north Germany, the Netherlands and Scotland, thus serving the whole north of England at reasonable prices. Again, it is difficult to know how far such pleadings corresponded to reality, but York men are certainly found taking fish to Leeds and Doncaster to sell. Freshwater fish, by contrast, was probably traded over more restricted areas, and much of York's supplies came from the Ouse, though fish was also sold there by men of Thorne and Crowle, well to the south.

Fuel and salt were two more indispensable commodities which York imported and no doubt re-exported to its region. Late medieval salt supplies came chiefly from Bourgneuf Bay in France, and the occasional salter found in the freemen's register (1497–8, 1517–18) may have been a provincial distributor of Bourgneuf supplies; but by Elizabeth's reign salt was being imported through Hull from Newcastle and (South?) Shields. Fuel was originally taken from local woods, but wood was becoming scarce by mid-century, as in many other parts of England, and substitutes had to be found. Turves from the 'marshland' round the lower Ouse formed the greater part of York's fuel by 1597, and there was a growing coastal trade in Newcastle coal. In the eighteen months ending at Michaelmas 1600, York men brought 544 chalders of it to Hull, and it became easily the biggest item of the city's coastal trade.

There was also a great variety of manufactured goods flowing into York, the counterpart of her own exports. They included such diverse items as cloth from the West Riding, Cumberland, Westmorland and even Coventry; butter and stockings from Swaledale and Wensleydale; and window-glass from Essex. But more important to York's trade than anywhere else outside Yorkshire was London. Even in the fifteenth century this was becoming significant, with York dyers, fishmongers and merchants owing money to London grocers. Most of the recorded transactions between Yorkers and Londoners involved London wares bought for cash, but if this were all there would be a net currency loss from the north. Perhaps we can envisage a roughly triangular pattern of trade, with Londoners buying lead, cloth and foodstuffs from Yorkshire and selling goods to York merchants, who then resold them throughout the county. The goods coming north were very mixed, two cargoes from London in 1566–7 including oil, soap, haberdashery wares, iron, currants, raisins, wine, copperas, hemp and candles. (Goods going in the reverse direction were much less diverse: beans, wheat and malt.) All such bulky goods came by sea, though smaller items like trunks, bales of books, and money could be sent overland from London by the York carriers.

Clearly, from the size of some London transactions, the Yorkers were buying to sell again over a much wider area than their own city. About 1577, in a single purchase, two York men were said to have bought, from a London skinner, soap ashes worth £176 3s. 4d. In 1585 a York alderman and draper died owing over £1,700 to four London merchant tailors for clothes, £727 of this to a single creditor, Edward Kempton, while five years later another York draper was owing Kempton £100. These, as so often, are examples taken from lawsuits, and we have no way of knowing how typical they are or even whether the statements were true, though they must at least have been credible to be put forward. Only for one untypical period do we have a more comprehensive picture of trade with London. On 8 July 1603 the York corporation banned trading contacts with London and other plague-stricken areas, and in a series of interrogations in the autumn they tried to establish how many goods were imported in defiance of the ban. The results, almost certainly incomplete, are none the less useful. Eleven men confessed to receiving wares from Londoners during the four and a half months concerned. Some had bought the goods at their own shops from the Londoners' agents, but in four cases the offenders had gone to Cowick, a small parish near Snaith, to buy from 'Mr Hill' of London. The wares involved were mainly fabrics and Venice gold and silver. They included some 216 yards of taffeta, as well as an unspecified quantity of taffeta and black damask bought for £80. One of the transactions shows very well York's entrepôt role. A mercer who bought 22½ yards of taffeta from Hill said they had been ordered for a country gentleman, and had been taken direct from Cowick to the customer's house at Nappa without passing through the city.[13]

V. FAIRS, MARKETS AND LOCAL SERVICES

Cowick, a place of no special importance, was probably chosen for the sake of secrecy. More usual locations for transactions with Londoners were the great fairs of Beverley and Howden, both regularly attended by York men. Their importance can be judged from the fear of them shown by the York corporation, who in 1584 instructed their M.P.s to sue to have them both suppressed. Howden, like Stourbridge, was a small place graced by a fair of national importance, a yearly gathering for merchants from London and the West Riding. Its speciality was cattle, and it is interesting that York should have started pressing for new cattle fairs in 1585, the year after the abortive attempt to suppress

Howden. We know something of Yorkers' dealings there in 1593, when, as in 1603, merchants were placing profit before plague precautions. One of the city's sheriffs, no less, went there to sell cattle, and also sent a servant there to buy two parcels of 'paper cards and such like'. Another York merchant, Robert Myers, was torn by conflicting feelings. He stayed away from the fair, but the Londoners there wrote him several letters expressing surprise at his absence, and telling him that his fellow-citizen John Watson was doing much trade there. They told Myers they would leave goods at Howden for him, and he, fearing lest Watson 'should draw away his custom', agreed.[14]

Howden and Beverley were only two, though perhaps the most important, of many Yorkshire fairs, between which there was a great deal of traffic. How far afield Yorkers went to fairs and markets has to be pieced together from occasional references in toll disputes and bans on visits during epidemics. These show that, apart from Stourbridge and Gainsborough, fairs over the greater part of Yorkshire were patronised by York men, from Richmond in the north to Barnsley in the south. One casual record, implying nothing out of the ordinary, is of two York pewterers, apparently partners, who at Michaelmas 1485 rode off to fairs fifty miles apart, at Barnsley and Bedale. An especially favoured town was Ripon, where twenty-two city crafts were trading in 1557, presumably at the markets or fairs. They included such diverse trades as merchants, drapers, pewterers, goldsmiths, tanners, butchers, bookbinders and armourers.

York had its own fairs, notably the three-day Lammas fair of the archbishop, which William Harrison listed among the principal fairs of England. There were also two six-day fairs run by the corporation beginning respectively at Whitsun and at SS. Peter and Paul. These three fairs were all in existence throughout the Tudor period. Two extra civic fairs authorised in 1502 ceased to be held by the 1590s, but in 1590 fortnightly cattle fairs from Palm Sunday to Christmas were instituted, and proved more enduring. With such a complement of fairs, York must have drawn many visitors. Unfortunately nothing seems to survive of the records which we know were kept at them, though we know that the Whitsun fair could draw a cloth-buyer from as far away as Louth. Their normal catchment area may be indicated by the list of markets where the corporation advertised their new fairs in 1502: a score of Yorkshire towns scattered all over the county except for the high Pennines, and ranging from the Humber and North Sea to Skipton, and from Guisborough in the north to Rotherham in the south. The range of goods available at the new fairs in 1502 was very wide, including cattle, sheep, horses, cloth, meat, beer, leather, silver, hats, gloves, hemp, iron, pewter, beds, and bows and arrows.

At the local level York was a market centre for its immediate hinterland, though it is impossible to draw a sharp line between this function and its wider role in regional trade. The distribution of market towns, plotted by Professor Everitt, shows that to south-west and south-east York's neighbouring markets were less than fifteen miles away, and in one case (Tadcaster) as little as nine, whereas to north-east and north-west the distance was nearer twenty. But a catchment area cannot be inferred from such a map, especially as York was more important than any of the surrounding markets. All that can be said is that there were other markets close enough to risk permanently capturing much of York's trade given the right opportunity. In 1604 a severe plague carried off nearly a third of the city's people, and the markets were closed down. Several wealthy merchants (including four future mayors) fled to Tadcaster, Selby and other nearby market towns. When the plague abated, the corporation threatened them with heavy fines, as they were still staying there and drawing away trade. This not only impoverished those tradesmen who had stayed in York, but also tended to draw gentry and other customers away from the city.

York had two large general-purpose markets, held every Tuesday, Thursday and Saturday, one in Thursday Market (now colourlessly renamed St Sampson's Square) and the other in the wide central street called Pavement, though by this period it was also spilling over into the adjoining streets of Coppergate and High Ousegate. In addition, at least six specialised markets were held in other streets or in the common hall (the present-day 'Guildhall'): malt, leather, seafish, freshwater fish, swine, and Kendal and West Riding cloth, the last a new market started in 1546. Of these the first two were also held thrice weekly. Furthermore the Shambles, the street of butchers' shops, ranked as a meat market; there was a cattle market on Toft Green; and besides all these civic markets there was apparently yet another held by the dean and chapter in the cathedral close. This is a huge complement for a provincial city, and the absence of any market records is very regrettable. We cannot even trace the fluctuating volume of toll receipts in the city's financial records, since it was usual to farm out the tolls for a fixed sum. All we have is a few indications, such as that maltmen of Pocklington (another specialised corn market) came regularly to York, and that villages from York's hinterland were, as we should expect, very frequent visitors. In 1494-5 evidence was given in a lawsuit by several such villagers. One Heworth man said he had 'come to York every market day' for twenty-four years or more, and an Osbaldwick man aged sixty-three, 'having livelihood in York', testified that 'since he had any discretion he hath used to come to York weekly'.[15] In 1537 Robert Aske, the leader of the Pilgrimage of Grace, was hanged on a market day, presumably to demonstrate the penalty of rebellion to the largest possible crowd.

More systematic indications of York as a local centre – whether for markets, shops or services – can be gleaned from the churchwardens' accounts of neighbouring towns and villages. A good example is Sheriff Hutton, whose wardens were often at York between 1538 and 1559, to buy goods, to attend the assizes or the church courts, or to appear before the royal visitors, or the Council in the North. It was at York that they bought buckskins, a cross, a lectern, service-books, a rood and censers; there that they sold a bell in 1552; and from there that crafts-men were summoned to mend a glass window, a chrismatory and the organ. Likewise, between 1595 and 1601 the churchwardens of Howden were at York three times on legal business, and in 1600 they called in a York man to look at the organ. Of purchases of secular wares there are also a few hints. The cordwainers (shoemakers) are known to have made a habit of hawking in country churchyards on Sundays, and one of their number, dying in 1589, was owed money by local countrymen of Selby, Shipton and Cliff, as well as by York citizens. A tapiter in 1553 had debtors in nearby Kexby and Rufforth as well as more distant places like Frodingham and Newark. A useful check on the custom of the city's armourers and associated crafts, taken in 1569 on the day the northern rising erupted, showed that armour and arms were being supplied to local gentry at Sutton, Acaster, Kexby, Copmanthorpe, Brandsby, Wighill and Naburn, as well as the more distant Carlton in Coverdale. Some of these goods were made in York, but coats of plate seem to have been made to measure at the customers' homes.

York, where nearly one freeman in ten was a builder, was also an important centre for building and repairs. It was a York bricklayer who was sent in 1545-6 to Temple Newsam, a new brick mansion near Leeds, to advise on repairs, and it was probably York men who built the brick houses just outside the city, at Bishopthorpe and Heslington. York carpenters and bricklayers were summoned to Kirkby Misperton (25 miles out) in 1581-2 when a new rector wanted an estimate for repairs to his house. And finally, York was a specialised centre for services as well as goods and craftsmen, for it own local area and much of the north. Its lawyers, notaries and surgeons had wide practices; its grammar schools, both before and after the Reformation, took in as boarders the sons of country gentry from as far away as Patrington, the other side of Hull. We can perhaps also include as a 'service' the money-lending which York's merchants and craftsmen practised as a side-line. Their clients included not only local gentry, but even such distinguished neighbours of the city as the fifth and sixth earls of Northumberland.

VI. A REGIONAL CAPITAL

Mention of the great Percys, who had various connections with York, brings us to the final aspect of the city's trading activity: its role as a regional capital, and therefore a centre of consumption for many who came on visits often unconnected with trade. As the seat of an arch-bishopric, York was the administrative centre not only of the large diocese of York itself, but also of the entire northern province, which after 1542 was extended to include the whole of the six northern counties as well as Nottinghamshire and Cheshire. There would be a constant demand for the services of shops and inns by clergy coming on business. Apart from any individual visits they might make, the parish clergy of the diocese gathered there in synods twice yearly, and the corporation was well aware of the need to keep such large numbers of visitors well supplied. In 1495 they imprisoned all the city butchers for shortages of meat at various times, and particularly on the synod day after Easter. There were pilgrims to various York shrines and relics, notably to the tombs in York Minster of St William and of Richard Scrope, centre of an unofficial local cult ever since his judicial murder in 1405. There would also be many visitors for important church services: on one such occasion Archbishop Lee preached in the Minster against the Pope, reporting afterwards that in the congregation 'were a great number of sundry parts of the country, which never lack in that city'.[16] Large numbers must also have come to attend the various church courts, either as litigants or as witnesses. In Elizabeth's reign a single one of these courts (Chancery) was hearing over 400 cases a year.

Before the Reformation there were other religious institutions attract-ing visitors to York. The city itself had a large complement of religious houses, including St Leonard's, the largest hospital in England, and St Mary's Abbey, the richest house in Yorkshire and the mother of cells stretching from Cumberland to Suffolk. The prior of one of these, Wetheral in Cumberland, is found trading in hemp at York in 1482. Of the four city friaries, at least three were heads of provincial groupings of their orders, the dependent priors of which met regularly at the York houses. In addition, at least thirty-six Yorkshire religious houses, together with the more distant Durham and Furness, owned property in York on the eve of the Dissolution, and some at least are known to have patronised the city's traders. York men sold wine, wax and oil to Newburgh, books to Byland, and corn, fish, pottery, spices, raisins, sugar and paper to Durham.

Religious changes destroyed this monastic patronage by 1540, but they also brought compensations. The Pilgrimage of Grace spurred the government to reconstitute the King's Council in the North in 1537, and although initially the Council moved from place to place to suit the convenience of successive presidents, it was in 1561 permanently established at the King's Manor in York. Its counterpart, the Ecclesiastical Commission for the Province of York, was set up at York in the same year. For the next eighty years the city was the home of two powerful and busy government agencies controlling the whole of the north. Both handled a great deal of business: the Council in the North was hearing between 1,000 and 2,000 cases a year at the turn of the century. This enormous figure justifies the vice-president's claim in 1560 that without the Council York would soon decay, and explains the city's repeated requests after 1641 for its re-establishment.

York was also of course the county town of the largest shire in England, the headquarters of the sheriff and the seat of the county gaol, and the scene of the twice-yearly assizes and occasional county elections. One such election in 1597 drew a crowd of close on 6,000, equivalent to more than half the city's population. And as if all this were not enough, the city was also the home of an admiralty court and (spasmodically until 1553) of two mints, royal and archiespiscopal. It is therefore not surprising that gentry from all over the north should have been familiar with York, as we should suspect from the large number found joining the city's Corpus Christi gild. A slander case in 1557 reveals casually that a whole northern party, then staying in York, included four esquires of Cumberland and Westmorland and the constable of a Northumbrian castle, and that one at least was very well known there.

Not all visitors met in York on business, for already it was developing that social life for the gentry which reached its apogee under the

Georges. The first recorded horse-race at York, between two Yorkshire esquires, was run in 1530. In 1568 the corporation agreed to the request of 'divers worshipful gentlemen' for a cockpit to be made in York, for the hard-headed reason that it would 'cause much money to be spent both among victuallers and other craftsmen'.[17] There were also a number of bowling alleys available, and occasional archery contests were held by county gentry. A contemporary ballad, 'York, York for my money', preserves details of one such series of matches, lasting a week, organised by the earls of Essex and Cumberland in 1584 for 'knights, squires and gentlemen'. The ballad indicates how welcome such meetings must have been to the shopkeepers:

> And never a man that went abroad,
> But thought his money well bestowed,
> And money laid in heap and load,
>   As if it had been at London,
> And gentlemen there so frank and free,
> As a mint at York again should be. . . .[18]

There is little direct evidence of purchases by the gentry in York, though it is significant that the mercers (in 1495) forbade any member to go through the streets with goods to sell unless he was sent for by any lord or knight. But occasionally we can measure the time some gentry spent in the city. Lady Margaret Hoby of Hackness (40 miles away) spent thirty-seven nights in York between 1599 and 1603, mainly on medical and legal business, and in her only extant letter she asks her husband to order starch if he comes home through York. The Hobys, like some other nobles and gentry (including Lord Burghley), owned property in the city, but others relied on inns and, before the Dissolution, on religious houses. Even so important a neighbour of the city as Sir William Fairfax, the sheriff of the county, used to lodge at a York inn in preference to buying or renting a house. Likewise the earls of Northumberland, whose favourite homes at Wressle and Leconfield were not far away, no longer kept up their family mansion in Walmgate. Instead they took lodgings, sometimes in a priory, and at least once in an alderman's house.

It is scarcely surprising that the city's inns should have flourished. In 1537 a report made for an expected royal visit showed that 1,035 beds were available in the city for strangers, apart from those in private houses and religious liberties. Likewise stabling was available for 1,711 horses. And this census was taken before a great rise in the number of

York innkeepers ('innholders'), which began suddenly about 1560, a rise probably connected with the establishment at York of the two great government commissions in 1561. Forty-seven innkeepers were made freemen between 1500 and 1560, but 101 between 1560 and 1600, a growth in numbers which made them the fifth largest trade by the last quarter of the century. The city and its dependent rural wapentake contained 86 inns in 1577 – over a third of the Yorkshire total – and the city alone had 64 in 1596.[19] And with growth came respectability. Early Tudor aldermen were not allowed to keep inns, but from 1540 innholders were elected to the bench without restriction.

We have now seen something of the variety and scale of York's trade. To quantify it, even roughly, is not possible. Dr J. N. Bartlett and Miss B. M. Wilson have shown, for the periods 1450–1550 and 1600–60 respectively, a generally declining city trade, but this refers mostly to overseas traffic. We cannot really know, short of new discoveries such as merchants' account books, whether regional or national trade was increasing to compensate for this. One piece of evidence suggests that they were, and even that depends on the dubious assumption that the wealth of the tax-paying population is an index of general prosperity. In 1334 York was taxed more highly than any provincial town except Bristol. By the 1520s its ranking had fallen to fourteenth, below what its population would have warranted, and below even the much smaller but wealthy cloth town of Lavenham. In 1662, taking the different basis of hearths taxed, it was back to second place, ahead of Bristol and just behind Norwich. This is not a conclusive indicator of urban wealth, but it is suggestive. Other indicators point the same way, towards a late medieval decline, culminating in the (for York) economic disaster of the Reformation, and then a recovery under Elizabeth and the Stuarts. New building on any scale died away around 1500 and began to pick up again after 1570. Population shrank from a peak of perhaps 12,000 in the early fifteenth century to only 8,000 in the mid-sixteenth, after which it regained its old level by about 1630. So it is reasonable to postulate an economic recovery in the century after 1550 to match the decline of the century before. If overseas trade was still doing badly after that date as it was before, we can suppose that internal trade and the patronage of the city by visitors were more than compensating for it.

3. The Buildings of Burford: A Cotswold Town in the Fourteenth to Nineteenth Centuries

MICHAEL LAITHWAITE

BURFORD is a decayed town on the eastern edge of the Cotswolds, noted nowadays for the picturesque quality of its old stone houses and its setting in the Windrush valley; 'an enchanted backwater', one writer has called it. But to the historian it presents a rare opportunity to study the housing of a small town between the fourteenth and the seventeenth centuries, for after that few entirely new houses were built in Burford until a housing estate and a scatter of other houses appeared on its fringes in the present century. Of course, much alteration and addition was done to older houses in the eighteenth and nineteenth centuries, but this had the effect of disguising rather than destroying, and in the late nineteenth century, when so much was rebuilt in other towns, building seems to have ceased almost entirely. In this essay I want to consider the fabric of the town as a whole, analysing the forms of houses as they evolved down to the seventeenth century, and discussing what the continual process of alteration has to tell about the social and economic history of the town during the whole period from the fourteenth to the nineteenth century.

I. HISTORICAL BACKGROUND

The documentary evidence for the history of Burford is very sparse indeed, especially before the middle of the sixteenth century. There can be little doubt, however, that it has always been one of the smallest places that could be called a town. Its population in 1545 has been estimated at about 800,[1] and between 1801 and 1901 it never rose above the 1,644 recorded in 1841. None the less it managed to retain the principal characteristics of a town until at least the middle of the nineteenth century. Its charter, granted by the lord of the manor, dates

from somewhere between 1088 and 1107, and by the early sixteenth
century it had a corporation consisting of an alderman, a steward, two
bailiffs and fourteen or fifteen burgesses. Economically it was both a
market and an industrial centre, with a useful inn trade resulting from
its position on the road from London to Gloucester. A weekly market
was held, and by the end of the fifteenth century there were two annual
fairs. In the late sixteenth century there were markets for corn, sheep
and wool, and in a Cotswold town there can be little doubt that the
latter was of long standing by this date. Italian merchants bought wool
at Burford fair in 1392,[2] but although there are references to woolmen
belonging to the town in the fourteenth and fifteenth centuries, none
seems to have been of the stature of Grevil of Chipping Campden or the
Forteys of Northleach. It has been suggested that Burford was more
concerned with the manufacture of woollens, and certainly the town
was dominated by this trade in the late sixteenth century. Between 1550
and 1599 about a fifth of the occupations shown in wills and inventories
are of men concerned with woollen manufacture. There was at least one
fulling mill at this date, and four or five clothiers, among whose wills
are references to looms out on loan in weavers' houses. The woollen
manufacture was still regarded as important in the late eighteenth-
century directories, but from the seventeenth century onwards tanning
and malting had been developing as subsidiary industries.

The inn trade was already well established in the fifteenth century.
In 1423 the 'Novum Hospitium Angulare'[30]* (later the Crown) was
bequeathed to the town as a going concern, and by the end of the century there were two other inns, the George [29] (first certain mention in
1485) and the Bear [12] (later the Angel, 1489). More were established
in the late sixteenth and seventeenth centuries, notably the Bull,[11]
re-founded on its present site c. 1610 and largely rebuilt c. 1620.[3] The
George, the most important of the medieval inns, also showed signs of
growth around this period and built on a whole new wing c. 1608.
Increased traffic on the roads no doubt led to this minor spate of building, but another factor may have been the popularity of Burford races,
which are known to have taken place as early as 1621 and were patronised by royalty in the late seventeenth century.

There are hints, however, that the town was less prosperous in the
seventeenth century than it had been in the early sixteenth century.

* The numbers in bold type between square brackets in this chapter refer to
the plan of the town on p. 63. Plans of houses show original work in black,
and later additions stippled or hatched.

The lay subsidy returns of 1523–4, though difficult to interpret, suggest that Burford was remarkably wealthy in relation to its size, and that the wealth was well distributed compared with some other small towns in which one man contributed most of the subsidy. Burford was surpassed in wealth among the Oxfordshire towns only by the considerably larger towns of Henley and Oxford.[4]

The ship-money assessment of 1635 presents much the same picture, but in 1637, when the assessments were revised, its payment was reduced, leaving it in fourth place behind Banbury.[5] Comparison of lists of chief rents implies a similar decline in prosperity, for whereas in 1552 the principal property-owners were Burford men, by 1652 and 1685 much property had passed to outsiders.[6] The *Universal British Directory* of 1791 nevertheless treated the markets and manufactures with respect. Economic collapse did not come until the first half of the nineteenth century. The Charity Commissioners, reporting in 1823, put it thus: 'For several years there has been no trade carried on here, and the road has been lately [1812] diverted, so that persons travelling in that direction [between Oxford and Cheltenham] do not pass through the town.' Other sources suggest that this was putting it a bit strongly, but in 1852 the railway by-passed the town by five miles and the subsequent decline in population was marked. The corporation was finally abolished by Act of Parliament in 1861, and in the 1870s even the market faded out. Industry of the factory kind had gained only one foothold in the town, the small Reynolds' (later Garne's) brewery,[32] founded in Sheep Street in the 1840s. A writer of 1902 was able to describe Burford as having 'gone entirely to sleep'.

II. TOPOGRAPHY

Most of the houses front on to the long, wide High Street that runs from the bridge over the river Windrush straight up the south side of the valley to the A.40 (the 1812 by-pass) at the top. The remaining houses lie mainly in Witney Street and Sheep Street, which are placed at right-angles to the High Street half-way up on the east and west sides respectively and were originally part of the London–Gloucester road. The High Cross formerly stood at the point where the three streets meet. These streets really formed the built-up area of the old town, apart from a few buildings in the minor streets, notably Guildenford Lane, Church Lane, Lawrence Lane and Priory Lane. The market was probably held in the lower part of the High Street, north of Witney

FIG. I. PLAN OF BURFORD

Based on the Ordnance Survey of 1881. The numbers relate to the buildings discussed in the text

Street and Sheep Street; certainly a photograph taken *c.* 1900 shows the fair occupying this position.[7] The sheep market, of course, was in Sheep Street, at least in the mid-sixteenth century.

The date of the street layout is unknown, but there can be little doubt that more or less the whole length of the High Street was laid out by the fourteenth century, and much of it by the thirteenth century. The bridge at its foot was in existence, and already in need of repair, by 1322, and fourteenth-century buildings can be found distributed evenly up and down the street. The third house above Sheep Street [37] was actually described as a half-burgage in a deed of *c.* 1250, suggesting that not only was this part of the town laid out by the early thirteenth century, but that pressure on space was already causing the original burgage plots to be divided up.[8] Too much emphasis should not be laid on the shortage of space, however. Title deeds show that wide-fronted plots remained common into the seventeenth century, and after the early Middle Ages there never seems to have been sufficient pressure to warrant taking land from the town's open fields. Possibly the population was cut back by the Black Death, and by the time it built up again in the seventeenth century, economic decline had enabled a number of larger plots to be divided between several families. One factor that must have helped considerably was the absence of large areas of land within the town given over to big lay and ecclesiastical properties, as often happened in other towns. There was no resident lord of the manor until the seventeenth century, and the medieval Hospital of St John (now called the Priory) [25] occupied quite a modest site in the north-west corner of the town, outside the built-up area. The parish church [18] too was tucked away well behind the building-line in the north-east corner. Deeds show there were houses on both sides of Witney Street by the late fourteenth century, and in Sheep Street by the fifteenth century. Much of Sheep Street, however, remained undeveloped until a much later date, possibly owing to its use as a sheep market. Two large closes at the west end of the south side [34, 33] remained unbuilt on until 1598 and *c.* 1628–52 respectively, while a large area in the middle of the north side [32] was taken up by a farmhouse, yard and several barns until well into the nineteenth century. A point worth making is that in the built-up parts of the streets odd plots do not usually seem to have been left empty. The gaps that can now be seen in the building-line are mostly the sites of houses demolished in the nineteenth century, when declining rents made it uneconomic to rebuild. The only gap which can be proved to have existed any earlier is the one which still exists on the west side of the High Street, referred to as the Cowpen Close [42] in the middle of the seventeenth century.

In the main streets the tenements, or building plots, are mostly very deep, up to 400 ft, but with relatively narrow frontages. In a trading centre competition for frontage was obviously important, and in fact the frontages in Burford are wide by comparison with, for example, the central areas of Oxford. Most are between 20 and 40 ft wide, but the range extends to 55 ft; a few go as low as 15 ft, but these are very much the exception. There is nothing to suggest there was ever a burgage plot of standard width. In some cases the depth of plots is limited by orchards, in separate ownership, lying fairly close behind the building-line, and while many of these were no doubt parts of the tenements that were sold off in the eighteenth or nineteenth century as the medieval tenement pattern began to break up, one of them, Bruton's orchard,[28] was in existence by 1580 and possibly by the fifteenth century.

III. THE BUILDINGS

To the casual viewer, modern Burford looks like a jumble of cottages and small houses, built mostly of stone, but with patches of rather mutilated timber-framing. Occasionally a grander classical façade or a fine piece of medieval carving stands out, but architecturally the over-all effect is quaint rather than impressive. It is only when one investi-gates the interiors of the houses and analyses the title deeds surviving in private possession and in record offices that it becomes possible to visualise Burford as it was in its heyday. For economic decline in the nineteenth century caused many of the larger houses to be divided into cottages and sometimes partially rebuilt, while in more recent times painstaking restoration has exposed the structural alterations of many generations in a way that was never originally intended.[9]

Another reason for the architectural unpretentiousness of Burford is its lack of grand public buildings. The parish church [18], very fine fifteenth-century with a Norman tower, and the Priory [25], rebuilt as a manor house in the seventeenth century, both come into this category, but they are secluded from the main part of the town. Otherwise there are only the Tolsey [36], or market house, a small sixteenth-century timber-framed building raised on stone columns (first mentioned in 1561), at the corner of High Street and Sheep Street, the Great Alms-house[17] founded in 1456) and the Grammar School[19] (founded in 1570). The latter are both modest architecturally, and are hidden away in

Church Green. A rather obscure reference points to there having been a gildhall, but it no longer exists, and in the seventeenth century the town hall is said to have occupied the upper floor of the Grammar School.

(a) Building materials and construction

The principal building material is the local limestone, which was used both for walls and stone roofing tiles. The manorial accounts show that the town had its own quarries both for freestone and tiles by 1435–6. In practice, however, the medieval builders relied for freestone mainly on Taynton quarries, two miles away to the north-west. These produced a hard, coarse stone that weathers well and which was much used in building the Oxford colleges. Burford stone was much less popular at this period, except for interior work, for it is soft and chalky in texture, and better for fine carving. But by the late fifteenth and early sixteenth centuries it was coming to be used increasingly for exterior work, as fine detailing came to be preferred to durability, and from the late seventeenth century it was used almost exclusively.[10] It is generally accepted, however, that earth and timber preceded stone as building materials, even in the stone belt,[11] and one is bound to ask at what stage this change took place in Burford. Stone was well established by the fourteenth century, for the surviving houses of that date are wholly stone-built, even if they are perhaps rather untypical survivals. But three points stand out. Firstly, the presence of fifteen wholly or partly timber-framed houses of the fifteenth, sixteenth and seventeenth centuries; secondly, the absence of workmen's cottages dating from before the late sixteenth century; and thirdly, the very great rarity of ancillary buildings, such as barns, brewhouses and stables, dating from before the eighteenth century, although of course probate inventories, which survive for Burford from the 1590s, show them in large numbers.

The timber-framing might be regarded as the remnant of a largely timber-framed town of the Middle Ages, and there is certainly a parallel for such a change among the farmhouses of Monmouthshire.[12] But in Burford the fourteenth-century houses do not contain timber-framing, and in most of the later examples it takes the form of a timber-framed front to an otherwise stone-built house. Shortage of timber might be the explanation for this, but Burford is on the edge of Wychwood Forest and moreover the timber used is of high quality; there is no sign that these are the tail-end of a timber tradition.[13] On the other hand it is apparent that houses of this mixed timber and stone (or in Norfolk, timber and brick) tradition are a feature of towns the whole length of the country, from Cornwall to Westmorland, between the fifteenth and seventeenth centuries. The nearby town of Banbury, which seems to have flourished after the Civil War, built stone houses with particularly exuberant timber fronts in the 1640s and 1650s. In Burford it is the better-class houses which tend to be of this type, and in fact the house originally containing the largest amount of timber-framing, Castle's shop [8] (Plate II), is one of the grandest in the town. But from about the middle of the seventeenth century, when the town appears to have been declining economically, they disappear altogether, in marked contrast to Banbury. The inference seems to be that timber-framing in Burford was a purely decorative or prestige feature, imported from outside and associated with the strong urban consciousness that resulted from its wealth at the end of the medieval period. The appeal of timber-framing must have arisen from the system of narrow-fronted plots that gave rich townsmen little chance to make an architectural display of their wealth, except on the façades of their houses. Carved stone in large quantities was evidently beyond the means of most of them,[14] but timber was not, and besides, its lightness gave scope for dramatic features such as over-hanging upper storeys. Obtaining craftsmen skilled in timberwork cannot have presented much of a problem, for the lowland areas of Oxfordshire and Berkshire, where timber remained the usual building material down to the seventeenth century, were not far away. It is clear that craftsmen were coming into Burford from these areas, because 'rafter' roofs and clasped purlins characteristic of south-east England are occasionally to be found,[15] and even examples of pargeting, or external decorative plasterwork.

Burford, like other towns, thus attracted styles of timber-framed building and roofing quite alien to its region.[16] Moreover its proximity to quarries of fine building-stone brought to it masons of more than local experience. In 1438–43 All Souls College, Oxford, had between fifteen and twenty-three masons in Burford, working stone for the college buildings;[17] and in the late seventeenth century Christopher Kempster, Wren's mason at St Paul's, had a house at Upton quarries in Burford. It is therefore dangerous to apply to Burford the generalisation sometimes made about the Cotswolds, that it was an area where architectural styles were slow to change. How far, if at all, the town was the agent in spreading building styles into the surrounding countryside is a subject that I have not yet been able to explore. It is not easy to find out the extent to which its craftsmen worked outside the town itself, but there is one case in 1654 in which two plumbers, John and Edward Scriven, had eight contracts for repair work within a radius of fourteen miles.[18]

The absence of early cottages and ancillary buildings poses more fundamental problems about the history of building in the town. Such buildings are not easily recognised, for they are the most easily altered, being the plainest architecturally and lacking the decorative detail by which grander buildings are dated. Nevertheless it is difficult to obtain evidence of them even in buildings thoroughly stripped down for restoration, and they are equally lacking in other places.[19] Burford is in fact unusual in having identifiable cottages firmly datable as early as the late sixteenth century, together with two remarkably fine ancillary buildings of the seventeenth century. If a vanished tradition of timber-framing comparable to that in Monmouthshire is ruled out, then there seems little alternative but to assume that these missing buildings, and probably many vanished dwelling-houses besides, were of earth mixed with straw and other binding materials, or some inferior and short-lived wood construction. Evidence for either is lacking, although it is worth noting that earth houses survive on the fringes of the Northampton-shire stone belt in places where neither stone nor timber were in good supply.[20]

Information about the cost of building, or of who actually organised the work, is almost completely missing. Landlords seem to have pre-ferred to grant building leases rather than build houses themselves. In 1649, for example, the trustees of the estate of Dame Elizabeth Tanfield leased a house in Sheep Street (now the Bay Tree Hotel) to Thomas Baggs, yeoman, on preferential terms in consideration of the fact that he had 'puld down and reedified' it. And in 1615 a Chancery case refers to three houses in Witney Street 'beinge soe ruynous & in decay that none would be tenante thereunto to repayre the same'.[21] One exception seems to have been Symon Wisdom (d. 1586), clothier and alderman, who owned eighteen properties in Burford at the time of his death.[22] Four buildings in the town bear his mark and the date, the earliest of them, now Roger Warner's shop, being the largest and almost certainly his own dwelling-house. Clearly, therefore, he built the others for tenants, and a plaque on one of them, a row of three cottages near the bridge (Plate V), records that he 'newly reedyfyed and buylded' them in 1576.

(b) The houses

The remarkable feature of Burford is the high proportion of houses that survive from before *c.* 1550, which is roughly the date when medieval architectural detail went out of fashion in small houses. There are six houses or parts of houses of the fourteenth century, and two that are either of this date or the early fifteenth century. What remains is mostly fragmentary, but its architectural quality and the fact that it remains at all are both impressive. Of the later fifteenth and early sixteenth centuries, there are no fewer than twenty-two houses or parts of houses surviving, and the quality of them makes it clear that this was a period of great and widespread prosperity in the town, confirming the evidence of the 1523–4 lay subsidy. It was at this time that the fashion for timber-framed fronts came in, exhibiting, as I have already suggested, a strong urban consciousness. The relatively wide plot frontages meant that few houses were built gable-end on to the street, in the distinctively urban fashion typical, for example, of central Exeter,[23] but gables were nevertheless introduced for largely decorative purposes. Castle's shop (Plate II), perhaps the most sophisticated house of this period, has a row of three gables, two of them with original carved barge-boards, and before alteration Calendars (Plate IV) had a gabled wing projecting strongly from one end of its upper storey. Structural evidence suggests that two other houses of similar type, Hill House and Reavely's, were remodelled to include the same feature. More important, in terms of improved living standards, was the introduction of fully two-storeyed houses in place of the single-storeyed ones that appear, on the surviving evidence, to have been characteristic of the fourteenth century. This is an interesting development because it shows the town a good half-century ahead in adopting a fashion that was to become general in the countryside from the late sixteenth century.[24] Exactly when the change began cannot be pinned down closely, but there is a distinct group of at least half a dozen houses built two-storeyed at the end of the fifteenth or early in the sixteenth century. Other houses seem to have been of the common late medieval type consisting of an open hall with a two-storeyed section at one end, but at Hill House and Reavely's, the two most certain examples, the two-storeyed section appears to be an alteration to an earlier house. The architectural detail of this period is particularly fine, with a wealth of carved stone doorways, some of them visible from the street, and five chimney-pieces carved with quatrefoils and trefoil-headed panels (Figs. 2 and 9(a)). Curiously, though, window-glass, another index of rising standards of housing, does not appear to have become established at this time. It was still being treated as a movable fitting in one of the most important houses in the town as late as 1607, and in the house of a rather impoverished barber even in 1636.

Most of the remaining houses are basically of the late sixteenth and seventeenth centuries, the period of the famous 'Cotswold' style.[25] But Burford has no really grand examples of Cotswold architecture. The building that comes nearest to it is Falkland Hall (Plate III) in the High Street, a great three-storeyed house built for Edmund Silvester, a leading local clothier, in 1558.[26] Yet this has a very medieval-looking oriel window in the middle of its second storey, and it really seems to represent the final fling of the town's prosperity in the early sixteenth century. Elsewhere in the town leading citizens were adding wings to existing houses rather than rebuilding in the new fashion. The smaller houses and cottages, however, were reaching the improved standards attained by the larger ones at the end of the Middle Ages. Probate inventories show nothing resembling a single-storeyed house at this period, and surviving houses originally of that type have clearly had an upper floor inserted at this date. The nearest documentary reference I have found to a single-storeyed house is in the inventory of Simon Horton, glazier, in 1627. It lists only a hall and 'the loft over the hall', and may have been a one-roomed single-storeyed house with a loft contrived in the roof-space. But Horton almost certainly lived on the edge of the town, in Guildenford Lane, where social change was probably slowest to penetrate.

An equally important aspect of this period is the fact that so many houses of the middle and lower classes have survived, suggesting that they had achieved a much improved standard of construction. Moreover new ground was being taken to build them, particularly on the two closes in Sheep Street already mentioned as remaining open until 1598 and c. 1628–52. Also, rows of cottages were beginning to go up, such as the three near the bridge (Plate V), built, according to a plaque, by Symon Wisdom in 1576. The inventory of one occupant, an ostler called Laurence Holdinge, was worth only £7 18s. 2d. in 1616. It shows that he had a hall, in which he clearly lived and cooked, and a chamber above, which he used for sleeping and storage. Unfortunately it is difficult to reconstruct the original appearance of the cottages, as they were converted into a single house and extended (by a tanner making use of the adjacent river) as long ago as 1693.

Clearly the upper classes were content to make use of the admirable

building stock left to them by earlier generations, and the obvious conclusion is that they were less wealthy. By the middle of the seventeenth
century it is apparent that the demand for larger houses was actually
decreasing, probably because the wealthier men were tending to leave
the town. In 1656, for example, one of the clothiers, Thomas Silvester,
moved to Witney, which was becoming increasingly prosperous with
the blanket manufacture. The 1652 list of chief rents shows that several
larger houses had already been divided up between two or more
tenants.[27] Burford, in fact, was becoming increasingly cottagey, more
like a village, and nothing illustrates this better than the Great House
in Witney Street,[14] and what is now the Methodist Chapel[15] in the
High Street. These two grand houses, towering above their neighbours,
were newly built in the late seventeenth and early eighteenth centuries
respectively, not for clothiers or the local gentry but for John Castle, a
physician, and John Jordan, a lawyer.[28]

Because of the relatively wide plot frontages, Burford houses were
usually built with their roof-ridges parallel to the street, and in fact up
to the seventeenth century they differed little in plan from contemporary
farmhouses, although of course the constricting shape of the plots
sometimes made variations necessary. Occasionally there was space for
the full medieval three-room ground plan (Fig. 7), consisting, to use
the terminology of architectural historians, of a 'hall', or dining-room,
flanked on one side by a 'parlour' or living-room, and on the other by a
cross-passage and a 'buttery' or service-room.[29] But the most common
types were reduced versions of this plan comprising a hall, cross-passage
and buttery (Fig. 5), or just a hall and cross-passage (Fig. 3). A point
where Burford plans often differed from those of farmhouses, however,
was in a tendency to have the hall fireplace in the rear wall, rather than
in one of the shorter end-walls, a feature usually associated with the
houses of the gentry.[30] There is only one example of the plan one would
most expect to find in this area, that with an axial stack backing on to
the cross-passage (Fig. 7).

These plans persisted from the fourteenth century down to the
seventeenth century, but they tended to move down the social scale. Thus
a one-roomed house in the Middle Ages might, from the quality of its
architectural detail, be the home of a man of some wealth, and yet by
the seventeenth century a house of similar size would be relatively plain
and suitable only for a workman or small craftsman.

Where additional rooms were needed, the three basic plans were
extended by building out a wing at the back to give an L-shaped plan.

Many of these wings were added in the late sixteenth or seventeenth century to accommodate a kitchen, a feature apparently lacking in houses of any class before this date. Possibly in some cases cooking had previously been done in outside kitchens long since demolished, as in the example which still survives at the nearby manor house of Stanton Harcourt, but often it was probably done in the hall. Rear wings intended for purposes other than cooking were already being built in the fourteenth century, and the one complete house of this date, Bull Cottage (Fig. 4), was built with an L-shaped plan from the first. But with the possible exception of the Rampant Cat,[39] none of the medieval rear wings appears to have been an open hall attached to a storeyed front range, as occurs, for example, in King's Lynn.[31]

Stuart Thomas's shop [26] in the High Street (Fig. 2) is the earliest of the one-roomed houses, though re-fronted in the nineteenth century, given an upper floor in the late sixteenth or seventeenth century and a two-storeyed rear wing in the late fifteenth or early sixteenth century. In the wing the ground-floor room nearest the street was clearly intended as a parlour, for it has moulded ceiling-beams and an elaborately carved stone chimney-piece. At the far end was a lobby or passage 4 ft 6 in. wide, probably with a door into the yard, and beyond that a further room. Unfortunately, however, that part of the house has been rebuilt. The whole of the front range is now comprised in the shop, and access to the rear of the plot is by a side-passage taken out of the next house. But in the rear wall of the shop, at the south end, is a two-centred stone arch which originally led out into the backyard, and which probably represents the rear end of a cross-passage. There is no structural evidence of the latter, but this is often the case in the medieval houses, possibly because the partitions were of a type that left no trace behind them.[32]

Stonehurst[16] is a fifteenth-century example with a rear wing added in the sixteenth or seventeenth century. It has an elaborately moulded two-centred arch at one end of the façade, and evidence that there was formerly an overhanging upper storey of timber-framing above, although at the other end part of the ground-floor room was probably open to the roof. Rose and Crown Cottage[27] bears the date 1578 and Symon Wisdom's mark; its front wall has been removed to insert a bay window and a rear wing added, but otherwise the original plan is well preserved. Basil Cook's Cottage [2] is almost certainly seventeenth-century, and was occupied c. 1643–76 by a mason, Roger Daniell, as tenant to the Grammar School. It is much the humblest of the three examples and had only one ground-floor room originally, with no cross-passage, although there is a surprisingly ornate ceiling of chamfered and stopped

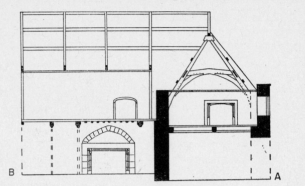

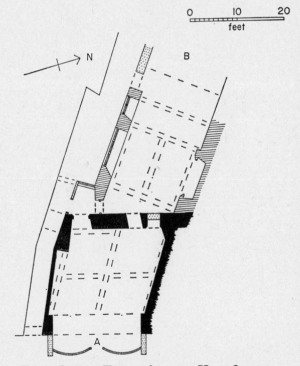

FIG. 2 STUART THOMAS'S SHOP, HIGH STREET
Ground-floor plan and section

joists. A rear wing was added in the eighteenth or nineteenth century, and later still a separate cottage was built on behind that.

Bull Cottage [13] is the earliest of the 'two-room' plans, although it had a rear wing from the first. It is the easiest of the single-storeyed houses to visualise in its original condition, for it is well preserved through having been absorbed into the stables of the Bull Inn during

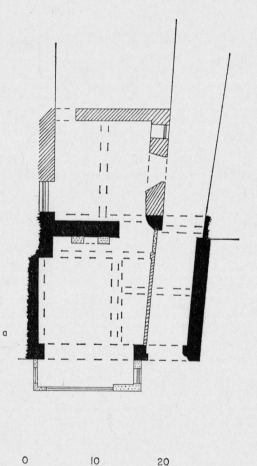

feet

FIG. 3 HOUSES IN HIGH STREET

Ground-floor plans: (a) Stonehurst (b) Rose and Crown Cottage
(c) Basil Cook's Cottage. See p. 75 for (b) and (c).

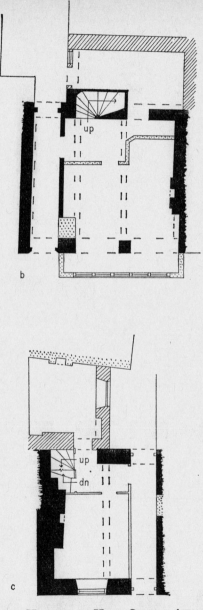

FIG. 3 HOUSES IN HIGH STREET (CONT.)

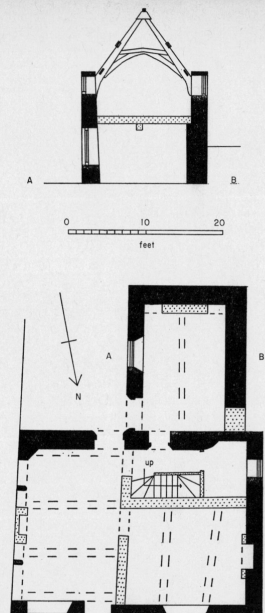

FIG. 4 BULL COTTAGE, WITNEY STREET
Ground-floor plan and section (partly restored)

the nineteenth century. A modern restoration has given it imitation 'Cotswold' windows, but a water-colour of 1840 (Plate I) shows the original doorway and the lower part of an original window with ball-flower carved on the jambs. The window must have been cut down and given its rather incongruous wood lintel when the upper floor was inserted in the late sixteenth or seventeenth century. There are no original chimneys in the house; the ornate medieval chimney-pot in the water-colour actually belonged to the next house. The internal walls (Fig. 4) are all later in date, except the one dividing the front range from the wing. An original stone doorway links the two ranges, and there are slightly plainer versions of it leading from the yard into the front range and the wing respectively. Against the eastern wall of the front range is a row of arches which must have been intended as a kind of reredos, for their heads are rebated as if to contain panels. Judging from the arrangement of the doorways, this ought to be the service end, so the original plan of the house is difficult to understand. But whether it was designed with two rooms or three, it demonstrates how modest was the accommodation required by a wealthy citizen in the fourteenth century, for that is what the architectural detail suggests the occupant was. In fact the house ties in well with the Colchester houses described in inventories of 1301, which show that only a few of the wealthiest citizens had as many as three rooms in domestic use.[33]

Later examples of the two-room plans are shown in Fig. 5. The largest of them, the Highway Hotel [6] (Plate II), was originally a two-storeyed range lying along the street frontage, but its external appearance has been altered by boxing out the roof to form a third storey. A south wing was added in the late sixteenth or seventeenth century, and a short north wing in the late seventeenth or early eighteenth century. Calendars [35] (Plate IV), somewhat altered since Buckler drew it in 1821, is a smaller version of the Highway Hotel at about the same date, but with a rear wing which may be a slightly later addition. The plan shown is a reconstruction of its original appearance, based on evidence uncovered during restoration. The third example, a cottage [43] still owned by the Grammar School, is a very modest version of the plan, probably built in the seventeenth century; a wash-house has been built out at the back, probably in the eighteenth or nineteenth century when it was divided between two households. The occupant in 1653–71 was a carpenter, Edmund Greenhill.

From about the middle of the seventeenth century two-room plans tended to have the cross-passage in the centre, flanked by rooms of equal size. Fig. 6(a) shows one of the earlier examples, the Bay Tree

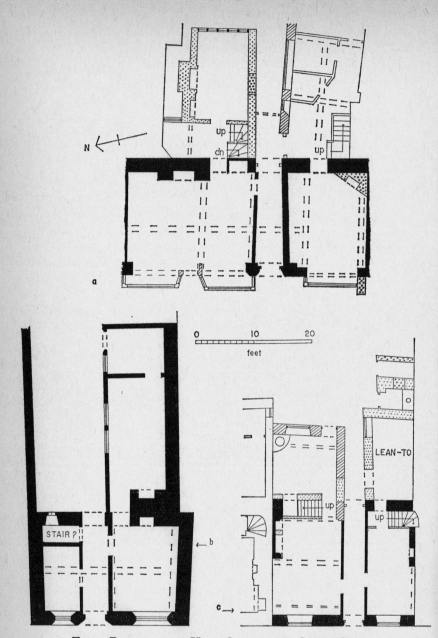

FIG. 5 BUILDINGS IN HIGH STREET AND SHEEP STREET
Ground-floor plans: (a) Highway Hotel, High Street (b) Calendars,
Sheep Street (restored) (c) Grammar School Cottage, High Street

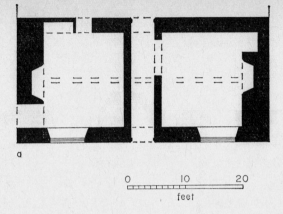

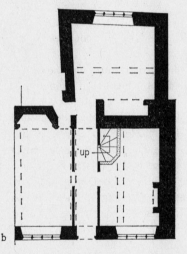

FIG. 6 BUILDINGS IN SHEEP STREET AND HIGH STREET
Ground-floor plans: (a) Bay Tree Hotel, Sheep Street (b) The Gabled
House, High Street (partly restored)

Hotel,[31] built in 1649. It has been much extended at the back, but the
original ground-floor plan was of only two rooms. Its first occupant
was Thomas Baggs, who described himself as a yeoman. The Gabled
House [41] (Fig. 6 (b)) is similar in plan, but with a narrower frontage,
and an original rear wing containing the kitchen. It was the house of a
tailor, William King, in the late seventeenth century. Obviously these

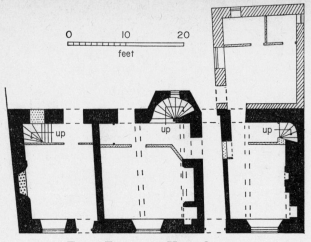

FIG. 7 EDGEHILL, HIGH STREET
Ground-floor plan

plans have been influenced by the Renaissance fashion for symmetry, although the style of the elevations remains solidly in the medieval tradition.

Only one example of the full three-room ground plan exists, Edgehill [44] (plate VI; Fig. 7), long since divided into three cottages. Its appearance and plan are thoroughly rural, and I have already remarked on the positioning of the hall fireplace. But despite its rather modest exterior, the stone chimney-pieces inside are in the best Cotswold manner, and its hall has a ceiling of chamfered and stopped joists. It was formerly a Grammar School property, occupied from at least *c.* 1643 to 1667 by a surveyor, Mathew Winfield, and may well have been built by or for him.

The tendency for larger houses to be split up into smaller units, and often partially rebuilt, from the seventeenth century onwards, makes them difficult to identify, and then only with the help of title deeds. For example, a 'mansion house', referred to in the 1652 list of chief rents as lying on the west side of the High Street, now appears to be represented by four separate houses of different dates [40] and with a total frontage of over 60 ft. Some owners of the wider plots in fact preferred a more spacious two-room plan, as at Hill House,[3] with a frontage of 55 ft.

But apart from the house types already described, there are four houses that stand apart as being grander than the rest. They take two forms: two are courtyard houses and two are 'double-depth' houses. The former have buildings round four sides of a courtyard, but unlike examples in other towns they do not have the hall and service-rooms in the rear range.[34] Roger Warner's shop [7] (Plate II), which was re-fronted in the early eighteenth century, really seems to have started from a long (44 ft) range on the street frontage and grew into a court-yard house by stages during the sixteenth and seventeenth centuries. Its continued growth was probably due to its having been the home of Symon Wisdom in the sixteenth century, followed by a succession of prosperous mercers, including the Bartholomews, who were the only seventeenth-century Burford family rich enough to have graduated into the gentry. The other example is, or was, Cob Hall,[22] now represented only by a piece of wall in front of the vicarage garden, but shown by drawings [35] to have been a courtyard house with a carriage-gate in the front range. Both the rear and side ranges contained medieval work, but references in the inventory of Richard Norgrove in 1636 show that then, at least, the hall was in the street range. It must have been the largest house in the town, and possibly it was socially a cut above the rest. Certainly in 1591 it was unusual in being the home of a gentleman, George Symons. He seems to have been related to the lord of the manor and was therefore a great rarity in Burford, a 'real' gentleman, as opposed to a professional man. The house passed to the town on Symons's death in 1592.

The double-depth houses have front ranges two rooms deep, and they seem to look ahead to the 'double-piles' of the late seventeenth century. Falkland Hall [24] (Plate III), of 1558, seems to have aimed at some such effect with its deep front range and central stack,[36] although it was still roofed in a single span. Castle's shop [8] (Plate II; Fig. 8), built in the late fifteenth or early sixteenth century, is a truer example, for the rooms at the back of the front range are roofed by three gables set at right-angles to the main roof. The wall carrying the division between the main roof and gables is supported at ground-floor level by a beam resting on two thick posts. The original layout of the ground floor is difficult to work out because of the many alterations made in the eighteenth and nineteenth centuries, including walling off the southern part to form a separate house. Both the front and back walls of the street range were originally timber-framed, but at the front all but two posts have been cut away to insert a shop front and the rear wall has been largely rebuilt in stone. One moulded post of the original front door

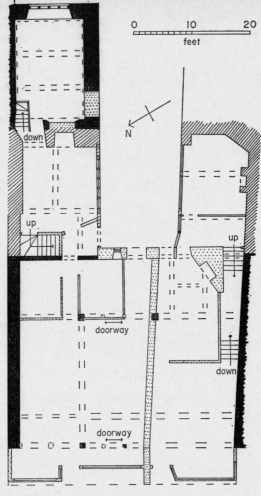

FIG. 8 CASTLE'S SHOP, HIGH STREET
Ground-floor plan

remains, and in the beam marking the rear end of the main roof are the
two disused mortices of former doorposts, suggesting that there was an
off-centre cross-passage. It was the usual two-unit plan, in other words,
but two rooms deep. The rooms at the front were clearly shops, for the
remaining posts and the moulded beam over them show that there was

a continuous row of unglazed windows, the timbers being rebated to take shutters when the shops were closed. The first floor appears to have been divided into three rooms at the front, corresponding to the three gables. Of these the southern room was evidently the most important, because it has an arch-braced collar-beam truss in the roof, put in more for decoration than structural necessity. There were originally no rear wings, but on the north side of the tenement there was a detached, two-storeyed building of stone with a cellar beneath. It contrasts curiously with the timber-framed front and back walls of the street range, and its original purpose is not clear; the detailing appears too fine for it to have been a kitchen. In the late sixteenth or early seventeenth century a kitchen was built, linking this building to the main house, and in the seventeenth century a second wing was added on the south side of the tenement. A reference in a deed of 1607 suggests that the house formerly belonged to the Bishops, one of the leading Burford families in the fifteenth century.

I have left to the last one final house type, because it appears to belong to a tradition quite alien to the town (Fig. 9). This has a frontage varying from 16 ft to 22 ft in width, allowing space for one room and a cross-passage at the front with a rear wing the width of the front room: an L-shaped house, in other words, but with a very narrow courtyard giving a minimum of light to the wing. In other towns the wing tended to contain an open hall, but not in Burford, unless perhaps at London House, where the wing has been much rebuilt. The front ranges are unusual for Burford in being three-storeyed, and narrow enough to be gabled; although in fact only one example (now hipped back) was originally so treated. Houses of this kind are relatively common in Oxford, King's Lynn, Tewkesbury [37] and elsewhere, but in Burford site constriction was not sufficient to make them necessary, particularly as they are houses of some quality. It is worth noticing, therefore, that they come in pairs,[4-5; 9-10] suggesting, perhaps, that wider sites have been split up by some speculator, aware that houses like those in larger towns might appeal to fashion-conscious townsmen. London House [9] (Plate II; Fig. 9(a)) is the grandest of them, built probably in the fifteenth century and with a timber-framed front. It has a fine stone-vaulted cellar with a central column, the only such cellar in the town and another thoroughly urban feature. On the first floor is a magnificent stone chimney-piece carved with quatrefoils. Symon's Close [4] (Plate II; Fig. 9 (b)) is a later example which, perhaps significantly, bears the initials and mark of Symon Wisdom, and a date in the 1580s (the last

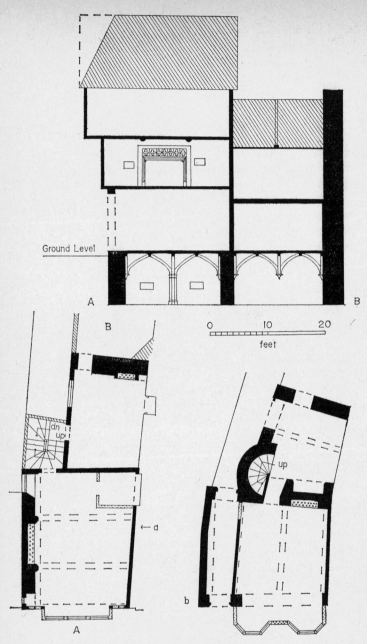

Ground Level

0   10   20
feet

FIG. 9 BUILDINGS IN HIGH STREET
(a) London House: first-floor plan and section (b) Symon's Close:
ground-floor plan

figure is defaced). The timber-framed front has suffered some alteration, probably the result of under-building an overhanging third storey
with rather inferior framing, prior to plastering it all over. A sawn-off
beam at eaves-level suggests that there may have been a projection at
the top of the house, perhaps a pair of gables.

(c) *Inns*

Burford was a place of numerous small and medium-sized inns, rather
than a few really big ones. Many are barely distinguishable from
ordinary houses. For example, the former 'Novum Hospitium Angulare' [30] (now Reavely's shop) originally consisted of a rather grand
single-storeyed structure of two rooms, one of them with a simple version of a hammerbeam roof. Likewise the former King's Arms,[20]
largely remodelled in the seventeenth century, has an L-shaped plan of
two rooms, differing from a house only in having a gate for carts in the
street range.

The medium-sized inns have usually had a longer history as inns, and
have consequently been much altered. The former Bear Inn [23] (Plate
III; Fig. 10), which was built in the seventeenth century, is the best
preserved. There is some evidence that its front room incorporates part
of the house adjoining on the north, but in effect it is a purpose-built
structure of one date. It lies at right-angles to the street, part of it behind
the frontage of the neighbouring house on the south. On the ground
floor is a wide gate for carts, beside which, one behind the other, were
originally two rooms of some quality, to judge from their chimney-
pieces. Behind them lay the kitchen, with a large fireplace, and beyond
that again the stables. At right-angles to the latter was the cart shed,
and this had another gate through it, for like every inn of consequence
in Burford, the Bear had a back exit into a side street, so that vehicles
could drive in one way and out the other. Galleries like those familiar in
drawings of the old Southwark inns are not found in Burford, but the
Bear had an outside staircase and a short gallery giving separate access
to what must have been the bedrooms on the first floor.

(d) *Eighteenth and nineteenth centuries*

Although classical architecture was in use in Burford by the 1670s, it
was mostly a matter of putting new fronts on to older houses, and
inserting new panelling and framed staircases with balusters – the latter,
rather curiously, not being found in Burford before this date. Apart
from the Great House, the Methodist Chapel and a group of rather

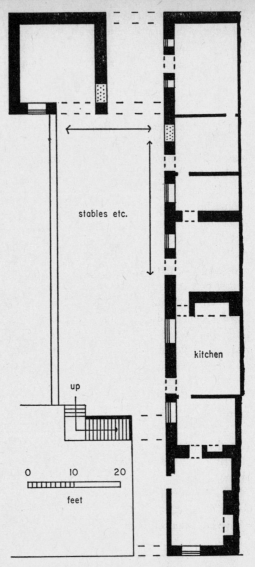

stables etc.

up

0   10   20
feet

kitchen

FIG. 10 THE BEAR INN, HIGH STREET
Ground-floor sketch plan (partly reconstructed)

grand mid-nineteenth-century houses, little else seems to have been
entirely newly built at this period. Interest centres rather on the

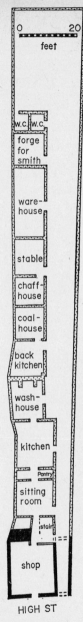

0   20
feet

W.C. W.C.

forge
for
smith

ware-
house

stable

chaff-
house

coal-
house

back
kitchen

wash-
house

kitchen

Pantry

sitting
room

stair

shop

HIGH ST

FIG. 11 TAYLOR'S SHOP, HIGH STREET
From a plan of 1898 belonging to Brasenose College, Oxford

P.E.H.—4

development of minor industrial buildings and rows of cottages in the backs of tenements, a feature of many small decaying towns at this period and of the centres of larger ones, where prosperous citizens were tending to move to new suburbs. In Burford this process was stimulated by the decay of the inn trade, which provided capacious yards suitable for development. In 1824, for example, the New Inn [39] (now the Rampant Cat) was sold to a baker, John Bowl, who built on a bakehouse, combining baking with innkeeping. But already in the late eighteenth century the Three Goats' Heads [38] had combined a rope-walk and a straw-hat manufactory with the inn.

In *c*. 1837 the George Inn [29] closed down, and in 1841 the census return shows nine families, containing forty-six people in all, occupying the 'George Yard'; largely, that is, the former stables, now converted into cottages. In Burford such developments were commonly referred to as 'colleges', a name sometimes used for almhouses and other institutions for the poor. 'Colleges' occur several times in the eighteenth-century land-tax returns, and a deed so describes one house as early as 1658.

Fig. 11 is a plan of a gunsmith's premises [37] in 1898, illustrating the curious plan that could evolve through building small workshops, etc., in the back of a tenement. It is basically a house of one-roomed plan built in the late sixteenth or early seventeenth century, and enlarged by stages from the late seventeenth century onwards. John Templer, the clothier who leased the property from Brasenose College, Oxford, described it in his will of 1625 as 'a shoppe & chamber with a backeside thereunto belonginge'. Possibly the shop was the workshop of one of his weavers.

Fig. 12 shows Crown Cottage, [1] until its recent conversion probably the last of the cottage developments to survive. It is basically a two-roomed house with cross-passage, built possibly in the sixteenth century, to which a kitchen wing was added in the seventeenth century. For some years in the middle of the eighteenth century it became an inn, or perhaps an alehouse, called the Crown, but by 1798 a cottage had been built on behind the kitchen. By 1803 the whole property had been divided up to make four cottages, two in the added range, one in the former kitchen and one occupying the street frontage. Still later the street frontage was itself subdivided to make a fifth cottage. In 1841, when the cottages had become a lodging-house, the census return shows them occupied by seventeen people.

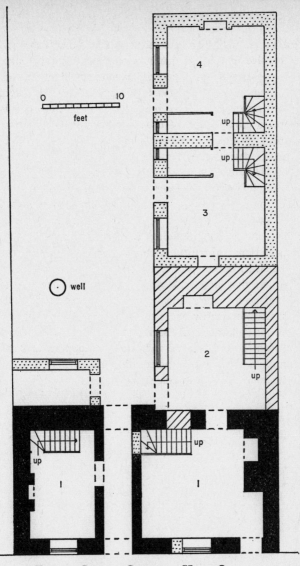

FIG. 12 CROWN COTTAGE, HIGH STREET
Ground-floor sketch plan (partly restored)

IV. CONCLUSION

So detailed an analysis of the fabric and documentation of a town is very expensive in time. Its justification is that only by such methods can the complex and closely packed layout of an old town be understood, and its changing shape and social character be properly interpreted. It is sometimes assumed that the buildings of an old town can be studied as a sort of cross-section of urban architectural history, with equal weight being given to examples from each period. But in fact towns can alternate dramatically between periods of prosperity and decline, producing, in relation to contemporary architectural standards, buildings of widely varying size and quality from one period to another. 'Historic' towns are almost by definition ones that have had a great period of prosperity followed by periods of either modest prosperity or decline, and the best buildings can easily be disguised by later refrontings and internal refittings. One of the snags about declining towns is that the larger buildings of earlier periods tend to become redundant, and it is here that large-scale study of documents can help to provide a more balanced picture. Finally, it needs to be stressed that urban buildings are more easily understood by seeing them against the background of the buildings of the surrounding countryside, for the relationship between the two is close and often overlapping, and moreover it is becoming increasingly apparent that towns played an important role in the innovation of building styles.

4. The English Urban Inn 1560-1760

ALAN EVERITT

I. THE PATTERN OF URBAN INNS

(a) Introductory

THE English inn has given rise to a very considerable literature over the past century and more, but it is no paradox to say that its history has never been written.[1] There are any number of books and articles on the Romance of the Road, in which a few precious facts may at times be found embedded among a mass of popular sentiment and Pickwickian nonsense. There are a few worthy if rather superficial general works about inns, dealing chiefly with their physical appearance, usually from the picturesque angle. There are a number of local studies of inns and inn signs, some of them quite useful as far as they go, and there is Larwood and Hotten's monumental *History of Sign-Boards*, published as long ago as 1867. There are also one or two useful works, like Joan Parkes's *Travel in England in the Seventeenth Century* (1925), containing a good deal of miscellaneous information, culled from contemporary tracts and the like. And there is a handful of scholarly monographs dealing either with particular aspects of the subject, like Dr W. A. Pantin's seminal essay on the structures of medieval inns in E. M. Jope's *Studies in Building History* (1961); or with the inns of particular towns, like Robert Dymond's 'The Old Inns and Taverns of Exeter' in the Devonshire Association's *Transactions* (xii, 1880). Apart from these and similar works, the historian will find the literature of the English inn for the most part a wretched farrago of romantic legends, facetious humour and irritating errors. There is no serious, systematic study of the *functions* of inns, of what exactly went on within them, and of why, in the days before railways and reform movements, they became the centres of so much of the social, political and economic life of the nation.

The present essay is no more than an attempt to indicate some of the very varied functions of the urban inn generally in the seventeenth and

eighteenth centuries, and in particular some of the salient features of
the innkeeping fraternity in a not untypical provincial borough during
this period, the Midland town of Northampton. It is hoped that this
essay may encourage local historians elsewhere to undertake similar
studies of inns and innkeepers in other provincial towns in more detail
than is possible here. In doing so other students will find certain parallels with Northampton, and no doubt many differences too: in short,
all the variety of human experience that makes the history of provincial
society so absorbing a study.

The golden age of the English inn may be said to have lasted from
the reign of Queen Elizabeth to that of Queen Victoria. Of course it
neither began nor ended during these years and the period of efflorescence varied a good deal in different parts of the country. There were
many extensive and important inns in medieval England, like the
George at Glastonbury and the Angel at Grantham. One of the largest
was the Chequers at Canterbury, built as a hostelry for pilgrims and
containing a dormitory with 100 beds.[2] It was later converted into nine
distinct premises, but it still survives, strung out along the length of
Mercery Lane. In Queen Victoria's reign, similarly, there is no precise
moment at which it is possible to say that the golden age of the English
inn has come to an end. There is no doubt, however, that many of the
historic inns of England rapidly declined in importance with the coming
of the railways and with the building of public halls, corn exchanges,
auction rooms, banks, town halls and county halls, which transferred
much of the traditional business of provincial inns to these and other
specialist buildings. By the middle of Queen Victoria's reign or there-
abouts it may be said that the age of the inn has given way to the age
of the hotel.

The hotel is a kind of building often of course much larger and more
elaborate than its predecessor, but essentially more limited in its functions. The origins of the word 'hotel' in England and its gradual spread
through the provinces are themselves interesting social phenomena
which need a few comments in passing. In its modern connotation the
word 'hotel' did not come into use until about 1770 and was still very
rare in 1800. The first hotel in England was built in Exeter in 1768
and was simply called 'The Hotel': it still survives, though altered in
1827, as the Royal Clarence Hotel. A few years later, by the summer
of 1774 or before, a hotel had also appeared in the rising watering-place
of Margate. The Margate Hotel was described in the *Kentish Gazette*
of the following year as the 'New Inn, Tavern, and Hotel' on the Parade:

the fact that it was described as an inn and tavern as well as a hotel shows that the new word was as yet scarcely naturalised.[3]

In the Midlands it would probably not have been understood at all at this date. The first hotel in Leicester did not appear until the year 1792, and was unsuccessful in establishing itself. Within a few years it had gone out of business, though happily its remarkably sophisticated assembly room, designed by the local architect John Johnson, still survives in Hotel Street. Even as late as 1884, when Leicester was a town of nearly 130,000 inhabitants, there were still only nine hotels in the whole borough out of more than 450 licensed establishments. The fact that in 1970 there were at least 111 establishments in Leicester describing themselves as 'hotels' is a nice comment on provincial attitudes in the twentieth century.[4]

(b) Distribution

How many inns, taverns and alehouses were there in fact in England in the sixteenth to eighteenth centuries – this golden age of the inn? There are no really reliable figures for the country as a whole, though with patience it is sometimes possible to reconstruct figures for particular towns or districts. The most complete survey is a census of inns drawn up in 1577 in connection with musters. This census is in the State Papers in the Public Record Office and lists more than 14,000 alehouses, 2,000 inns and 300 taverns. It covers only twenty-seven counties, but another document in the State Papers reckons that there were nearly 3,600 inns, alehouses and taverns in the remaining thirteen shires. The total of about 20,000 hostelries of all kinds in England must of course be regarded with a good deal of caution. The figures were collected locally and in consequence, like all statistics of the time, probably varied a good deal in their basis from place to place. It is hard to believe that there were only five inns in the whole of Nottinghamshire, yet more than 1,000 alehouses; still harder to accept that there were more than twice as many hostelries in this small Midland county (1,028) as in a large and populous shire like Essex (493).[5]

Nevertheless the figures in the census of 1577 are of great interest. Yorkshire, not surprisingly, comes easily at the top of the table with nearly 3,700 alehouses and 239 inns. The city of York itself, as an important legal and ecclesiastical capital and headquarters of the Council of the North, may well have contained more inns than any other provincial town at this date. As early as 1537 there were more than 1,000 beds in the city inns and stables for more than 1,700 horses. In 1596 the corporation licensed as many as 64 innholders and more than 100 tipplers in the city.[6] Also high in the county list was Middlesex, with 720 alehouses in 1577 and 132 inns. Rather more surprisingly, the two small inland shires of Hertfordshire and Buckinghamshire contained between them nearly as many inns as the whole of Yorkshire: 152 in Hertfordshire and 72 in Buckinghamshire. The fact that the former shire, though one of the smallest in England, contained within its borders more inns than any county but Yorkshire is indicative of its importance in the 'thoroughfare trade'. On many of the roads northwards out of London the first night's stage was in Hertfordshire. In the small town of St Albans alone there were at this date as many as 27 inns – one of the highest figures for any town in England at this time.

Two later censuses of inns, drawn up for military purposes in 1686 and 1756, may be found in the War Office Miscellanea in the Public Record Office (WO 30/48; WO 30/49). These are not precisely comparable with the Elizabethan list, for they do not give the number of inns but the number of beds and the extent of stabling available in each town and village. Nevertheless these and other sources indicate the remarkable expansion of innkeeping between Queen Elizabeth's reign and George III's. By the end of the seventeenth century in the county of Wiltshire alone nearly 200 towns and villages boasted at least one inn. There were nearly 100 beds in the inns of the little town of Devizes, 143 in the inns of Marlborough, 163 in those of Chippenham and 548 in Salisbury. Altogether these four Wiltshire towns alone could probably accommodate well over 1,000 guests and 2,000 horses at this date. In the town of Derby a local enumeration of about the same period (1693) records that no fewer than 120 of the 684 houses in the town were alehouses. This figure seems incredible and is certainly hard to accept; but in the town of Northampton, where the census of 1577 had listed only 17 inns, there were by George II's reign at least 62 inns and an undiscoverable number of alehouses. In Canterbury at about this period there were 98 inns; and in Loughborough during George III's reign – a town of fewer than 4,000 inhabitants about this period – there were 43 inns in the year 1770 and 50 in 1783.[7] The number of provincial inns and alehouses continued to increase, moreover, with the rapid growth of population during the following decades. In Northampton in 1845 there were 74 inns, 53 smaller public houses and nearly 40 beer-sellers. And in 1870 a directory of Kent listed nearly 4,000 inns and beerhouses in the county, or one to every 185 inhabitants.[8]

The growth of provincial hostelries between Queen Elizabeth's days and Queen Victoria's was particularly striking in 'thoroughfare towns', that is, those situated on the principal roads of England. As more roads became turnpiked and as traffic in goods and people increased, these towns were placed at an advantage over those on minor routes and gradually absorbed a good deal of their trade. Hanoverian travellers like Dr Pococke, absentee bishop of an Irish see whose *Travels* around the year 1750 were published by the Camden Society in 1888–9, frequently remarked upon the importance of the inn trade in thoroughfare towns. Tamworth in Staffordshire, said Pococke, is 'a pretty large town, with a good market, and abounds in inns'. At Blandford in Dorset, on the 'great thoroughfare to the West', there were 'many good inns and shops in the town'. Llandilo in Carmarthenshire was a little town but 'as it is the high road from many parts to Brecknock, Hereford, and many great towns on the Severn, there are good inns in it'. Very similar remarks were made by Pococke about places like Warwick, Gloucester, Cardiff, Machynlleth, Lambourne, Fairford and Kington.[9]

The growth of inns in thoroughfare towns was particularly evident on routes like the Great North Road and the roads to Dover, Bath, Chester, Exeter and Manchester. Their importance in the case of Burford, on the Gloucester road, is mentioned by Mr Laithwaite in the previous essay. Until the second quarter of the eighteenth century (on some roads the third or last quarter) the usual 'stage' many coaches could accomplish daily was about 25–35 miles, so that the chief coaching centres often tended to be spaced out about this distance apart.[10] There was often a smaller intermediate town half-way between them, partly for the midday stop and a change of horses, and partly for the sake of the slower stage-wagons and carriers' carts which often travelled no more than about half the daily distance of the passenger coaches. On the Manchester road the chief coaching centres were normally Dunstable, Northampton, Leicester, Derby, and Ashbourne or Buxton, all of them between 25 and 35 miles apart; while intermediate stops were made in such towns as Loughborough and Market Harborough.[11] All these towns had of course been established market centres for several centuries before the age of the stage-coach; but stage travel tended increasingly to concentrate traffic in these towns and draw it away from places less conveniently situated.

On the Great North Road some of the most impressive inns in England were to be found in towns like Stamford, Grantham and Newark, and even in small coaching centres like Wansford and Stilton. A number of these great inns, like the Haycock at Wansford, the George at Stamford and the Angel at Grantham, still survive. On the Chester road both Towcester and Stony Stratford depended heavily on their inn traffic during the eighteenth century: there are still eleven hostelries strung out along the High Street of the latter town. A few miles north of Towcester, where the same road is crossed by the prehistoric droveway called Banbury Lane, the village of Foster's Booth owed its very existence in the seventeenth and eighteenth centuries to innkeeping. In origin it was no more than a 'forester's booth' in the wooded country bordering Buckinghamshire and Northamptonshire, and it never developed into an independent parish. It sprang into prominence during the sixteenth and seventeenth centuries, at the boundary of Pattishall and Cold Higham parishes, very much as Stony Stratford had originated, four centuries earlier, at the junction of Calverton and Wolverton further down the same road. By Queen Anne's reign Foster's Booth had become 'a fair street of inns', according to the Northamptonshire historian John Morton. At this time there were as many as twelve or thirteen hostelries along either side of Watling Street, and the place continued to exist by its road traffic until it was by-passed by the railway early in Queen Victoria's reign. After the railway Foster's Booth rapidly declined in importance, and nowadays only two of the original inns, the George (built in 1637) and the Red Lion, survive to commemorate its heyday.[12]

On the Dover road the most remarkable example of an innkeeping town, though few people would now suspect it, was Sittingbourne. Like most of the settlements along the Kentish section of Watling Street, apart from Rochester and Canterbury, Sittingbourne was a late one. It is not mentioned in Domesday, and the first documentary reference to it in J. K. Wallenberg's *Place-Names of Kent* relates to the year 1200. In all probability it originated as a street-migration from the much older settlement of Milton Regis, and its early fortunes no doubt owed something to its position as a halting-place for Canterbury pilgrims. At the beginning of Queen Elizabeth's reign it was still little more than a village, however, with a mere 88 houses and a population of perhaps 400 souls. Then in 1566 it acquired the right to hold a market, and in 1599 the queen actually granted it a charter of incorporation with the privileges of electing a mayor and jurats and of returning two members to Parliament. Strangely enough this charter never appears to have been implemented, no doubt because of the insignificance of the new town. During the following two centuries, however, Sittingbourne rapidly developed as one of the most important coaching centres in the south-eastern counties, owing to its convenient position midway between Dover and London. Its fortunes were also stimulated, no doubt, by the fact that it became the favourite resting-place of George I and George II on their way to Hanover.[13]

Chief among the numerous coaching inns of Sittingbourne in the Hanoverian era were the Red Lion, the Bull, the George and the Rose. The Red Lion was a medieval establishment, once visited by Henry V on his return from France, and it remained the principal hostelry of the town until it was eclipsed in the eighteenth century by the Rose. The origin of the Rose Inn at Sittingbourne is an interesting one. It had been built as a rather grand private house in the town in the year 1708, by one Robert Jeffs, and called Rose Place. Its life as a private dwelling, however, was brief. Within a few years it had been converted into an inn and it rapidly became celebrated for its lavish hospitality. In the 1770s Edward Hasted remarked that the 'principal support of [Sittingbourne] has always been from the inns and houses of refreshment in it for travellers', and 'the principal inn now in it, called the Rose, is perhaps the most superb of any throughout the kingdom, and the entertainment afforded in it equally so . . .'. Perhaps the supreme moment in the history of the Rose came in 1825 when the future Queen Victoria and her mother stayed there, and it was renamed the Royal Victoria Hotel. By that date Sittingbourne was a small but busy market town of about 2,000 inhabitants. Within a generation, however, its principal industry, the coaching trade, had come to a sudden end with the building of the railway. Most of the grand old inns of the town were either split up into shops and tenements, or converted to other uses. Only one, the Bull Hotel, still retains its original function.[14] Yet, to quote *The Buildings of England* for Kent, 'in spite of the mutilation of nearly every house by modern shopfronts, one can still sense the prosperity of the Georgian town'.

(c) Siting

The precise topographical situation of an inn was often an important factor in its fortunes. One of the commonest sites was in the market place, a situation which enabled many hostelries during the seventeenth century to attract urban commerce to themselves, so that in effect they became covered or private market places, often of a rather specialised kind. There were at least six inns round the market place of Hanoverian Northampton, including one of the largest in the town, the Peacock, whose frontage extended for eleven bays along the eastern side of the square, and whose yard extended for more than 200 ft behind the inn.

There were seven inns round the market place of Jacobean Shaftesbury in Dorset: the Raven, the Lamb, the George, the Bush, the New Inn, the Lion and the Star.[15] In Warwick, Newark, Leicester and many other towns something of the same concentration can be traced.

The market place was not always an ideal site for a large inn, however, once the coaching era had begun. With the growth of the coaching and carrying trades in the seventeenth and eighteenth centuries the chief requirement was a long site with room to build extra chambers and warehouses, and a back entrance so that wagons and coaches could enter the yard and leave it without turning or backing – always an awkward problem for a horse-drawn vehicle. The topography of a town like Stony Stratford, with back lanes running parallel to the High Street on either side, was ideally suited to this requirement. Several of the Stratford inns have or had very long yards, with back entrances: that of the White Horse extended for 260 ft from the High Street to the Market Place, and that of the Cock for nearly 400 ft to Vicarage Lane. In Exeter three of the major inns in the High Street – the Green Dragon, the Half Moon and the New Inn – had entrances also in Catherine Street.[16] In Grantham the stable yard of the Angel runs back for some hundreds of feet from the High Street to Swinegate. In Maidstone the yard of the Star extends for more than 400 ft from the High Street to its back entrance in Earl Street.

In some towns, for a variety of reasons, groups of hostelries also came to be established, particularly from Queen Elizabeth's reign onwards, outside the old town centre, in extra-mural suburbs. Sometimes, where urban streets were narrow and tortuous, as in Leicester and Canterbury, this development enabled coaches to avoid passing through the centre of the town. In other places, as in the extra-mural suburbs of Cotton End and St James's End outside Northampton, these inns developed in connection with the droving trade; for innkeepers on the edge of a town were able to provide meadow grounds where drovers might pasture their sheep and cattle overnight before selling them next day to the stock-dealers. In many cases these suburbs had probably originated in the medieval period. It is interesting to note that in several cases – for example at Leicester, Northampton, Godstone and Billesdon – they were associated with an inn called the White Hart, a name that often derives its origin from the medieval White Hart society.

Though often medieval in origin, however, inn-suburbs of this kind developed principally with the growth of carrying and coaching during the seventeenth and eighteenth centuries. Speenhamland in Berkshire seems to have originated in this way, as an extra-mural suburb of Newbury linking the town with the Bath road. As a chapelry of the independent Speen parish, Speenhamland was outside the jurisdiction of the borough of Newbury, and as late as 1906 it was still described as 'a kind of suburb of inns and posting houses'. In Essex a striking example of the same kind of phenomenon was Moulsham, a suburb immediately outside Chelmsford. Like Speenhamland, Moulsham never became a parish in its own right and it was not made a separate chapelry until 1838. It seems to have come into existence as a characteristic commonland settlement, composed of squatters' cottages and hedge-alehouses, and it developed rapidly with the growth of Chelmsford itself as a coaching centre and as the county town of Essex during the seventeenth century. By 1628 there were as many as 7 inns and 22 alehouses in Moulsham. Like extra-mural hostelries elsewhere, these were a frequent source of trouble to the local constables and J.P.s and ultimately all but five of them were declared 'superfluous'. According to the Stuart justices, the Moulsham inns and alehouses had encouraged gaming, dicing, dancing and brawling, and were veritable nests of pickpockets and highwaymen. They were also accused of increasing the problems of local poor-relief because they offered pawn facilities to poor people who then became a charge upon the parish. Obviously the justices' evidence was tendentiously expressed; but it does point up the more shady and dubious characteristics of some of these extra-mural alehouse settlements.[17]

Another example of an innkeeping suburb very similar to Moulsham developed at Leicester, in the area known as the Bishop's Fee, outside the medieval walls of the borough, along Gallowtreegate and Humberstonegate. The jurisdiction over this area had long been a matter of dispute between the corporation and the bishop of Lincoln (and his successors) and was not finally settled until the nineteenth century. It was doubtless for this reason that part of the area came to be called No Man's Land. Very much as the unappropriated commonland outside Chelmsford had facilitated the development of Moulsham, so the disputed jurisdiction in the Bishop's Fee facilitated the growth of a cluster of suburban inns in No Man's Land outside Leicester. In this case, however, the reasons for the development were rather more complex than at Moulsham. Most of the earliest inns of Leicester had in fact been situated well within the walls, particularly along Highcross Street, the original route from London by way of Northampton and Welford. With the growth of the coaching and carrying trades in the seventeenth century this route proved impracticable for wheeled traffic owing to the narrowness of the town gates. Instead more and more traffic through Leicester came to use the alternative London road by way of Market Harborough and Gallowtreegate, which passed immediately outside the walls. The old inns in Highcross Street gradually declined as a consequence, while the new extra-mural ones in Gallowtreegate, Humberstonegate and Granby Street rose in importance until the celebrated Three Crowns and Three Cranes became two of the largest coaching inns in the Midlands. Eventually, for these and other reasons, the commercial heart of Leicester itself gradually moved outside the walls, and the removal of the town gates in 1774 was unable to halt this development. Thereafter Highcross Street subsided (until recent years) into a comparatively quiet backwater, whilst the extramural Gallowtreegate has remained ever since the principal trading street of the borough. In the early seventeenth century, before this move had taken place, the numerous inns and alehouses in the Bishop's Fee at Leicester were a frequent source of trouble to the corporation, very much as those at Moulsham were to the justices of Essex. They were accused of encouraging illicit trading, immorality, nonconformity and political subversion.[18]

One final point regarding extra-mural or extra-parochial inns is worth noting. There is some reason to think that they played a part in the growth of illegitimacy in the early nineteenth century. Many of the illegitimate births recorded in the parish registers of Ringwood and Fordingbridge in Hampshire are said to have been associated with two extra-parochial inns, the Fighting Cocks at Godshill and the inn at Picket Post outside Ringwood.[19] It would be interesting to know whether this association occurred in other towns.

(d) Scale and status

In size and status the inns of Stuart and Hanoverian England must not be thought of as mere village pubs. Many of them were no larger than this, of course; but at the top of the hierarchy, in the great coaching towns particularly, a number of hostelries were remarkable for their scale and splendour. This is evident both from surviving buildings and from documentary sources such as probate inventories and newspaper advertisements. The frontage of the Bath Arms at Warminster, for example, extends to eight bays of building; that of the Crown at Salisbury and the George and Dragon at Marlow to nine bays. The Three Tuns at Thirsk, originally built as a manor house, also extends to nine bays; the Peacock at Northampton (until its destruction in 1958) to eleven bays; and the Lansdowne Arms at Calne (Wilts.) to thirteen. In the seventeenth century the Rose and Crown at Northampton extended to thirteen bays in width and three storeys in height. The Castle Inn at Marlborough, originally built as a private house for the duke of Somerset and now forming part of the College, is a splendid brick mansion fifteen bays in width. One of the largest of provincial inns was probably the George at Sittingbourne, which at its fullest extent appears to have stretched for no fewer than twenty-one bays along the south side of the High Street. Probably as large as the George at Sittingbourne was the Three Crowns at Leicester. This building no longer survives – it was replaced by the National Provincial Bank building in 1870 – but its façade is said to have been three storeys high and to have contained fifty windows. In Northampton the three greatest inns of the town – the George, the Red Lion and the Peacock – all seem to have contained about forty rooms. The most celebrated of the three, the George, was described by Defoe in his *Tour* as 'more like a palace than an inn', and is said to have cost more than £2,000 to rebuild in 1675, or perhaps something like £70,000 in modern terms. No wonder Thomas Baskerville, visiting Northampton about this time, remarked that its leading inns were 'such gallant and stately structures the like is scarcely elsewhere to be seen'.[20]

The extent of the stabling in many English inns affords a further indication of their scale at this time. Many of them in the eighteenth century could accommodate 40 or 50 horses and some a good many more. The Clinton Arms at Newark is said to have had stabling for 90 horses in 1800. The Angel at Stilton, in the days of the notable Miss Worthington (the famous eighteenth-century innkeeper who first introduced Stilton cheese to the world), accommodated more than 300 horses for coaching and posting. Some of the London coaching inns were still larger. One of the most famous, the Bull and Mouth, is said to have had underground stabling for no fewer than 400 horses. The inns on Hounslow Heath, the first stage out of London on the Great West Road, were capable of accommodating between them as many as 2,500 horses at this period.[21]

In the case of Northampton, figures have survived in advertisements in the local newspaper, the *Northampton Mercury*, for the stable accommodation of eight of the 62 Hanoverian inns in the town. These range from standings for 20 horses in the smallest of the eight to standings for 150 in the largest, the Saracen's Head in Abingdon Street, which was the town's posting-house. The total number of horses that could be accommodated in these eight inns amounted to more than 450. None of the three chief hostelries in the town – the George, the Peacock and the Red Lion – is included in these figures; but if the sample is otherwise typical, it is possible that about 3,500 horses could be stabled in the inns of Northampton by the beginning of George II's reign. In addition to the facilities offered by inns, many alehouses and commercial premises in the town had converted their backyards into stable accommodation by this date. A local glazier, for instance, had erected standings for 18 horses behind his premises, and a baker for as many as 40.[22] Altogether it is probable that there was stabling for between 4,000 and 5,000 horses in Hanoverian Northampton. As these figures will suggest, it is quite a delusion to imagine that traffic problems are an essentially modern phenomenon. They were very acute indeed in towns like Northampton at this date. It was with a view to alleviating them that the western arm of All Saints' church was demolished and several of the main streets were widened and straightened after the fire of 1675, which destroyed four-fifths of the town.

Some further idea of the scale of activities in which the landlord of an important inn might be called upon to engage may be gathered from the accounts of feasts and banquets occasionally to be found in eighteenth-century newspapers. When Frederick Montagu, on his election in 1759 as M.P. for Northampton, gave the town 'a present of a new lock' on the river Nene, 119 people sat down to a great banquet in his honour at the George Inn. At Leicester in 1770, after a concert at the Assembly Rooms, as many as 200 gentlemen adjourned to dine at the White Hart Inn. On the occasion of the hundredth anniversary in Leicester of William III's landing in England, as many as 627 people are said to have sat down to the Revolution Club's dinner in the Lion and Lamb and two other inns in the town. Even more remarkable were the great Venison Meetings of the Leicester Constitutional Society. These were held at the two principal Whig inns, the Three Cranes and the Three Crowns, and on one occasion it is said that 900 people sat down to the Venison Feast at these hostelries.[23]

Probably the most lavish and ambitious celebration ever organised by a provincial innkeeper in the eighteenth century took place in connection with the Shakespeare Jubilee at Stratford upon Avon in 1768. John Payton, the innkeeper of the Red Lion, was entrusted with supervising the catering for this event, and for this purpose he is said to have employed 300 waiters and ordered 300 dozen plates, 300 dozen knives and forks, 100 dozen spoons, 50 dozen stewpans and kettles, and ten pipes of wine, or probably more than 1,000 gallons.[24] The fact that these arrangements were organised by the innkeeper of a town of fewer than 3,000 inhabitants may give the student of provincial society in the eighteenth century pause for thought.

The position of landlord in one of the greater trading inns of Hanoverian England was in fact one that required a degree of flair and an organising ability of no mean order. It is therefore not surprising that in inland entrepôts like Northampton the principal innkeepers often became aldermen and mayors and were among the richest men in the town. This is evident from some of their wills and probate inventories. One of the richest Northampton innkeepers was probably James Bordrigge of the Red Lion. When he died in the year 1743, the personal property listed in his probate inventory was valued at more than £1,045 and the goods and furniture in the inn itself at more than £600, or perhaps something like £20,000 in modern values.

With the growth in scale of inns in this era the social status as well as the wealth of the leading innkeepers was enhanced. James Bordrigge was not untypical of his class in stemming from a family of minor gentry, in his case probably originating from Yorkshire. Other inn-keeping dynasties, like the Lyons and Peaches in Northampton, either originated as sons of wealthy local tradesmen or married into a wealthy urban dynasty, and successfully pushed their way up into the lower levels of the urban gentry. The same phenomenon may be observed in many provincial towns, sometimes even in quite small ones. When Thomas Baskerville, a Berkshire squire, visited Daventry in 1673, he remarked that 'we lay at the Sign of the Swan, near the church, Mrs Bostock, a widow, a proper gentlewoman, the landlady of it . . . and formerly the wife of a handsome tall gentleman of that name . . .'. When Daniel Defoe visited Doncaster in the early eighteenth century he found that his 'landlord at the Post House was mayor of the town as well as postmaster, that he kept a pack of hounds, was company for the best gentlemen in the town or in the neighbourhood, and lived as great as any gentlemen ordinarily did'. When Fanny Burney, the diarist, visited the Bear Inn at Devizes with Mrs Thrale she noted that the landlord's wife, Mrs Lawrence, was a ladylike woman, that her two handsome daughters were accomplished pianists, and that the house itself was full of books, paintings, drawings and music. It was not altogether inappropriate that such a household should give birth to the Regency portrait painter, Sir Thomas Lawrence – the celebrated brother of the two pianists.[25] Some of the leading innkeepers of the eighteenth century were in fact men of considerable substance and sophistication as well as force of character.

II. THE FUNCTIONS OF URBAN INNS

(a) Trading functions

From Queen Elizabeth's reign onwards the inns of England developed many new functions in society, so that by the eighteenth century they had come to perform a whole range of services in addition to the basic one of providing lodging and refreshment. One of the most important of these new functions was their development as trading centres. With the growth of inland trade from the 1570s onwards, with the development of wholesale commerce and dealing by sample, and especially with the rapidly growing numbers of travelling factors and merchants, a great deal of market activity migrated during this period from the open market place to the provincial inn. In some branches of commerce, particularly in the wool and cloth trades, this activity in some areas probably began a good deal earlier than 1570. In 1389 the York corporation forbade 'foreign' poulterers to sell their goods in the inns of the city, and in 1492 'foreign' cloth was being sold in York inns. Nevertheless it was chiefly from Queen Elizabeth's reign onwards, so far as most products were concerned, that trading inns became particularly widespread.[26] The advertisement pages in many early provincial newspapers show that during the eighteenth century it was a very common practice.

By this time, for example, much of the hop trade had come to be centred in inns. Hop factors travelled extensively, purchasing in all the principal hop-growing regions – Kent, Sussex, Surrey, Hampshire and Worcestershire – and selling to the public through the inns they frequented. In Northampton the hop trade was associated in the eighteenth century with the Woolpack Inn. In October 1751 a hop merchant from Market Harborough announced in the *Northampton Mercury* that he had 'bought a large quantity of Kentish hops of the right Canterbury growth [reputedly the best], at the lowest market that has been this season, and proposes to be at the Woolpack Inn in Bridge Street, Northampton, for several market days, where he will sell . . . as cheap as in London and in any quantity above 20 lbs. weight', for ready money or three or six months' credit.[27]

Much of the trade in agricultural seed was also centred in inns at this time. By the end of the seventeenth century sales of wheat, barley, potato and turnip seed were taking place in the courtyard of the Cock Inn at Stony Stratford. In 1758 one of the numerous nurserymen of Northampton was selling his seed not only in local inns but in those of Towcester, Daventry and Stony Stratford. In Northampton itself, which was the principal centre for the distribution of seed in this part of the Midlands, the Hind Inn in the Market Square and the Woolpack became marts for turnip seed, the Old Goat in Gold Street for clover seed, and the Chequer in the Market Square for clover, trefoil and grass seed.[28] Products like these may seem trivial in themselves, but they played a decisive part in the agricultural developments of the time.

Much of the trade in corn and malt was also commonly centred in inns in the seventeenth and eighteenth centuries. When the river Soar was made navigable to Loughborough in the eighteenth century, the town rapidly developed as the chief centre of the grain and malt trades in Leicestershire – trades which always followed in the wake of navigational improvements – and by 1770 much of this commerce was taking place in Loughborough inns. An angry contemporary described the development as due to the 'artful management and iniquitous combinations of avaricious farmers'. More probably it was chiefly due to the greater convenience of dealing in an inn than in a windy market place, and to the provision of corn-chambers by the innkeepers. Certainly the bakers and traders of Leicester who frequented Loughborough for their supplies of corn and malt must have found it more convenient than purchasing in the traditional way, and it had the additional advantage of enabling them to avoid payment of market tolls.[29]

The provision of corn-chambers was a service frequently offered by innkeepers at this period. In early nineteenth-century Preston, the principal market of north and central Lancashire, great quantities of grain are said to have been stored in the corn-houses attached to local inns, particularly the Castle, the Boar's Head, the King's Head, the White Horse and the George. In Hanoverian Northampton there were corn-chambers attached to several of the inns, such as the Fleece in Bridge Street and the Chequer in the Market Square. In Croydon there were corn-chambers at several inns in the seventeenth century, and in the early nineteenth century local farmers brought their corn into town on other days than market days, stored it in rooms hired for the purpose in the inns round the market, and then sold it to their customers, either in or outside the market, by samples carried in their pockets.[30]

The cloth trade was another branch of inland commerce associated with provincial inns. At Exeter the great seventeenth-century cloth fair was held at the New Inn, and that at Norton St Philip at the George. In London the lace markets were held at the George in Aldersgate and the Bull and Mouth in St Martin's by Aldersgate. At Halifax a French traveller in 1788 remarked that on market day he saw cloth displayed for sale not only in the streets and squares but in every inn in the town, so that 'the whole town on Saturdays becomes one huge white cloth hall'. In Leicester much of the cloth trade at this date was centred in the Old White Hart Inn in Humberstonegate. According to an advertisement in the *Northampton Mercury* in 1758, this inn was 'much frequented by Yorkshire, Manchester, and West Country gentlemen and traders . . . particularly dealers in the woollen manufactory'. The new landlord announced that 'as I have served an apprenticeship in a branch of the wool trade, and been a sorter of wool some years, I shall be willing to do any business in that way by commission. All commands of this kind will be most carefully and faithfully executed.' [31] This is a nice example of how the landlord of an urban inn might himself foster the trade with which his house had come to be associated.

In the case of a cloth-merchants' inn at Putloe in Gloucestershire, a tract of 1675 affords an interesting account of how the connection with the cloth trade had come about. A soldier from Cromwell's army had married a Scottish wife while stationed in Scotland during the Interregnum, and on his return to England after the Restoration he took a small house in Putloe 'and therein sold drink and entertained passengers and travellers that had occasion to lie there as a little inn; and particularly, his wife being a Scot as aforesaid, divers persons of that nation who usually travel from thence into England with Scotch cloth and other commodities resorted thither, and chose rather to lodge there than elsewhere for her sake, as being their countrywoman'. Personal connections of this kind often determined the channels of trade at inns in the seventeenth and eighteenth centuries. In this instance the inn at Putloe seems to have become a centre for the gathering of Scottish cloth merchants in Gloucestershire. [32]

In Northampton, owing to the survival of an unbroken run of the *Northampton Mercury* from its foundation in 1720, there is a good deal of information about these trading inns. When an inn came up for sale or to let, it was customary to insert an advertisement in the *Mercury*, and these often afford details of the speciality for which the inn was noted. In other cases the travelling factors themselves inserted an announcement informing the public when they would be in Northampton and which inn they would frequent. From this information it is clear, for example, that by George II's reign the Dolphin Inn had become a cheese mart, attended by dealers in Cheshire and Warwickshire cheese and no doubt other varieties. The principal trade in Northampton at this period was the horse trade – in Defoe's phrase it was 'the centre of all the horse-markets and horse-fairs in England' – and this too, for obvious reasons, came to be associated with local inns. Most of the horse-dealers' inns in Northampton were situated either in Bridge Street (the London road) or in Marefair and the Horsemarket. One of these, the Blue Boar, was in fact run by a 'horse-courser' during Charles II's reign. Probably the most important horse-dealers' inn in the town was the King's Head, which had standings for 60 or 70 horses and was described in 1751 as 'the most commodious house for the reception of [horse] dealers, etc., at any time'.[33] The other staple industries in the town were connected with the leather trades, particularly shoemaking, and until 1723 the Star Inn in Abington Street was the centre of the Northampton leather market. In that year the inn was sold and, after an abortive attempt to move it to the Talbot, the shoemakers and curriers, most of whom were at that time small craftsmen, endeavoured to get the market moved back again to its traditional site in the Market Square. But the tanners and leather-dealers, who were among the wealthier section of the community, evidently refused to agree, and on 11 May 1724 at a general meeting 'of all the dealers in leather it was unanimously agreed that the fairs and markets [for leather] be for the time to come kept at the Peacock Inn in Northampton, where all tanners are desired to repair and meet their chapmen'.[34]

By this date several inns in Northampton were also providing accommodation for travelling surgeons and oculists, for auctions of house property and market gardens, and for sales of jewellery, silverware, glass, books, pictures, furniture, carpets, upholsteryware, linen and drapery goods. It was chiefly the larger inns, like the Peacock, the Red Lion, the Unicorn and the Saracen's Head, that afforded these facilities.[35] At the Unicorn in Bridge Street in 1758 a typical drapery sale included muslins, men's neck-clothes, pelong satins, flowered silks for waistcoats, cotton and thread stockings, printed and bordered silks, soo-soo handkerchiefs, scarlet cloaks, women's plain, flowered, leghorn and chip (straw) hats, and 'clear, quarter, checked, striped, spotted, flowered and mignonetted lawns'. Another centre for the visits of travelling mercers was the Toll House Inn in St James's End, where, for a sale in 1737, an advertisement of two merchants lists more than forty different varieties of cloth, from rich brocades to Dutch velvets and Italian mantuas. The Northampton furniture sales were held on market days, by Jasper Haworth Quenby, a local 'appraiser' or valuer, at his sale-room at the Angel and Star in the Drapery. These sales consisted of a great variety of furniture, including beds, curtains, tables, chairs, mirrors, bureaux and chests of drawers.[36]

Finally, there were the numerous drovers' and carriers' inns of Northampton. For obvious reasons many of the former were situated on the edge of the town, either in Cotton End, where the London road crossed the river Nene, or in St James's End, where the routes from Wales and the west entered the town. On both routes the water-meadows by the river afforded the pasturage necessary for the drovers' flocks and herds. A hostelry like the Bull's Head in St James's End made a point of providing ample grass 'for all sorts of cattle in several pasture grounds'.[37] Many of the carriers' inns were to be found, also for obvious reasons, either in Bridge Street and the South Quarter (the London road) or else in Sheep Street, the route to Leicester and the north. In a typical advertisement of 1749 the Fleece in Bridge Street was described as 'a very good, commodious, and accustomed carriers' inn, with good granaries, a large yard, and convenient stabling . . .' The granaries, of course, were for the use of corn-carriers, for the Fleece was one of the centres of the grain trade of the town. Later in the same year a neighbouring inn to the Fleece, the Lion and Lamb, was advertising as 'an old-accustomed carriers' inn, with convenient stabling, brewhouse, . . . and rickyard'. The rickyard with its stacks was an important adjunct to an inn of this kind, for when a train of carriers' wagons arrived of an evening, after a tiring day's journey, there might well be thirty or forty horses to feed. The wagons were normally drawn by up to six or eight horses, and the carriers usually travelled together in trains of half a dozen or more for mutual protection on the road. In 1739, for example, six Northampton wagons were travelling together with three others on the London road when they were stopped by highwaymen near St Albans and robbed of £40.[38]

In an inland entrepôt like Northampton the carrying trade was one of great importance to the community. For provincial towns generally it is very difficult to track down the origin of this carrying trade. It certainly goes back before the early seventeenth century, when it is clear from John Taylor's *Carriers' Cosmography* (1637) that London at least was linked by carrier's wagon with virtually every substantial town in the kingdom. It is not until the days of country newspapers, however, that it is possible to obtain much idea of the network of long-distance carriers' routes around provincial towns. By the 1750s, when detailed information first becomes available for Northampton, the pattern was so intricate and extensive that it was obviously no innovation but must have been gradually built up over a long period, no doubt during the preceding century and more. An advertisement inserted in the *Mercury* by the landlord of one of the carriers' inns in 1754 – William Dodd of the Bull's Head in Sheep Street – makes it clear that the town was then linked by carriers' wagon with Cambridge, St Neots, Wellingborough, Oxford, Daventry, Coventry, Birmingham, Warwick, Nottingham, Derby, Lancaster, Kendal, Carlisle, Newcastle and Durham, 'or any part of those counties'. There were also indirect services, by way of Cambridge, to Newmarket, Bury St Edmunds, Yarmouth, Norwich 'or any part of that side of the country'. If we had similar advertisements for other carriers' inns in the town the network of routes would of course be a good deal more extensive.[39]

One important concomitant of the growth of trading activities at provincial inns was that, before country banking developed towards the end of the eighteenth century, innkeepers themselves sometimes acted in a rudimentary banking capacity. The problem of conveying money safely about the countryside was a very real one. Sometimes it was conveyed by drovers, carriers and travelling factors, and it was partly no doubt to protect themselves when carrying money that these travellers usually journeyed in groups rather than alone. Sometimes, however, it seems that travelling traders preferred to deposit their money with an innkeeper rather than face the risk of attack by highwaymen. In this case the factor and innkeeper entered into bipartite bonds with each other, or some similar sort of agreement, and when the factor returned to the same inn for further trading activities during the following year he would utilise his credit with the innkeeper for transactions in the town. This kind of arrangement was doubtless an important reason for the growing association of certain types of trade with certain inns during the seventeenth and eighteenth centuries. As these specialist factors returned to the same inn year by year and there met others like themselves from different parts of the kingdom, they developed insensibly into a distinct and self-conscious community in their own right. The innkeeper played an important role in bringing them together, in imparting local commercial information to them, and in opening up the channels of trade.[40]

(b) Administrative and political functions

Quite a different function performed by the urban inn was its development from Queen Elizabeth's reign onwards as the principal centre of local administration, county business and provincial politics. The place of the inn in parliamentary elections in the days before the Reform Bill is too well known to call for comment here.[41] But elections were merely the occasional highlights in the day-to-day political life of the shires. What is not so well realised, though in a sense it was more significant, was the use of inns as the regular meeting-places of political clubs and the centres of country administration. In part this development was due to the rapid expansion in the duties and activities of country justices; in part to the growing political self-consciousness of the country gentry; and in part to the development of the armigerous class in each shire, through increasing wealth and frequent intermarriage, into a single great 'county cousinage', or 'county commonwealth' in Namier's memorable phrase. The centuries from the sixteenth to the nineteenth were, for good and ill, the great age of county society, and in a very real sense this society was centred not only in the manor houses of the gentry (though the manor house was its chief centre, of course) but in a group of great inns in each of the forty or so county towns of England. It is rather surprising, in a sense, that the 'county inns' of England have never been seriously studied by historians from the political viewpoint. They were the centres of much of the social and political development of this country from the early seventeenth century to the Napoleonic wars.

Until the building of county halls in the nineteenth century it was inevitable that a good deal of county business should be transacted in inns: they were usually the only places where it was possible for considerable numbers of people to congregate on secular matters. True, there are some fine examples of late seventeenth- and eighteenth-century 'county halls' still surviving in England, for example at Warwick, Aylesbury, Derby and Northampton. But these county halls were generally assize courts rather than administrative centres. By the early seventeenth century, however, one finds that in many county towns one or two leading inns have become the recognised meeting-places of the justices and deputy lieutenants upon county business. At Chelmsford, for example, the justices' inn in the seventeenth century was the Black Boy. At Nottingham the principal meeting-place of the county aristocracy until well into the nineteenth century was the Blackamoore's

Head, owned by the duke of Newcastle, and the largest inn in the town. At Maidstone it was the Star Inn in the High Street – still the principal hotel in the town – where the great county room called the Justice Chamber had come into existence before 1640. Whenever the Kentish assizes were held, this room became a kind of 'parliament chamber' for the shire, and it was there that the Kentish petition of 1642 which sparked off the Civil War was organised. At Exeter the great inn of the county community, from Queen Elizabeth's reign until the 1780s, was the New London Inn. There too the meetings of the gentry on the business of the shire were held in the County Chamber, and when this room was redecorated after the Restoration, the arms of the leading families of Devon were incorporated in the new plasterwork.[42]

In Northampton very much the same function in the mid-seventeenth century was fulfilled by the Swan Inn in the Drapery. It was from here that the Northamptonshire petition of 1642 was launched, approving the Grand Remonstrance and attacking the 'malignant party' and the 'popish lords and bishops' in Parliament. Throughout the later seventeenth century until about 1690 the Swan Inn remained the principal stronghold of the powerful Whig party in Northamptonshire. Here the London newsletters was regularly received and discussed, and every Saturday in the early 1680s up to fifty or so Whig leaders, 'under pretence of dining together', held their 'meetings, clubs and cabals' for the 'alteration of the succession to the crown'.[43] This, at least, was how the Tory gentry represented the facts, adding that Friend's Coffee House was another forum of the local Whig cabal. The Tories themselves appear to have organised a rival political club, meeting probably at the Goat Inn in Gold Street. Both inns and coffee-houses played a prominent part in the political troubles of the time, chiefly because they were places where the London newspapers and letters were received and discussed. In 1683 the Grand Jury of Northamptonshire had presented all 'unlicensed coffee-houses or places where false and seditious news is invented and spread', and demanded stricter regulation of inns and alehouses because of their 'great temptation in spreading seditious news'.[44]

By the end of the seventeenth century the Goat and the Swan had lost ground in Northampton as the principal meeting-places of the country gentry, and had been succeeded by the George, the Red Lion, the Peacock, or occasionally one of the coffee-houses of the town. The county meetings of the gentry at assize time or on militia business, for example, were normally held at one of these three inns. The great meeting of the gentry under the earl of Halifax in 1745, galvanising the county to defend itself against the Young Pretender, was held not at the Swan but at the George. The Goat Inn appears to have remained a centre of Jacobite activity, however, and certainly it was still running its long-established news-room. These news-rooms at provincial inns played an important role at this time in the dissemination of political news, the growth of political clubs and the development of party consciousness. When Sloswick Carr, the landlord of the Red Lion, opened a coffee-room and news-room at his inn in 1748, he specifically announced that it was established there 'at the desire and by the encouragement of the gentlemen of the town of Northampton and parts adjacent . . .'.[45] It is not difficult to envisage how these news-rooms led to debates and discussions and to the formation of local political clubs.

At Leicester, as in Northampton, there was a succession of different 'county inns' from the sixteenth century to the nineteenth. In this case each change reflected the gradual movement in the topographical centre of the town as well as a change in the scale of county requirements. In the sixteenth century the gentry appear to have been content to meet generally in the Talbot or the Blue Boar in Highcross Street. These were both very ancient inns, but comparatively modest in scale, and as Highcross Street gradually ceased to be the principal thoroughfare of the town during the seventeenth century they declined in status and the gentry began to meet instead at the Angel or the White Lion in Cheapside. In the eighteenth century a further move took place, when these inns were in their turn eclipsed by the palatial Three Cranes and Three Crowns, both of which were situated in Gallowtreegate, the principal thoroughfare from the north and from London. These two latter inns were also centres of political organisation in the county, particularly of course during parliamentary elections.[46]

As well as the more formal business of the county, important business meetings of all kinds were commonly held in inns. In Northampton they usually took place in either the George or the Peacock. In 1743, for instance, the gentry and clergy of the town and county were meeting at the George to organise the foundation of the new County Infirmary; the Annual General Meeting and Infirmary Feast continued to be held either there or at the Peacock or Red Lion in subsequent years. In the 1740s to 1760s the George was also the scene of numerous meetings for extending the navigation of the river Nene, first to Oundle, then to Thrapston, and eventually to Northampton itself. These and other inns, such as the Angel and the Bull, were utilised for meetings of the Puritan *classis* in Queen Elizabeth's reign, for the election of the Verderers of

Rockingham Forest, for the business meetings of the Charity School Trustees, for the celebration of royal birthdays, for the gatherings of freemasons and for meetings to organise a new water supply: in short, for almost any of the countless business events that took place in the town between 1570 and 1800.[47]

The holding of business meetings at inns was not of course a peculiarity of Northampton. In 1791, for example, the scheme for the building of the Ellesmere Canal in Shropshire was launched at a public meeting at the Royal Oak at Ellesmere, and the Canal Company Committee continued to hold its meetings in the same place for the next fifteen years, until Telford's Canal Office building was completed. At Leicester the meetings of the corporation about the navigation of the river Soar and regarding problems of the woollen manufacture in the town during the eighteenth century were held at the old Angel Inn. The foundation of the Leicester Infirmary in 1766 and of the Leicester Literary Society in 1791 were both inaugurated by public meetings at the Three Cranes. When the Infirmary was eventually opened, in 1771, a great public banquet was held, at the Three Cranes for the gentlemen who had promoted the scheme and at the Three Crowns for their ladies.[48]

(c) Social and cultural functions

The efflorescence of cultural and social life in provincial towns in the seventeenth and eighteenth centuries is an interesting and strangely neglected aspect of English history. It was due to many complex causes, but put in the simplest terms its origins may be said to be twofold. On the one hand it was associated with the rise of the gentry to a dominating position in county society, and hence with the expansion of a leisured class and their increasing sense of solidarity. In some shires a vigorous intellectual life among the country gentry had sprung up as early as Queen Elizabeth's reign: in Kent, certainly, from the time of William Lambarde in the 1570s. In some parts of England the development came later, but probably in all it was in some degree apparent by the time of the Civil War. In this development the county towns played an influential role as the forums of county society; and their influence was very much increased with the establishment, particularly during the second half of the seventeenth century, of a regular annual social season, when for several weeks the country gentry migrated to their town houses or to the great county inns in the shire capitals.

On the other hand the efflorescence of cultural life was closely associated with the growth of the leisured and professional classes in the towns themselves, particularly from the mid-seventeenth century onwards. The underlying reasons for the rise of what may loosely be termed the 'pseudo-gentry' in provincial towns – a class of people supported by independent sources of income but unsupported by a country estate – lie beyond the scope of this essay. It must suffice to say that by 1700 there was usually a sizeable and expanding group of leisured urban gentry and partly leisured professional families permanently resident in most considerable provincial towns, particularly in cathedral cities like Canterbury and county towns like Derby, Preston and Northampton. These families formed a perfectly well-recognised social group in the eyes of their contemporaries. In Northampton and other towns they were referred to as 'the town gentry' or 'our town gentlemen', in contradistinction to 'the country gentry' from the surrounding county.

During the Hanoverian period the numbers of the urban gentry rapidly increased. The social life of almost every Georgian town of any size, except the new industrial centres, came to be headed by its own local nexus of leisured families. There is any amount of architectural evidence for the existence of these families in the many Georgian and Regency houses of provincial towns, even of places as small as Ashford and West Malling in Kent, Blandford in Dorset, and Louth in Lincolnshire. And it was usually this class who played the dominant role in the social and cultural life of the urban community. In George III's reign even the most pedestrian little towns, such as Loughborough in Leicestershire, with its 3,000 or so inhabitants, maintained an elaborate annual round of balls, assemblies, concerts, lectures, card-parties and florists' feasts, not to mention cockfights, anti-slavery meetings and other excitements. Nearly all these activities in Loughborough itself were based on the inns of the town and were organised by its innkeepers, with the gentry principally, though of course not exclusively, in mind. There are many references to these events in the *Leicester and Nottingham Journal* of the time.[49]

One of the most usual ways of facilitating the development of social and cultural activities was to build an assembly room. Except in a few of the largest towns, most of the early assembly rooms were built by innkeepers and formed part of the inn itself. The first of them were probably erected towards the end of the seventeenth century; by the end of the eighteenth there were few towns of any size without them. It is indeed astonishing to find how small were some of the places in which they were built. One of the earliest surviving examples, dating from the first years of the eighteenth century, is to be found in the tiny Kentish borough of New Romney, a town with no more than 755 inhabitants at the time of the first census in 1801 and probably barely 500 a century earlier. In the Weald of Kent, Viscount Torrington found in 1788 that new assembly rooms had recently been built by the landlord of the Queen's Head Inn at Hawkhurst, a market 'town' with probably fewer than 1,000 inhabitants at this time. Seven miles north-west of Hawkhurst there were also assembly rooms at about this time in the market village of Lamberhurst, whose population then probably numbered no more than 750 inhabitants. Nine or ten miles east of Hawkhurst, at Tenterden, a town with about 1,500 inhabitants at this date, assemblies were held in the new town hall (rebuilt in 1792) adjoining the Woolpack Inn. (Tenterden must also have been one of the smallest towns in England to have a theatre of its own at this period.)[50]

About ten miles east of Tenterden a flourishing social life came to be centred during the eighteenth century on the inns and assembly rooms of Ashford. In the 1790s Ashford was described by the Kentish historian Edward Hasted as 'a small but neat and cheerful town', the houses 'mostly modern and well built', the High Street wide and newly paved, and 'many of the inhabitants of a genteel rank in life'. The numerous tombs of the local urban gentry in the parish church and churchyard bear out Hasted's description. The town had already given birth to several well-known physicians, one of whom, Dr Rowzee, had made a name for himself by writing a treatise on spa waters. Ashford was also something of an educational centre at this time, with 'an exceeding good English academy', a boarding school for young ladies, a writing school for the sons of poor townsmen, and a grammar school at which 'most of the sons of the neighbouring gentry' received their early education. In short, with a population of no more than 2,151 at the first census in 1801, Ashford was already on the way to becoming a kind of miniature social capital for the Weald of Kent. The balls and supper-parties organised by the innkeepers of the town figure amusingly in the letters of Mrs Montagu, the celebrated bluestocking (1720–1800), when visiting her relatives a few miles away at Mount Morris.[51] Several of the inns and 'genteel houses' of her period still survive, together with the assembly rooms above the market hall (rebuilt before 1808), though these have now been mutilated and debased to other uses.

Although the extent of social and cultural life in minor towns like Ashford was sometimes surprising, it was naturally in county towns like

Preston and Northampton that such activities principally flourished. From the advertisement pages of the *Northampton Mercury* a good deal can be discovered about this aspect of the history of a provincial town.[52] In the eighteenth century the social life of the county gentry when in Northampton centred principally on the triumvirate of inns at the top of the local hierarchy, the George, the Red Lion and the Peacock, though until the 1730s the last sometimes gave place to the Rose and Crown. There seems to have been a kind of 'gentlemen's agreement' between these three to share out the spoils between them. The first great event of the season was the horse-races held in about the third week in September. The races were not entirely a county affair: the County Plate (given by the country gentry) was open only to the county gentry and the Town Plate (given by the corporation) to inhabitants of town and county; but the Earl's Plate (given by Lord Northampton) and probably others seem to have had no restriction on entry, so that peers and squires from all over the kingdom flocked into the town and put up at its leading inns. The Northampton races were in fact a great public occasion, as were the races at other towns. 'I much wonder Mrs Tate should choose to come to Northampton at so *public a time* as the horse-races', wrote Lady Jane Compton somewhat tartly, from Studley Royal in Yorkshire, to the countess of Northampton at Castle Ashby in 1737. 'I hear a great deal of her in *this country* not much to her advantage.'[53] The Northampton races lasted for three days and each day they were followed by a great banquet and a ball. On the first day the gentlemen dined at the Peacock, the ladies at the George, and the ball was held at the Red Lion; while on subsequent days the order of arrangement was carefully reversed. On special occasions this great gathering of the aristocracy in the town could be conveniently turned to other than merely social uses. In 1745, for example, the *Gentleman's Magazine* recorded that on 'the first day of the horse-race here we were honoured with the presence of that true friend and bright ornament of this country the E[arl] of H[alifa]x, who dined at the George with a great number of gentlemen of distinction, and immediately after dinner made a speech to them . . .'. The earl warned them of the 'unnatural rebellion now raised against his Majesty's person and government, and the infamous attempt which our enemies are making to ruin our happy constitution both in church and state and to reduce us to superstition and bondage under a popish pretender supported by the power of France'.[54]

Normally, however, horse-race week in Northampton was peaceable enough and it must have brought a good deal of money into the coffers of the tradesmen as well as the innkeepers of the borough. In all probability the social life of many of the local gentry then continued without a break throughout the autumn and winter months. During October 'public breakfasts', followed by balls and card-parties, were held at each of the three great inns. These were followed by the Northampton Assemblies, held every week during the succeeding months: in December at the George, in January at the Red Lion and in February at the Peacock. The gentlemen's tickets were sold for 7s. 6d. and the ladies' for 5s., and this entitled the holder 'to dance and play at cards from six in the evening till twelve'.[55]

Another very popular pastime among the Northamptonshire gentry during the annual season was cockfighting. This was organised by the landlords of a number of inns – for example the Fleece, the Old Goat, the Black Lion, the Wheatsheaf and the George, all of which seem to have had their own cockpits – and the prizes ranged from 2 guineas a battle to as much as 50 guineas for the final battle. Sometimes the antagonists were the rival gentry from two neighbouring places, such as Northampton and Daventry; sometimes they were supporters of two rival county families, such as the Samwells and Montagues; sometimes they consisted of the town gentry versus the county gentry; and sometimes the Northamptonshire gentry versus those of Buckinghamshire or some other neighbouring shire. These occasions always provided an excuse, of course, for convivial banquets.

In the summer months, among the most frequent events organised by the Northampton innkeepers were the Florists' Feasts, Carnation Feasts and Gardeners' Society meetings. Exactly when these events originated it is impossible to say. Certainly they had become fairly usual by the 1730s, but they may well have been in existence for many years before the *Mercury* was founded in 1720. The most usual venues were the George, the Red Lion, the Angel and the Peacock inns. The prizes were moderate – £2 or £3 was a common figure offered – and clearly they too afforded the usual excuse for conviviality as well as genuinely encouraging horticulture. In one other respect the Florists' Feasts of the time were of interest, in that they were often open to all kinds of gardeners, of whatever social status. Normally distinctions of class were inflexibly observed in Hanoverian and Stuart Northampton, more so perhaps than at any time before or since. But the Florists' Feasts were among the few occasions in the year when these barriers were temporarily lowered, and the market gardeners and tradesmen of the town exhibited side by side with the county gentry. Then, as now, the Englishman's love of gardening formed a curious bond between all social ranks and degrees, and no doubt provided as fertile a topic of conversation as it does in a modern village.

There were a number of events in Northampton every year designed to appeal to the popular passion for prize-fighting and the delight in marvels. Trials of skill between pugilists, wrestlers, swordsmen and the like were regularly put on at Northampton inns. In December 1721, for instance, a trial of skill at the quarterstaff, sword and dagger, and backsword was staged at the Hind Inn between Robert Blake, the Irish 'master of the Noble Science of Defence', who claimed to have fought 'most of the best masters in the three kingdoms', and William Flanders, the Northamptonshire prize-fighter, 'who never did refuse the best of masters that did appear in London'. In October 1731 'Mr Joseph Johnson the renowned Yorkshire champion' mounted the stage at the Goat Inn with 'the famous Mr Edward Sutton, the Kentish Hero . . . the only man in England having fought 225 battles with the greatest applause and always come off conqueror'.[56]

Then in 1752 there was much excitement in the town over the visit of the great fire-eater, Mr Powell. Mr Powell claimed to have exhibited before several members of the royal family, and 'most of the nobility and quality of the first rank in London: especially . . . before that learned body the Royal Society, who in testimony of their highest approbation made him a present of a purse of gold and a large silver medal which he wears in honour of them . . .'. After a few days spent at the Saracen's Head in Northampton Mr Powell announced that he was proceeding to Warwick, Coventry, Birmingham, Nottingham, Derby, York, Scarborough and other towns.[57] During the following year the town was greatly entertained by the performances of the Learned English Dog. 'Of all the extraordinary curiosities that have ever been exhibited to the inspection of the curious,' the *Mercury* announced in November 1753, 'none have met with such a general approbation and esteem as the learned English Dog, now at the Angel Inn in this town: for he actually reads, writes, and casts accounts; answers various questions in Ovid's *Metamorphoses*, geography, the Roman, English, and sacred history; knows the Greek alphabet; . . . tells, by looking on any common watch of the company, what is the hour and minute; . . . shews the impenetrable secret or tells any person's thoughts in company; and distinguishes all sorts of colours.'[58]

In meeting the more serious cultural interests of the townsmen, inn-

PLATE I Bull Cottage, Witney Street, Burford, in 1840 (Reproduced from a water-colour in the Dryden Collection by permission of the Northampton Public Libraries Committee).

PLATE II (a)   East side of High Street, Burford. From left, Upton's Shop, London House, Castle's shop, Roger Warner's shop, Highway Hotel (Photo: Michael Laithwaite).

PLATE II (b)   East side of High Street, Burford. From right, Symon's Close, the Gay Adventure, the Highway Hotel (Photo: Michael Laithwaite).

holders also played a prominent part. Lectures, concerts, plays, exhibitions and literary gatherings formed regular features of the activities they sponsored and were evidently well patronised by the town and country gentry. In November 1737, soon after the opening of the gentry season, the *Mercury* announced that there was to be a concert at the Peacock Inn 'by the best masters from London'. It was to be followed by 'several antique and French dances and a ball, after the performances are ended'. In December 1752 (also during the gentry season) an exhibition was held at the Ram Inn of Mr Motet, the French sculptor's, 'six inimitable pieces of marble sculpture', representing 'our Saviour's life from the institution of his last supper to his resurrection, in upwards of 400 fine figures in relievo'.[59] In January 1755 a well-known scientific lecturer, Mr Griffis, began his course of public lectures, at the Hind Inn in the Market Square, on experimental philosophy and chemistry. In the summer of the same year a committee was formed which met from time to time at the Red Lion Inn for promoting the publication of Bridges's *History and Antiquities of Northamptonshire*. This was a venture of widespread interest to the gentry of both town and shire, though it was many years before publication of the project was in fact accomplished. At a public literary gathering at the Chequer Inn in October 1758, among a series of papers read were 'an essay on the standard of taste and judgement', 'a critical dissertation on the Roman and English Histories', a comparison of English and French courage, and (to lighten the diet) a 'whimsical impromptu on the Brussels, London, and Amsterdam gazetteers'. So far as drama was concerned, there was a theatre in the town by the end of George II's reign, and before that date public performances were taking place at some of the leading Northampton inns, particularly the Hind. In January 1724, for example, Dryden's comedy *The Spanish Friar, or The Double Discovery* was put on at the Hind, and this was followed in February by *Hamlet*. Both were probably performed by travelling groups, though the part of Torrismond in the former play was taken by an anonymous gentleman 'for his own diversion'.[60]

These examples of cultural activity in Hanoverian Northampton represent only a few among many which might be cited. Of course by no means all the intellectual activity of the town was centred on its inns. Nothing can be said here of more serious ventures like Philip Doddridge's celebrated Academy (1729–51); of the activities of the Northampton Philosophical Society, an early scientific body founded in 1743;[61] or of the many educational establishments in the town at this period – boarding schools, writing schools, finishing schools, riding schools and private academies. Virtually all of these have long since disappeared, and they owed little or nothing to the initiative of innkeepers in the town. But in the more general cultural awareness of both town and county, Northampton innkeepers played an enterprising and decisive role between the Restoration and the Reform Bill. In this they were probably not untypical of landlords in many other towns in the provinces.

III. URBAN INNKEEPERS

What kind of men were the innholders who organised these highly diverse activities? It is by no means easy to generalise about so amorphous a group of people, but by examining the innkeeping fraternity of a single provincial town in detail it is possible to detect certain outstanding characteristics. In the following pages Northampton is once again taken as a case study. Though in some respects unique, its general experience was probably not untypical of other inland entrepôts, such as Worcester, Salisbury or Shrewsbury, or of county towns like Exeter, Chester and Canterbury.

(a) The nobility of innkeepers

The first point to note is that the innkeepers of Northampton were among the most mobile elements in the community. It was not unusual for an innkeeper to migrate from one town to another at least once during his working life, and occasionally two or three times. There is abundant evidence of this fact in the advertisement pages of provincial newspapers like the *Northampton Mercury*. It is not really surprising, since the communications system of the country was essentially based on its inns and operated principally by its innkeepers. Well before Queen Anne's reign a widespread network of coaching, posting and carrying services had come into existence, channelling all kinds of news and information as well as goods and passengers through provincial hostelries. Naturally included in this news was information about profitable openings in the inkeeping world; and these openings the victualling fraternity was not slow to follow up.

Migration was especially frequent in important thoroughfare towns like Northampton, where inns were large and landlords numerous. The influx of new innkeepers into the town was a matter of grave concern to the Northampton corporation from the late sixteenth century onwards. In 1629 the constables and headboroughs of every ward were instructed to report to the mayor every month the names of all new-comers who were tapsters, chamberlains or ostlers, while a strict watch was kept on new innkeepers.[62] These regulations do not appear to have been very effective, and several attempts to limit the number of land-lords to those of the twelve recognised 'ancient inns' proved equally abortive. Gradually, it seems, the corporation had to reconcile itself to merely levying a freedom fine on 'foreign' innkeepers, usually of £10 or more, and acquiescing in their increasing numbers.

In 1642, for example, Thomas Holland, the influential landlord of the George, was 'questioned' by the corporation for keeping an inn without permission. Their questioning, however, had no effect and two years later the corporation declared that Holland had 'much intruded the liberty of this town by keeping of an inn, he being not a freeman of the same town, and hath . . . kept a tavern . . . without consent of the corporation'. On his submitting himself to them and paying a fine of £10, however, the corporation was perforce content to let him continue his house.[63] By that date alien innkeepers must have been recognised as a source of considerable profit to the community. Innkeeping was a trade, moreover, in which opportunism and mobility were essential, and by the middle years of the seventeenth century the innholders of North-ampton were too wealthy and numerous a body to antagonise. Many of them in fact were now becoming members of the corporation themselves.

During the eighteenth century it is evident that a considerable number of innkeepers had originated outside the borough.[64] In the smaller inns some of them had been servants in a great house, like John Day of the Three Tuns who had formerly been a servant of the earl of Rockingham and groom to Viscount Cobham. In the larger inns they had more usually graduated from another hostelry, either in Northampton or in some other place. John Stoughton, the landlord of the George in 1732, had formerly kept the Swan at Kettering; Robert Atkins, of the Elephant and Castle, had formerly kept an inn in Coventry; Hugh Curtis, of the Black Boy, came from the White Hart in Wellingborough; and William Davis, of the Angel, from the Crown at Dunstable.

A number of other Northampton innkeepers at this time came from much further afield. James Bordrigge of the Red Lion, for example, seems to have stemmed from a family of minor gentry in Yorkshire. Several, like Obrien Alliston, may have been of Irish extraction and a few, like René Laforce, were of European origin. After the union of the Scottish and English crowns in 1707 a considerable number came from north of the border. Among these were Neil McNeill, who at one time kept the Plume of Feathers and later moved to the Unicorn; and probably Sloswick Carr, one of the best known of Northampton's innholders during George II's reign, who eventually became landlord of the Red Lion.

Though most of the 'foreign' innkeepers in Georgian Northampton came to stay, a number moved on after a few years to other towns. John Hitchcock of the Peacock, for example, moved on in 1735 to the Swan at Newport Pagnell; Josiah Key of the George moved in 1736 to the White Horse at Dunstable; Daniel Dowell of the Angel moved in 1749 to the Angel at Kitts End near Barnet. A number of inn-servants from Northampton eventually became landlords in other towns too. George Winckles, a servant at the George Inn, in 1733 became innkeeper of the Peacock at St Albans. John Earle, the drawer at the Peacock in Northampton, moved first to the Ship Inn at Wellingborough and in 1759 became innkeeper of the Swan Inn in the same town.

This kind of mobility among the innkeeping fraternity was not peculiar to Northampton. It was probably found in most thoroughfare towns. During George II's reign the landlord of the Ram Inn in Smithfield moved to the Bull at St Albans; Robert Matthews of the Crown at St Albans moved to the Crown at Dunstable; Francis Hall (originally a Northampton inn-servant) moved from the Rose and Crown in St John's Street, London, to the White Swan at Redbourn; Philip Thompson of the Chequer at London Colney moved to the Saracen's Head at Newport Pagnell; and John Wise, an innkeeper from Liverpool, took on the George at Markyate, near Dunstable.

Two common characteristics mark most of these examples of migration. In the first place virtually all movement took place between places connected with each other by major coaching and carrying routes. Wellingborough, Kettering, Coventry and Newport Pagnell were all on much-frequented roads radiating from Northampton. Barnet, London Colney, St Albans, Redbourn, Markyate, Dunstable, Newport Pagnell and Northampton were all stages on the road from London to Chester and Liverpool. The more distant connections between Northampton and Yorkshire, Scotland and Ireland may also be explained in this way; for most of the principal routes from London to Ireland, to the west of Scotland and to west Yorkshire also passed through Northampton at this time.

The second point to observe is that these migrations evidently marked a step upwards, as a rule, in the innkeeping hierarchy. When moving to a new inn in the same town the landlord sometimes stressed that he was doing so 'for the more commodious reception of his guests', and 'at the desire and by the encouragement of the gentlemen of the town'. When moving to another town he emphasised that his new hostelry had been 'wholly new fitted up and made much more commodious than formerly'. This does not mean, of course, that the upward movement was a universal phenomenon. There must have been many stories of failure and misfortune of which we know little or nothing. As a rule it is only the pushing and successful landlords that we hear about, either through their advertisements or from their wills and inventories. Nevertheless, when all allowance is made, there were a good many forceful and enterprising characters in the innkeeping world at this time, and success stories in the Stuart and Hanoverian era were not infrequent.

(b) The innkeeping hierarchy

In Northampton, and probably in many places like it, these successes operated within a distinct and clearly defined hierarchy of prestige. This hierarchy was not wholly inflexible, of course, in a town with so many inns and so flourishing an entrepôt trade. It was certainly possible for a gifted and enterprising landlord to raise the status of his inn in the scale of respect. And yet the scale of respect was felt to be a reality, and each inn occupied a more or less settled place in the hierarchy. Urban communities at this time, it must be remembered, were as concerned with questions of status and degree as the landed gentry in the country-side around them.

At the top of the scale in eighteenth-century Northampton were the three 'county' inns already mentioned. These were particularly patronised by the gentry of the shire, by titled magnates on their travels from one part of the kingdom to another, and by the corporation or other public bodies on festive occasions. The George was always regarded as the first among equals, and after its rebuilding following the great fire of 1675 was described by Defoe as 'more like a palace than an inn'. Defoe's remarks were echoed by many of his contemporaries, and in 1739 it was described as 'the best and most commodious inn for noblemen, gentlemen, and travellers between London and West Chester'.[65] Among the many important visitors to the George around this period were the duke of Tuscany, the duke of Devonshire, the earl and countess of Egmont, the earl of Chesterfield on his way into Ireland as lord lieutenant, and General Wade on his way to Scotland in 1745.[66] Some idea of the scale and splendour of the George around this period can be gained from the probate inventory of one of its landlords, Henry Lyon.[67] When Lyon died in September 1698 his personal estate alone was valued at nearly £800, or perhaps £30,000 in modern terms. The George then contained forty-one rooms, most of them with names like the Globe, the Mitre, the Rose and the Mermaid. (The numbering of rooms in hotels was of course a much later development.) The total value of the furnishings in the inn then amounted to more than £500, or perhaps £15,000–£20,000 in current values. The linen and the brass and pewterware were each worth more than £80, or possibly more than £3,000 in modern figures. The contents of the principal bedroom, the Queen's Head Chamber, were assessed at about £30 (say £1,200) and of the King's Head, the Mermaid, the Crown and the Two-Bedded Chamber at £16–£20 each (£600–800). The value of the goods in the wood-yard, probably consisting chiefly of fuel for the coming winter, was estimated at £67 (£2,500 or so), and that of hay in store for visitors' horses at more than £100 (say £3,000–£4,000 worth). It is not surprising to find that the landlords of inns like the George were described as 'gentlemen' by their contemporaries.

In scale and status the George was closely rivalled in Northampton by the Red Lion in the Horsemarket. It is evident from James Bordrigge's inventory (June 1743) that this also contained forty-one rooms, and though not quite so lavishly appointed as the George, its furnishings were valued in 1743 at nearly £450 (or perhaps about £14,000 in modern terms), and its stock of wine and spirits at more than £90 (£3,000). The silverware in the inn was assessed at more than £100 and there was a splendid collection of kitchen goods valued at nearly £35 (say £1,000 in current values). Among these kitchen goods were 16 dozen plates, 13 dozen soup plates, 160 dishes and 10 roasting spits, together with all the usual kitchenware of the time such as tea kettles, cauldrons, fish kettles, frying pans, saucepans, chafing dishes, warming pans, plate-warmers and coffee pots. Many of the rooms in the Red Lion were lined with hangings and pictures, and in the Dragon Chamber, the dining-room and the Queen's Head Chamber there were nearly 90 yds of tapestry. Among the more interesting items of furniture were a mahogany dining-table, several Japanese tea-tables, Chinese wall-papers, Virginia chairs, gilded sconces and the family coat of arms over the drawing-room chimney-piece.

Of the innkeepers of the Red Lion in the Stuart and Hanoverian era more is known than of those of any other Northampton inn.[68] In William III's reign the inn was run by one William Burt, whose family gave at least three innkeepers to the town about this period. Burt had probably died by 1704 when the inn had evidently been taken over by one of the Lyon family, who also provided at least three innkeepers in Northampton during the late seventeenth and eighteenth centuries. It is possible that Charles Lyon managed the inn in association with Burt's widow Elizabeth; for in her will of 1706 Elizabeth Burt was still described as dwelling at the Red Lion. After his death in 1704 or 1705 it was continued by *his* widow, Mary Lyon. It is clear that Mary Lyon was a woman of some character, for in addition to running the Red Lion for more than twenty years she seems to have been the first innkeeper in Northampton to run a daily stage-coach service to London (most ran only on alternate days). This was a service which she founded in 1724 and continued to operate after her retirement from the inn in the following year. She was succeeded at the Red Lion by Mr Pratt, a member of another long-standing victualling dynasty in the town, one of whom had been an innkeeper as far back as 1519.

The next innkeeper we hear of at the Red Lion (probably Pratt's immediate successor) was the Yorkshireman James Bordrigge. When he died in 1743 he was one of the richest innholders in the town. He did not own his inn (very few Northampton innkeepers did) and his will has not survived, so that we have no knowledge of any real property he may have possessed. But his personal estate was valued at £1,045 and his probate inventory was one of the longest and most elaborate of any townsman in the seventeenth or eighteenth century. After his death an announcement appeared in the *Mercury* that the whole contents of the inn were to be sold; but before the sale took place they had been purchased lock, stock and barrel by the landlord of the Goat Inn, Sloswick Carr.

Carr was probably of Scottish extraction and he may have come to Northampton in or about the year 1739, when, as landlord of the Goat Inn, he paid £10 for his freedom fine. He was clearly an obsequious kind of man and from the first he was well in with the corporation, who in the year of his freedom decided, somewhat unusually, to hold their annual feast at his comparatively minor inn instead of at one of the three great inns or at the Angel or Hind, their usual rendezvous. He may already have been a member of the common council by this date, and before long he became an alderman and finally, in 1750, mayor of the town. When he moved up the innkeeping scale from the Old Goat to the Red Lion in 1744 he also gained the patronage of the gentry. In 1747, 'at the desire and by the encouragement of the gentlemen of the town of Northampton and parts adjacent', he opened a coffee-room at the Red Lion, where the public papers were taken. Typically, there were also to be had 'at the same place red and white ports, Lisbon, Canary, Madeira, Mountain, rum, and brandy'.[69] It was by measures such as these that an inn like the Red Lion developed into a kind of club for the county gentry, its coffee-room their centre of debate and its dining-room of their conviviality. Like so many anglicised Scots, Sloswick Carr must have been a prosperous as well as an ambitious man, for when he died in 1751, during his year of office as mayor, he was hunting his own pack of beagles, and the Mercury described him as one 'whose examplary conduct as a magistrate had gained him the general esteem, and whose death is much regretted'.[70]

Sloswick Carr's widow, like those of his predecessors, kept on the inn herself for a number of years after her husband's death. It was during her tenure that a new and much faster coach service to London began to operate from the Red Lion and George. It was performed by light coaches, called the Northampton Flying Berlins, and these covered the 66 miles to London in twelve hours, setting out at 6 a.m. (the ordinary stage set out at 3 a.m.). In August 1752 the new service occasioned an amusing advertisement in the Mercury:

By particular desire of several of our customers [the proprietors announced], we are to acquaint the public that the Berlin will set out exactly at six o'clock; and it is therefore humbly hoped that no one will take it amiss if, after this notice, they should lose their earnest [deposit] . . . in case they are not ready punctually at the time . . .; for so much time is lost in going about the town [for those who have overslept], and those whom we take up at first are so much displeased at being carried about, and at sitting to wait for others who too often are not ready, that every one is now desired, for the general good, to walk down to the George or Red Lion a little before six. And that nothing may be wanting on our parts, a porter shall be sent to each person's house to give proper warning.[71]

Beneath the level of the Red Lion, the George and the Peacock there was a second group of inns in Northampton, comprising about ten or fifteen in number, and including such hostelries as the Saracen's Head, the Angel, the Swan, the Bull, the Hind, the Dolphin and the King's Head. These inns, in addition to catering for the gentry and the corporation, were also patronised by travelling factors and merchants connected with the wholesale and retail trades of the town. The Saracen's Head in Abington Street had the advantage over other houses in the group of being also the post office, and hence possessing, in theory at least, the exclusive right to hire out post-horses.[72] It was rarely able to maintain this monopoly, but it certainly operated an extensive hiring service and, as already remarked, its stables provided accommodation for as many as 150 horses. In status the Saracen's Head evidently ranked immediately below the Peacock, and on more than one occasion its landlord moved on to become landlord of that inn. The Hind Inn, with entrances in Sheep Street and the Market Square, was described in the 1740s as an old-established coaching inn patronised by gentlemen when travelling with their families and servants. It was also utilised, as we have seen, for public lectures and dramatic performances. The Bull, the Dolphin, the Angel and the Swan offered similar facilities, and they were also made use of by the corporation when entertaining important visitors and for the mayoral feasts, the sessions dinners and the annual Vernall's Inquest dinner. At times the scale of corporation entertainment at these and other inns became something of a scandal. In the 1690s an angry contemporary described the mayors as selling the town land for claret.[73]

One of the most interesting of the Northampton probate inventories, that of John Summers, relates to one of these inns, namely the Bull, in 1672. This was a large inn, with thirty-six rooms and at least forty beds. It had evidently been recently extended, since several of the chambers are described as 'new'. Its contents were valued at nearly £400, or perhaps about £16,000 in modern terms. Its dining-room was hung with tapestry and adorned with royal coats of arms, the portraits of the king and queen, and sixty family escutcheons. One of the interesting features of the inventory is its list of linen, which was valued at nearly £50, or possible £2,000 in modern terms. This included, *inter alia*, 38 tablecloths, 45 pillowcases, 122 sheets and 337 napkins.

It would be misleading to suggest that inns like these were entirely typical of the innkeeping trade even in a major thoroughfare town like Northampton. Beneath them there were a number of sizeable but unpretentious drovers' and carriers' inns, such as the Bull's Head in St James's End and the Fleece and the Lion and Lamb in Bridge Street. The landlords of inns in this class rarely moved up into the top ranks of the hierarchy, but there was a good deal of movement among themselves. In 1736, for example, Joseph Cook of the Sun in Bridge Street moved on to the Fleece Inn and Joseph Williams of the Raven took over the Sun. Three years later Joseph Cook had either moved again or possibly died, and Joseph Williams moved up from the Sun to the

Fleece, which was clearly one of the most important carriers' inns in the town.

Beneath the carriers' inns, at the foot of the scale, were many small inns of which little or nothing is known but their names and situations. Scarcely any of them survive today, but their modest scale is indicated by their landlords' wills and probate inventories. Nearly half the innkeepers whose inventories have survived in fact left personal goods worth less than £100. James Keyes, for example, who died in 1662, left barely £19 worth of goods in his simply furnished nine-roomed inn. Alexander Taylor, who died in 1715, left property worth less than £16, and his inn comprised only a parlour, a kitchen, a little drinking-room, a cellar, a brewhouse, three chambers and a garret. Abraham Matthews's inn, in the 1720s, was smaller still, consisting only of a kitchen, parlour, cellar, brewhouse and three chambers, while his goods were valued at no more than £15 19s. Hostelries of this kind clearly belonged to a different social and economic world from that of the George and the Red Lion, or the Saracen's Head and the Bull.

Within this hierarchy of inns in Northampton there was a good deal of movement up the scale from one house to another. Though the hierarchy itself over lengthy periods remained more or less fixed, there was plenty of scope within it for an ambitious man to better himself. This is evident from the fact that, when an inn became vacant, it was frequently taken over by the landlord of some inferior house in the scale, and quite often this move led to a general post among three or four other hostelries in the town. When Joseph Cook of the Sun Inn, for instance, moved to the Golden Fleece in 1736, Joseph Williams of the Raven moved to the Sun, and another innkeeper took over the Raven. Three years later Joseph Williams himself moved from the Sun to the Golden Fleece, and Robert Lucas, a former servant of Mr Pratt, took over the Sun. Five years later, in 1744, Joseph Williams bettered himself once more and moved on to the Old Goat Inn when its landlord, the Scotsman Sloswick Carr, took over the Red Lion following the death of James Bordrigge. Ten years later, when Sloswick Carr's widow retired from business in 1754, Joseph Hall, who had moved from the Black Boy to the Angel in 1748, moved once again from the Angel to succeed Mrs Carr at the Red Lion. When Joseph Hall himself retired from business in 1756, Robert Lucas, who had taken on the Sun in 1739, and then moved to the Woolpack around 1750, now made his last move – to the Red Lion. On Lucas's vacation of the Woolpack, the Woolpack itself was taken over by John Segary from the Chequer, and the Chequer by John Fletcher, a former coachman of the earl of Northampton. Although, as already remarked, it was rarely if ever possible for an innkeeper to run through the whole gamut of inns, beginning at the lowliest and ending up as landlord of one of the triumvirate at the top of the scale, there was a continual process of self-improvement among the innholders of Northampton and a powerful sense of cohesion among the innkeeping families of the town.[74]

(c) Innkeeping dynasties

The third feature to be noted about Northampton innkeepers is the development of distinct innholding dynasties in the town. The importance of these must not be exaggerated; they rarely continued their innkeeping activities over more than three or four generations and they comprised only a minority of the innholders of the town. Within this relatively mobile section of the community, however, they provided an element of permanence and continuity out of proportion to their numbers. They formed a kind of focus within the innkeeping fraternity and probably contributed much to its *esprit de corps*. If there were more early innkeepers' wills it is probable that some of these dynasties could be traced back a good deal further than is now possible. There are in fact only five landlords' wills dating from before 1660, compared with thirty-two for the century from 1660 to 1760 – a fact in itself eloquent of the rising numbers and status of the innkeeping fraternity in the town.[75]

One of the most noted of these innkeeping families in Northampton has already been mentioned, namely the Lyons. They were not the longest lasting: that honour must probably go to the Pratts, one of whom, John Pratt, was an innholder at the beginning of the sixteenth century (he made his will in 1519), while probably the last to keep an inn, another John Pratt became landlord of the Red Lion in the 1720s. But if not the longest lasting, the Lyons were certainly one of the wealthiest and most well known. The origins of the family are obscure, and since none of their wills survives the family tree cannot be reconstructed with complete certainty. Their history seems to begin around the mid-seventeenth century, with Henry, Samuel and Charles Lyon, who were possibly sons of a prosperous draper in the town in Charles I's reign, all of whom became prominent local figures. Henry Lyon was a very successful innkeeper who eventually became landlord of the George and who died in 1698 leaving nearly £800 worth of goods in his inn. His widow Katherine kept on the inn and a year after her husband's death married another innkeeper, Robert Key. The Keys also belonged to an influential innkeeping family in the area, one of whom (Harry) had apparently kept an inn at Watford (Northants.), another (John) was probably the John Key who became landlord of the Angel at Stilton (Hunts.) in 1731, while a third (Josiah) became landlord of the George in Northampton in the 1730s. Henry Lyon's brother Samuel may not have been an innholder, but Samuel's son John certainly was, and Samuel himself became a well-known alderman in the town and was twice elected mayor. The third brother, Charles Lyon, had probably become an innkeeper in Northampton by the 1670s, if not earlier, and when he died in 1704 or 1705 he was landlord of the second great inn, the Red Lion. As already remarked, his widow Mary Lyon kept on the inn in her own name for more than twenty years after her husband's death, and she also founded the Northampton Flying Stage Coach. Their son, Charles Lyon II, did not follow the family tradition of innkeeping but became an upholsterer and 'appraiser'. As such he drew up many of the probate inventories of the wealthier townsmen, including that of his uncle Henry in 1698. He was clearly a man of considerable property in his own right and his son, Charles Lyon III, became a well-known surgeon and apothecary in the town who for more than twenty years served as an alderman. This last Charles Lyon was still living and practising in Bridge Street in 1768, and he may have been the father of the final representative of the family, Mrs Elizabeth Lyon, who died in 1797, aged seventy-three, and is buried in the north aisle of St Peter's church. For four generations, extending over more than a century from Charles I's reign to George III's, the Lyons and for a time their kinsmen the Keys were among the wealthiest and most influential families in the town, and six or seven of them had been among the most prominent local innholders.

Quite as interesting as the Lyons, though for a different reason, were the Peaches. They were the principal example in Northampton – there were several others on a more limited scale – of the way in which a family founded by an innkeeper gradually acquired the freehold of quite a chain of inns in the town, putting in its own nominees as landlords.

The pedigree of the Peaches is an exceptionally complex one and, as with the Lyons, their origins cannot be established with complete certainty. The first of the family who can be definitely identified is Thomas Peach I, who in 1656 was described as a 'gentleman' and 'innholder', and who had acquired the freedom of the town, as well as his inn apparently, by marrying the widow of another innholder, George

Ecton. The fact that Thomas I's freedom fine amounted to £13 6s. 8d., an unusually high figure for this date, suggests that he was probably not a native of Northampton, but the name appears to have been a local one and he may have come from a nearby village. Thomas I was succeeded by Henry Peach I, whose occupation is not known and who probably died quite young (certainly before 1685), leaving two sons, Thomas II and John I. Both these sons became fellmongers and founded distinct and prosperous local dynasties of their own. The descendants of John, the younger brother, need not be traced in detail here: some became jersey combers and some woolstaplers, but most of them, like many go-ahead Northampton families in the eighteenth century, eventually turned to shoe manufacturing. (There was still a firm of Peaches manufacturing shoes in the town in 1898.)

It was Thomas II's branch that continued the family connection with innkeeping, though now by acquiring inn freeholds rather than by becoming innkeepers themselves. By the end of the seventeenth century it seems that comparatively few Northampton innkeepers actually owned their hostelries. Some inns belonged to the country gentry and some to town gentry and tradesmen. The George, for instance, belonged to the Drydens of Canons Ashby until it was rebuilt after the fire of 1675, when Dr Dryden (a canon of Windsor) converted the freehold into a charity for the relief of impoverished townsmen.[76] In many towns the motive for the acquisition of inns by county families like the Drydens was doubtless a political one: it afforded them a means of influencing parliamentary elections. But it is doubtful if this was the motive with the Peach family. Though frequently described as 'gentlemen' in their wills and in other documents, none of them ever became country landowners except in the most minor sense. They were, however, very astute businessmen, and for them an inn was clearly regarded as a profitable investment. By the middle of the eighteenth century the Peaches had acquired the freehold of at least ten inns in the town.

The first of the family to begin this process of acquisition on some scale was Thomas III, who was apprenticed by his father Thomas II as a fellmonger in 1701 and died as a 'gentleman' in 1744. His will is a remarkable and revealing document, an immense and elaborate parchment, clearly the work of a forceful and authoritarian mind, and also of a great-grandfather who, though aged, still keeps his numerous descendants firmly under his control. By 1739, when he made his will, Thomas III had purchased lands and tenements in Hardingstone, a parish just outside the town, where he was then living and was to be

buried alongside his late wife. (His executors were carefully instructed
to provide within six months of his death 'a neat monument of marble
with an inscription to be engraved thereon . . . to be set up in the corner
or some other convenient place against the walls of the said church as
near my grave as may be'.) He had also purchased property in the
Horsemarket in Northampton, and a substantial portion of his income
was evidently derived from the four important inns he had acquired:
the Angel, the Golden Fleece, the Black Raven and the Cock. By the
elaborate provisions of his will Thomas III's real estate was virtually
entailed on his numerous grandchilden and great-grandchilden, with a
life interest only, and that in no more than part of it, to his second son
Henry. All his household goods, including his silver, brass and pewterware, his chairs and tables, his escritoire and looking-glasses, his clock
and clockcase, were left to his two granddaughters, the children of his
elder son, Thomas Peach IV, both of whom were confusingly named
Elizabeth.

This son, Thomas IV, was himself not left penniless, however. He
must have already possessed considerable property of his own, for he
was a wealthy maltster, and his father left him all his money, mortgages,
bonds, credits and securities. Quite clearly Thomas IV was cast in the
same authoritarian mould as his father. For many years before his death
in 1761 he was referred to in the town as Thomas Peach the elder, to
distinguish him from his son and grandson of the same name. He added
considerably to the family patrimony. His will is even more elaborate
than his father's, extending to as many as seven sheets, and specifying
in minute detail the distribution of his estate among his three sons,
William, Thomas V and Robert, his three daughters and his numerous
grandchildren. To keep his real property intact Thomas IV adopted the
same ruse as his father, leaving only a life interest in most of it to his
immediate heirs. To the four inns acquired by his father he himself had
added another five: the Ram, the Woolpack, the Crosskeys, the Talbot
and the Three Pots. In addition to these he owned maltyards in the
Marefair and the South Quarter, several houses, gardens and workshops
within the town, and at least ten tenements and cottages in the town
fields and liberties. Of his three daughters one had married well, into
the prominent local dynasty of the Jeffcuts, and the two others into the
Hawkins and Hayes families. Henry Jeffcut was clearly in his father-
in-law's good books and was appointed one of his trustees. William
Hawkins, however, must have been less satisfactory as a son-in-law. In
the original will, dated 1758, the bequest of £500 to Hawkins's wife

Elizabeth was payable to her alone 'separately from her husband'; in a codicil dated just before Thomas IV's death this bequest was revoked and Elizabeth was left £25 a year 'to her own exclusive use, her husband in no wise to intermeddle with it'.

Altogether Thomas Peach IV's will is that of a possessive and dominating personality, perhaps not an unkindly man fundamentally, but certainly one entirely preoccupied with his own descendants. Not a single penny was left outside the family circle, and not a farthing to any kind of charity. Like his father before him, Thomas IV described himself as 'gentleman' in his will, and the designation was not inaccurate from the point of view of economic standing. But his was a form of gentility entirely urban in its origins, in no way rooted in the surrounding countryside, and wholly confined in its interests to the town. By the time of his death in 1761 both Thomas Peach IV and his two elder sons, William and Thomas V, had for many years been influential members of the corporation.

The further fortunes of the Peach family, though of interest in their own right, lie outside the scope of this essay. By the time Thomas IV died, his younger brother Henry had for several years been in possession of the Mitre – the tenth inn in the town to be acquired by the family. There may have been other inns that the family owned by this date of which no record now exists, since there are no other surviving wills of this period. Thomas IV was succeeded by his three sons William, Thomas V and Robert, of whom William and possibly Thomas continued the malting business and Robert was probably a cordwainer. By the 1770s it is probable that one branch of the family had tiptoed up into the ranks of the minor country gentry and acquired a small estate at Deenethorpe, a few miles from Oundle. The relationship of the Deenethorpe family to that of Northampton is not altogether certain; but if they were in fact kinsmen, it is interesting to note that the connection with Northampton was maintained when Conyers Peach of Deenethorpe returned to the town in 1774 to be apprenticed to a saddler and whip-maker. Essentially the Peaches remained throughout their history an entirely urban dynasty. They and their kinsmen the Jeffcuts were typical of a whole nexus of related families at the centre of Northampton life during the seventeenth and eighteenth centuries: families rarely rich enough to sever all their urban links and set themselves up as independent country gentry, but always backed by substantial property and a powerful sense of dynastic cohesion.

The Lyons, the Keys and the Peaches are examples of the way in which dynastic influence in the innkeeping world could extend itself in the male line. But in Northampton at least (and probably other towns), owing to local peculiarities of inheritance, it could also descend in the female line. By Northampton custom the freedom of the borough could be acquired not only by the normal processes of apprenticeship and inheritance from father to son, but by intermarriage with the widow or the daughter of a freeman. There is plenty of evidence that marriage with an innkeeper's daughter or widow was one of the commonest ways in which innkeepers from others parts gained a footing in the town. By doing so they entitled themselves not only to the freedom but also to the hostelry in question. Several examples of this process have already been mentioned in passing, and among many others were the following. In 1696 John Penavayre (whose surname suggests that he was not of local or Midland origin) acquired his position as landlord of the Dolphin and the freedom of the borough by marrying Mrs Lacey, the widow of the former landlord. In 1730 Josephy Halley, a trooper probably stationed in the town, became a freeman and the landlord of the important King's Head Inn on his marriage to the widow of the late landlord, Mrs Harrison. In 1694 a Frenchman, René Laforce – very possibly a Huguenot: the Edict of Nantes had been revoked in 1685 – acquired the freedom of the town by marrying the widow of Jeremiah Friend, and in addition to running his wife's inn ran one of the earliest and most influential coffee-houses in the town. These instances are sufficient to illustrate the way in which widows who kept on their husband's hostelries might play an influential role in the innkeeping fraternity. The gain was by no means all on the side of the fortunate male, for the custom put Northampton women in a powerful bargaining position, and the wills of many of them indicate that they were veritable matriarchs. Significantly enough, their wills are usually more detailed and more informative about their family connections than the often somewhat perfunctory documents drawn up by their husbands.

IV. CONCLUSION: THE INNKEEPING FRATERNITY

Quite clearly the innkeeping fraternity of a town like Northampton, though frequently augmented by additional members from elsewhere, was animated by a strong sense of cohesion and united by frequent ties of intermarriage. There is no reason to suppose that this *esprit de corps* was in any way peculiar to Northampton; it must have existed in many cities and boroughs. In some respects it was independent of and in others merely a local manifestation of that much wider sense of community among provincial innkeepers which, by George III's reign, had incorporated many of them in different parts of the country into a single brotherhood. The movements of landlords from inn to inn and town to town were among both the causes and the consequences of this sense of cohesion in the innkeeping world.

One form of connection linking many of the less reputable inns remains to be mentioned: the network of highwaymen and footpads that infested late seventeenth- and eighteenth-century England. Although these highway gangs seem to have been based chiefly on rural hostelries, no study of the urban inn would be complete without some reference to them. True, respectable pillars of the innkeeping establishment like the Lyons and the Peaches would never have considered themselves in any way associated with this network; yet there was a sense in which the highwayman was as much a part of the wayfaring world as the most reputable innholder. On the one hand he was necessarily a horseman, and the horseman's home was necessarily the inn; on the other hand a certain disreputable type of hostelry provided the highwayman with the readiest outlet for disposing of his ill-gotten gains and (if reports were true) with ample facilities for robbing wealthy travellers.

The highwaymen of the period tended to operate in certain well-defined types of countryside. They were particularly notorious in many old forest and woodland areas wherever these were traversed by major coaching routes; for the woodland cover provided the mounted horseman with a readily accessible place of refuge. One notorious haunt in the Midlands was the part of Rockingham Forest north-east of Kettering. Another was the wooded country bordering Buckinghamshire and Northamptonshire, where Watling Street and the A50 traversed the former Whittlewood and Salcey Forests. A third area, further south, was the countryside around Woburn, Brickhill and Leighton Buzzard, where the same route crossed the wooded greensand district bordering Buckinghamshire and Bedfordshire.[77] In Kent one of the most dreaded areas was the countryside between Canterbury and Faversham, where the Dover road passed through what was then the wild and unfrequented Forest of Blean. The newspapers of the 1730s and 1750s, like the *Northampton Mercury* and the *Worcester Journal*, contain many references to highway robberies in areas like these.

One of the more notorious of these gangs of highwaymen, operating on roads in Leicestershire, Northamptonshire, Warwickshire, Shropshire, Staffordshire and Worcestershire, was tracked down and brought to book in the year 1732. Its members, sometimes disguised as gypsies, had based their activities on a widespread nexus of Midland inns and disposed of their prizes chiefly through one William Manley, landlord of the Rose and Crown on the Lickey Hills near Bromsgrove. Manley himself was apparently looked up to by the gang as their 'captain' and he sold their prizes to a Londoner named William Ward, 'a pretended jockey' who every six weeks or so visited Manley's inn to collect his purchases. Apart from the Rose and Crown, 'the most usual haunts and residence of this wicked gang were the Swan, a mile beyond the turnpike from Birmingham . . . the Swan at Hinckley [Leics.]; the Cock in Stourton near Kinver [Staffs.]; at the Fox and Goose at Foxlydiate near Bromsgrove; the Fox and Goose at Redditch [Worcs.]; and the Cock at Meriden [Warks]. Clearly here was an elaborate network of highway robbery systematically organised by an innholder and his gang, and based on a chain of convenient hostelries, principally in or close to the smaller market towns of the area. The gang itself was eventually broken up by the discovery of Manley's activities and his execution at Stafford in 1732.[78]

More primitive in their organisation but equally effective were the activities of the landlord at Putloe (Gloucs.) already referred to. The story can best be told in the colourful language of a contemporary tract, *The Bloody Innkeeper, or Sad and Barbarous News from Gloucestershire* (1675). The guests at this inn, it will be recalled, were principally Scottish cloth merchants, and Putloe was a poor, decayed market village on the Bristol–Gloucester road. When the landlord and his wife first set up their inn, 'contrary to all expectations they began to thrive amain, furnishing their home rarely well with all sorts of household goods and convenient utensils, and having money on all occasions to lend his neighbours at a pinch, which all that knew them much admired at'. If we may believe the tract, these good neighbours 'had not the least suspicion or mistrust of the unhappy truth that this spring tide of fortune was swelled with blood, and his gains raked together with the barbarous hands of robbery and murther'.

The truth did not come to light until the innkeeper and his wife moved to a larger hostelry near Gloucester and the Putloe inn was leased to a blacksmith. The new tenant erected a shed in the garden for his smithy, and while he was excavating the ground beneath to set up his anvil, he suddenly came across 'the bones and part of the flesh of a man buried there, the sight whereof strangely surprised and affrighted him'. He took counsel with his neighbours and they, evidently not without a certain ghoulish pleasure, persuaded him to continue digging, coming along themselves to assist him. Eventually the bodies of seven persons were unearthed before the amazed villagers. But who could be to blame for 'so much inhumane barbarousness? . . . At last just heaven . . . wonderfully opened a way to the discovery; for as they were viewing more narrowly the bones and corps[es], and removing the earth and rubbish to behold them the plainer, they perceived a knife stuck in by the blade bone of one of their breasts'. On closer examination this fatal instrument was found to bear the incriminating initials, it seems, of the Bloody Innkeeper himself. He and his wife had been secretly robbing their unsuspecting guests for years and then, if suspicion was at length awakened, quietly knifing them and burying them in the garden, no doubt at night.

The melodrama of Putloe need not be taken as typical of the inn-keeping world in general – no doubt the majority of hostelries maintained a reasonable degree of respectability – but it was not untypical of its more sordid side. The provincial inn was pre-eminently a place where people *met*, whether in large groups or small, whether as peers or princes, as country gentry or clergy, as travelling merchants or lawyers, as doctors, quacks or highwaymen. And hence its history reflected innumerable facets of English life in the seventeenth and eighteenth centuries, from the highest to the lowest, from the most aristocratic to the most ignoble. The imagery of the inn and the way-faring life centred upon it became indeed a commonplace of the literature of the time, from the days of John Bunyan's pilgrim to those of George Borrow's *Lavengro*. Even contemporary sermons and religious writings are sometimes fraught with its imagery. The learned and saintly John Conant of Northampton, we are told by his biographer, ever looked upon himself as no more than a stranger and pilgrim on this earth, and on the world itself as nothing but 'an inn in our way to a better, an heavenly country'.[79] It was not a surprising view for a man to take who had spent much of his life ministering to the needs of one of the great innkeeping centres of England.

5. A Hanoverian Watering-Place: Margate before the Railway

JOHN WHYMAN

I. INTRODUCTION: MARGATE A UNIQUE SEASIDE RESORT

A CRAZE for sea bathing and seaside holidays grew out of the publicity given to the medical advantages of sea-water treatment in the 1750s and 1760s, and Margate was the first of the Thanet coastal towns to cater for visitors in search of health and pleasure by the sea. A guide-book of 1813 observed that 'It was merely a fishing town, and one dirty narrow lane . . . was the principal part of the town. From the salubrity of the air, and the convenience of sea bathing . . . it eventually rose from its state of insignificance into a handsome and even celebrated town. The cheapness and convenience of the packet boats have doubtless greatly contributed to the popularity of the place.'[1] This contemporary observation belonged to the coaching and hoy era of Margate's history. The eighteenth-century foundations of Margate as a seaside resort had been built up on communications by coach and hoy. Hoys were originally single-masted cargo sailing vessels, usually carrying corn into London and returning to Thanet with shop goods; accustomed to taking passengers, they gave way during the later eighteenth century to sailing packets and sailing yachts.

The first steam packet, the *Thames*, with one 16 h.p. engine, was brought into Margate harbour by Sir Marc Brunel in 1814, and this event ushered in the steamboat era, which reached its zenith, in the sense of being unchallenged by any other form of transport, during the 1830s. Margate during the 1820s and 1830s came to enjoy increasing renown as a well developed and popular steamboat resort. According to traffic evidence submitted in 1850 to the Select Committee on Ramsgate and Margate Harbours, the number of passengers arriving at and departing from Margate by water communication amounted to 2,219,364 over thirty-five years between 1812–13 and 1846–7, giving an annual average of 63,410 passengers. The number of passengers coming and

going annually during the three years prior to the opening of the South
Eastern Railway in December 1846 averaged 86,802.

The 1847 holiday season was the first to benefit Margate by means
of an influx of railway visitors travelling on the first railway link between
London and Thanet. Margate, however, was more than a century old as
a sea-bathing resort· by this time. It can claim to be unique among
English seaside resorts on at least three grounds.

First, in company with Scarborough and Brighton, it is certainly
one of the oldest of English seaside resorts. Of the three Thanet coastal
resorts (Margate, Ramsgate and Broadstairs) Margate has been renowned as a bathing resort for about two hundred and fifty years.
Indeed, sea bathing there preceded the publicity given to sea-water
treatment during the 1750s and 1760s, which will be discussed later in
this essay. Its origins can in fact be traced back to the 1720s, while an
alternative to open bathing in the sea was advertised as follows in the
Kentish Post and Canterbury News Letter of 17 July 1736:

> Whereas bathing in sea-water has for several years, and by great
> numbers of people, been found to be of great service in many
> chronical cases, but for want of a convenient and private bathing
> place, many of both sexes have not cared to expose themselves to the
> open air; this is to inform all persons that Thomas Barber, carpenter,
> at Margate in the Isle of Thanet, hath lately made a very convenient
> bath, into which the sea water runs through a canal about 15 ft long.
> You descend into the bath from a private room adjoining to it.
> N.B. There are in the same house convenient lodgings to be let.

The same source on 27 April 1737 informed 'all persons, that Thomas
Barber, carpenter, at Margate, . . . finding his bath (which was advertised last year) not large enough for the number of people which came
there to bathe in the sea water, he hath made another bath much larger
and more commodious than the other, and is so contrived, that there
is a sufficient quantity of water to bathe in it at any time of the tide'.
Mention at the same time was also made of 'lodging rooms, dressing
rooms, and a handsome large sashed dining room, and a summer house
on the top of the house, which affords a pleasant prospect out to sea'.
Mr Barber continued to advertise his sea-water bath at Margate in
May 1740, along with 'good lodgings and entertainment at my house,
which adjoins to the bath, and a good coach-house and stabling'. From
being an embryonic resort before 1750, Margate developed rapidly
during the eighteenth century, and won considerable publicity, coming

to prominence in numerous topographical works and newspaper reports from the 1760s onwards, as some of the source references in this essay will show.

Secondly, while communications have been decisive in the growth of most English seaside resorts, the pre-railway growth of Margate and Ramsgate into well-developed resorts was owing to a direct and low-cost water-communication link with London. Margate did not enjoy the sustaining influence of royal patronage which contributed enormously to the growth and popularity of Brighton and Weymouth. Once nature had marked Margate out as a suitable site for the establishment of sea bathing, the hoys initially brought the traffic and were replaced in their turn by steam vessels. Most seaside resorts underwent a great economic expansion as the result of the coming of a railway, and many owed their initiation to its presence, of which Blackpool and Bournemouth are examples; but not so with Margate, whose reputation was owing to direct and easy water communication from London using the natural highway of the Thames.

The contrasting explanation of prosperity as between Margate and Brighton was reported as follows by *The Times* of 1 September 1804:

> Margate, August 30 . . . has not been so full of visitors for eight years past, as it is this season. Every hoy or, according to the modern term, every packet is literally loaded. The smallest of these vessels brought down 120 persons yesterday morning . . . Though the town is so remarkably full, there are not here, at present, many persons of high rank and fashion.
>
> Brighton, Thursday, August 30 . . . is at present unusually full of company; and the presence of his Royal Highness has its obvious influence on the vivacities of the place.

The competitive position of Margate over other resorts was further strengthened by a lowering of the steamboat fares between 1820 and 1840, and it was from such facilities of cheap communication that the Thanet resorts underwent a considerable pre-railway expansion which placed them in a leading position over most other watering-places.

This lead, however, was not maintained during the middle decades of the nineteenth century. The opening-up of direct railway communication between London and the south-coast resorts, commencing with the Brighton line in 1841, destroyed the relative advantage of access from London enjoyed hitherto by the Thanet resorts. Railways placed English coastal resorts on a completely new footing. The very rapid growth of Brighton during the 1840s represented an intensifying competition between resorts so far as Margate was concerned. The almost exclusive advantage of a water highway to Margate was reduced as soon as railways were opened to the south coast. The growth of Margate was checked simply because railways revived or created rivals along the south coast.

It is possible therefore to recognise two periods of marked expansion in the development of Margate as a popular resort. The first lasted from 1730 to 1840, and this period forms the subject of this essay. The second began in the 1860s, when a more direct railway communication with London was established, and holidays and day excursions enjoyed an increasing demand owing to rising living standards among almost all sectors of society.

Thirdly, and this particular point becomes more apparent later on in this essay, there were few pre-railway resorts which had to cater for social groups below the level of the upper classes. Margate was an exception to the general rule that spas and watering-places were almost exclusively the resorts of the upper classes even before the close of the eighteenth century.

II. THE CHANGES BROUGHT ABOUT BY HOLIDAYMAKING

The growth of a holidaymaking function naturally brought about great changes in the economy, society, amenities and physical appearance of Margate. Those developments are best seen in observations extracted from an almost inexhaustible supply of contemporary topographical descriptions and newspaper reports. What was happening to Margate up to 1763 is reflected in part of the title to the first original guidebook of the area compiled in that year by John Lyons, a Margate schoolmaster: *A Description of the Isle of Thanet and particularly of the Town of Margate; with An Account of the Accommodations provided there for Strangers, their manner of Bathing in the Sea, and Machines for that Purpose, their Assemblies, Amusements and Diversions, public and private; the Antiquities and remarkable Places to be seen on the Island, as well as on some Short but pleasant Tours along the Coasts of Kent; . . . The whole illustrated with a correct map of the Island . . . and a Representation of the Machines for Bathing.*

An early newspaper report from the *Kentish Weekly Post and Canterbury Journal*, 28 August–4 September 1769, noted that 'Margate is now in great repute for its conveniences for sea bathing, by means

of most commodious machines, etc., which draws thither a great con-
course of company every summer, and has occasioned the town's being
lately embellished with several new buildings for lodging houses'. By
1770 it could be observed that

> There are several good lodging-houses, and their rooms, though
> frequently small, are neat. They may be said to be commodious too,
> if it is considered that many of them are now applied to a use for
> which they were not originally intended. However, many have been
> built of late years, expressly with an intention of their being hired
> for lodgings, and the old ones are daily receiving all the improve-
> ments they are capable of. There are, likewise, boarding-houses kept
> in a very decent, reputable manner, for the convenience of small
> families, or single persons, who rather wish to have a table provided
> for them at a certain and easy expense, than to be at the trouble of
> keeping one of their own.[2]

Margate had acquired by this time the first of its fashionable squares,
subsequently named Cecil Square. The supply of new accommodation
was expanding rapidly, to judge from an observation made in 1772:
'During the summer season this town is full of all sorts of people, whose
circumstances will permit them to spend money, and whose health requires bathing for its support . . . There are some good houses let in
lodgings, by which considerable sums are spent in the town; and since
the beginning of the present years (1771) several pieces of ground have
been let on building leases, and they are now erecting handsome houses
to accommodate the company.'[3] From a small town, Margate, it was
claimed in 1778, had 'now increased to a place of very considerable
magnitude, . . . adorned with houses fit for the reception of people of
the first rank, and with places of amusement and recreation'.[4]

Amusement and entertainment formed an important and growing
part of the apparatus of an expanding and popular resort. The facilities
and amenities of Margate at any one given point of time can be
abstracted from a great mass of guidebooks and topographical articles
and reports. Assembly rooms opened in Margate during the 1769 season
and attracted support from 930 subscribers at 5s. each. In addition to
five bathing rooms and 20–30 bathing machines, Margate could offer
visitors circulating libraries and such amusements as cards and dancing,
while during 1786 a theatre was constructed, at a cost of over £4,000,
offering performances four times a week.

On 17 July 1787 the *Maidstone Journal and Kentish Advertiser* reported that 'Margate has increased, and is still increasing, beyond all other sea-bathing places', and 'in point of building-speculation no place at present can vie with it – Booth with his theatre, Benson with his hotel, are both in great vogue with all the Margate company'. Margate expanded in size and stature with every passing decade, emerging in the 1800s as 'one of the most fashionable, and best frequented, watering places in the kingdom'.[5] The *Morning Chronicle* reported on 8 September 1810 that 'this place is crowded with company, and indeed may be considered as London in miniature, being in many circumstances an epitome of that vast metropolis'.

In 1819 *The Thanet Itinerary or Steam Yacht Companion* looked back as follows on the astonishing growth of Margate as a resort:

When the rage for sea bathing became general the vast metropolis poured forth her smoky thousands, who hastened to the sea coasts of Thanet. . . . The natural advantages of Margate soon obtained for it a decided preference over every other watering-place in the kingdom. Its convenient distance from London, its pure air and limpid waters, the delightful level of its fine sandy shore, and the high state of cultivation of the surrounding country, all conduced to make it the favourite summer retreat of nobility, gentry and citizens. . . . The effect was astonishing; squares were laid out, streets built, places of amusement erected, markets established.

III. MARGATE BEFORE SEA BATHING

In order to see the development of Margate as a seaside resort in perspective, it is necessary to know something of its earlier prosperity and of its other economic functions independent of its growth as a seaside resort. The economy of the Isle of Thanet up to the middle of the eighteenth century rested on commercial arable farming, which supported a small population settled in villages and farmsteads a little inland from the sea, some of which were connected with a small harbour and pursued independent or ancillary maritime occupations. Thus the small agrarian settlement of St John's, which contained the ancient church of Margate, stood close to another settlement which contained the harbour of Margate and was essentially maritime. This dual settlement, of St John's as an agrarian community distinguished from Margate as a maritime community, can be found in contemporary references to the area in the 1720s and 1730s. With the settlement expansion of eighteenth-century Margate these two separate communities merged into the single town of Margate.

It cannot be stated precisely when Margate ceased to be a village and became a town, for as late as 1763 the first Thanet guidebook observed that 'as Margate is only a large village, you cannot expect that it should be so regularly supplied with shops as a market town; not but that there are several good ones, and many very reputable tradesmen'. This deficiency, however, was 'in a great measure supplied by the numerous articles to be found in most of them, and by their ready and quick communication with London by the hoys'. The harbour of eighteenth-century Margate was prominent for its role in a substantial corn trade to London and as a port of embarkation and disembarkation to the Low Countries. Other maritime activities included fishing, smuggling and foying, the latter function embracing servicing and provisioning passing ships using the world's greatest commercial shipping route to and from London, going off to vessels in distress with anchors and chains, or rescuing crews and wrecks, particularly from the notorious Goodwin Sands.

Several contemporary references to Margate suggest that the town's fortunes were clearly not buoyant during the 1720s and 1730s. The Revd. J. Lewis, who was Thanet's eighteenth-century historian, took this point of view both in 1723 and in 1736.[6] In 1723, for instance, he was distressed at seeing Margate as 'a small fishing town, irregularly built, and the houses very low', which had 'formerly been of good repute for the fishing and coasting trade', for 'it seems owing a good deal to this decay of the fishing here, with the falling off of the foreign trade, and the removal of so many of the substantial inhabitants on that account from this place to London, that the charge of the poor is so much increased within those 80 years past'. The fortunes of Margate were probably at their lowest ebb during the 1720s. Lewis tells of a harbour which had been washed away by the sea, and for which the dues had not been and were still not being properly collected. Trading had decayed and merchant vessels were being constructed of a tonnage too large to lay up in the harbour. Daniel Defoe observed in the 1720s: 'the town of Margate is eminent for nothing that I know of, but for King William's frequently landing here in his returns from Holland, and for shipping a vast quantity of corn for London market, most, if not all of it, the product of the Isle of Thanet, in which it stands'. J. Harris in *The History of Kent in Five Parts* (1719) calculated 'that above 20,000 seams or quarters of all sorts of grain are sent to London, in a year, from this island, besides what is sent by the inhabitants, and sold to other places'. The great bulk of Thanet's corn output was grown as a cash crop for the London market. It was exported from Margate rather than Ramsgate. Margate lay nearer to London and avoided navigation round the North Foreland.

IV. MARGATE AND SEA BATHING

It was sea bathing that transformed Margate from a stagnant maritime village into an expanding and prosperous resort, from the mid-eighteenth century onwards, the effects of which were all too apparent in the course of a few decades at most. Brighton, like Margate, had declined during the seventeenth century, 'not again to hold up its head until the middle of the next century when it gradually became prominent . . . as a watering-place'.[7] According to Professor E. W. Gilbert, 'Before 1750 Brighton appeared but seldom in the main stream of English history, but . . . the practice of sea bathing brought new life to the decayed town of Brighton. After the doctors had prescribed sea water and sea bathing as a cure for numerous ills of mind and body and had commended the health-giving properties of sea air, Brighton became in due course a seat of the court and the social capital of the country.'[8]

The vogue for sea bathing and sea air, which developed quite dramatically during the eighteenth century, was crucial to the development of Margate. The initial growth of Margate as a resort resulted from a combination of three major developments: firstly, from the medical publicity which was given to sea water and sea air; secondly, from the sea-bathing facilities which Margate possessed and developed, so that sea-water treatment could be practised with comparative comfort; and thirdly, from the extension of inland and water transport linking London and the county to Margate. Of these key factors in the early rise of Margate as a watering-place, communications were clearly the most vital over the long term.

The cult of sea bathing, particularly for medical reasons, was very much an eighteenth-century phenomenon. During the two or three decades before 1750 several eminent physicians explored the possibilities of sea-water cures, but few people in the 1740s thought of applying sea water, both externally and internally, as a form of medical treatment. In the 1750s, however, the merits of sea water were given great publicity by the pen of Dr Richard Russel, F.R.S. (1687–1759), 'the father of all seaside watering places', and above all of Brighton.

He was undoubtedly the most active propagandist among the physicians working in this field, and the published work which made him famous at the age of sixty-three bore the title *A Dissertation on the Use of Sea Water in the Diseases of the Glands, particularly the Scurvy, Jaundice, King's Evil, Leprosy, and the Glandular Consumption.* It was published first in Latin in 1750, and in English from 1752 onwards.

Dr Russel, by means of this *Dissertation,* offered to the scrutiny of the medical profession and the reading public several instances of illness which he claimed had been cured by sea water, taken either inwardly or by means of bathing. The reader was introduced to thirty-nine cases illustrating the medical value of sea water. His findings were studied by the medical profession, including Dr John Coakley Lettsom, who was one of the principal founders of the Margate Sea Bathing Infirmary, the country's first hospital for tuberculosis. Russel's *Dissertation* also enjoyed an extensive readership among the public, who rapidly adopted the recommendations of sea bathing and the drinking of sea water. The work passed through a sixth edition during 1769, the third edition of the *Encyclopaedia Britannica* (1797) observing that 'It may be justly expected to contribute to the improvement of physic'.

It is well known that Dr Russel was not the only physician to be found working in this field in the early eighteenth century. There were other observers who were likewise convinced of the medical virtues of sea water, some of whom corresponded with Dr Russel. The independent researches of a Dr Speed culminated in a second work, *A Commentary on Sea Water,* which, drawing also on case evidence, was published during the 1760s.

Following Russel and Speed there was an extensive literature on the medicinal value of sea water, which continued into the nineteenth century and included a number of foreign contributors. This crusade in favour of improved health at the seaside won popular acceptance. It coincided with a time when people were unable to travel abroad because of wars. They were also heartily tired of the amenities of the inland spas, and wanted a fresh outlet for their activities. Brighton and Margate were among the first resorts to profit from these developments once the gospel of the sea was preached.

Contemporary evidence shows that the publicity given to sea-water treatment was put immediately into practice during the 1750s. A manuscript in the possession of Margate Public Library states in 1757 that 'of late years, since the physicians of London have in several cases prescribed drinking and bathing in salt water, the town of Margate has become much frequented in that account as the shore is flat and sandy'. Another contemporary referred in 1769 to 'an epidemical disorder that was formerly quite unknown and even now wants a name, which seizes whole families here in town at this season of the year. One would almost imagine that the people were all bit by a mad dog, as the same remedy is thought necessary. In a word, of whatever nature the complaint may be, it is imagined that nothing will remove it but spending the summer months in some dirty fishing town near the sea shore'. Bishop Pococke found himself in Margate in 1754 and described it as 'a fishing town . . . of late much resorted to by company to drink the sea water as well as to bathe; for the latter they have convenient cover'd carriages at the end of which is a covering that lets down with hoops, so that the people may go down a ladder into the water and are not seen'.[9]

During the nineteenth century the drinking of sea water gradually dropped out of medical practice, and emphasis in treatment changed to the value of sea air, ozone coming to be regarded as one of the chief health-giving elements. The concern of physicians with the medical properties of sea air had a long history extending back into the eighteenth century. A Dr Ingenhousz, for instance, made several experiments at Gravesend, in the middle of the English Channel, between the Kent coast and Ostend, and at three miles from the mouth of the Thames, to ascertain the salubrity of sea air. In 1780 he concluded 'that we may now with more confidence send our patients, labouring under consumptive disorders, to the sea'.

For the benefit of sea air and sea bathing, holidaymakers, well-off permanent residents, the medical profession and boarding schools were attracted to the seaside. The first original Thanet guidebook of 1763 noted of Margate: 'Two physicians usually reside here, during the summer season . . . there is a boarding-school for young ladies, kept in a very decent reputable manner; and another, where young gentlemen are taught arithmetic, mathematics, etc., so that gentlemen may now bring down their children for the benefit of the sea, without losing time in their education.' It was not long before physicians and surgeons took up permanent residence. In 1792 there were seven surgeons and physicians in Margate, or one doctor to every 681 inhabitants – an exceptionally high proportion compared with many other towns. The private preparatory school for children of wealthy Londoners and provincial families was throughout the nineteenth century a coastal institution.

In connection with sea bathing Margate had a number of distinct advantages. Margate Bay possessed fine sands and what contemporaries described as a 'weather shore'. The latter fact was given great stress in the *Gentleman's Magazine* in 1771:

> Another advantage peculiar to Margate is its being a weather shore, during the greatest part of the summer. . . . The southern winds, which generally prevail in that season, blow from the land; by which means the sea is rendered perfectly smooth, . . . whereas most of the places on the sea coast, in the English Channel, from the North Foreland to the Land's End, are on a lee shore, during the greatest part of the summer, and are incommoded very much by the southerly winds before mentioned . . . which never fail to occasion . . . a continual swell and surf of the sea on the south coast of England which not only makes the water there foul and thick, but annoys, frightens, and spatters the bathers exceedingly.'

These natural advantages must have been very reassuring to the invalids and timid bathers of the eighteenth century. Safe and convenient arrangements for sea bathing were of prime importance at a time when many were naturally terrified of the sea, which they had envisaged hitherto mainly from literary impressions or hearsay. Bathers demanded privacy in addition, and this was guaranteed by the bathing machine described thus by Zachariah Cozens in *A Tour through the Isle of Thanet, and some other Parts of East Kent* (1793):

> That sea bathing may be attainable with the strictest decency, there are near 40 machines employed in a season. . . . They consist of a carriage similar to that of a coach, but more simple, much stouter and considerably higher, that it may resist the waves in blowing weather; the wheels are high and strong. . . . In the front is a platform, from which you have admittance into the machine, which forms a neat dressing room, $6\frac{1}{2}$ ft long, 5 wide, and $6\frac{1}{2}$ high, with a bench on either side for the bathers to undress upon. . . . At the back opens a door, and, by means of a flight of steps attached to the machine, the bathers descend into the water, concealed from public view by a large umbrella of canvas stretched on hoops, which is let down by the driver, by means of a rope which comes to the front of the machine, until it touches the water, and forms a bath 10 ft long and 6 wide. . . . The proprietors employ very careful drivers, under whose guidance the machines are drawn out to the depth the bather may require.

The widely accepted claim that the bathing machine was invented in 1753 by Benjamin Beale, a Margate Quaker, is now disputed. Mobile chariots for bathing were put to use in Scarborough, Brighton and Margate well before 1753, and Beale's significance in the history of the bathing machine was to add the important refinement of a concertina-like canvas canopy to afford privacy to both sexes. In the words of *The Thanet Itinerary or Steam Yacht Companion* (1819), 'the screen – an umbrella of canvas, covering the whole hinder part of the machine – was an invention of one Benjamin Beale . . . some of whose relatives still carry on the business of bathers'.

The more refined bathing machine, which in Margate took the place of bathing from a tilted cart, was soon widely acclaimed. The *Kentish Gazette* of 15–18 June 1768 carried the following advertisement: 'Cornelius Jones, near the Rope Walk, Dover, begs leave to inform the public that he has lately provided a machine upon the same plan as those at Margate.' It was from the Margate model that bathing machines were introduced at Ramsgate and Broadstairs in 1754, at Lowestoft in 1768 and at Gravesend in 1796. They were even manufactured and exported to the East and West Indies.

Bathing rooms provided an alternative to open bathing in the sea, and the provision of a bath as early as 1736 in Margate provides another interesting example of early seaside enterprise. The bathing rooms of Margate became more elaborate in the course of time and particularly during the nineteenth century acquired every possible refinement. It was concluded of Margate bathing in 1770 that 'the sands are so safe and clean, and every convenience for bathing in the sea is carried to such perfection at this place, . . . it is no wonder that it should be frequented by such multitudes of people, who come hither either for health or pleasure'.[10]

V. MARGATE AND COMMUNICATIONS

Of longer-term significance than medical recommendations to the growth of Margate as a seaside resort were the physical means of getting there by land and water, which developed from the second half of the eighteenth century onwards. Until the railway arrived in Margate on 1 December 1846, the main forms of communication from London were either by coach or by boat, and before the middle of the nineteenth century water conveyance was by far the more important method. It was the most direct and by far the cheapest, and in its later years it was also the most comfortable. In a very real sense the journey to Margate presented no great problems, because hoys and, later, steamboats were able to operate frequent and cheap services by way of the river Thames. Whereas Brighton owed its prestige to royal patronage, water communication created the popularity of Margate. The development of this traffic before 1840 can be divided into two phases. The era of transport by coach and hoy lasted until about 1815, and that of the steamboat from 1815 onwards. The means of conveyance from London in 1793 included 'the indiscriminating hoy', 'the more respectable packet', stage-coaches and private carriages.

By land Margate was reached during the 1760s and 1770s by taking the Dover road from London to Canterbury where, since the Dover coach branched off, it was necessary to change to local coaches which took passengers the remaining 16 miles into Thanet. In 1770, for instance, two local coaches ran every day to Canterbury to meet the London coaches, and in 1779 two local coaches and a diligence. The coach journey from London to Margate was described in the *Gentleman's Magazine* in 1771. Stage-coaches set out from London every day, Sundays excepted, at 5 a.m., reaching Canterbury at 4 p.m., fare 12s. each passenger, or at 6 a.m. carrying only four passengers inside for 15s.: 'from Canterbury another machine, which runs all the summer, takes the passengers on to Margate the same day at 4s. each'. The whole distance of 72 miles was performed in 13–14 hours, the total fare coming to 16s. or 19s. Coaches left daily direct for London in 1796; for instance, from Mitchener's Hotel a coach left every morning at 4 a.m. for the White Bear, Piccadilly, carrying three inside at a fare of £1 6s.; or a night coach departed from the Fountain Inn at 5 p.m. arriving in London early next morning, carrying six inside passengers for £1 3s.

The coach journey of the 1790s from Margate to London took all day or all night, and cost between 22s. and 26s., a figure which may be compared with a minimum fare of 5s. on the hoys. When Joseph Farington, R.A., the topographical artist and diarist, after a stay at Broadstairs in 1804 returned by coach to London on 27 August, he left Margate at 5 a.m. and arrived in London at 7 p.m. In order to do this he had to spend the night of the 26th in a Margate hotel.[11]

Travelling by coach was costly partly for the reason that the total distance between London and Margate was about 25 miles further than from London to Brighton. Coaching was heavily taxed, moreover, and for the passenger there was much in the way of incidental expenditure in the form of tips to drivers and meals taken at inns. Even in 1830 the

PLATE III   Falkland Hall, High Street, Burford, in 1821. Bear Inn on right. (Reproduced from a water-colour by J. C. Buckler: Bodleian Library, Oxford, MS. Top. Oxon. a. 65, no. 138).

PLATE IV   Calendars (2nd. house from left), Sheep Street, Burford, in 1821 (Reproduced from a water-colour by J. C. Buckler: Bodleian Library, Oxford, MS. Top. Oxon. 65,a. no. 139).

PLATE V Wisdom's Cottages, adjoining the bridge, Burford. (Photo: Michael Laithwaite).

PLATE VI Edgehill, High Street, Burford. (Photo: Michael Laithwaite).

VESSELS USED ON LONDON TO MARGATE ROUTE

	Packets	Yachts	Hoys	Tons	Fares	
1763			4	80–100	2s. 6d.	
1770			5	80–100	2s. 6d.	
1780		1	5	80–100	2s. 6d.	
1789			6		4s.	
1792			6		10s. 6d., 6s., 4s.	
1796	8		3		10s. 6d., 7s., 5s.	
					Best cabin	Fore cabin
1802	9			80–120	7s.	5s.
1807	9		3		7s.	5s.
1809	9		2		9s.	7s.
1811	11		3		9s.	7s.
1812	7				7s.	5s.
1815	7–13				7s.	5s.

coach fares from London to Margate remained high: at 28s. inside and 15s. outside they had risen somewhat since 1796.

The famous Margate hoys of the eighteenth century were corn sloops which had a tradition of carrying passengers, the fare by corn hoy being only 2s. in 1757. The table above summarises the number of hoys, packets or yachts and the trend of fares on the London to Margate run between 1763 and 1815.

The number of vessels increased steadily between 1763 and 1811. Between 1811 and 1815, at the time of the Napoleonic wars, some of the packets were switched from passenger carrying to troop carrying. The minimum fare ranged from 2s. 6d. to 7s., falling back to 5s. in 1815, which was double that of 1763. One fare only obtained between 1763 and 1789, with complete stability until after 1780. The differentiation and rise of fares in the 1790s were associated with greater comfort. The packets were 'fitted up in an elegant and commodious manner, and furnished with good beds'.[12] Some of them had 'a state room or after cabin, which may be engaged by a select party for 5 or 6 guineas'.[13] Three of the packets operating in 1815 had private state cabins, which could be hired separately. Children in arms were conveyed at half fare in 1812; baggage was carried at under 6d. per cwt. in 1780 and at later dates 'proportionately cheap'.

The hoys carried more passengers than the coaches, and *The New Margate, Ramsgate, and Broadstairs Guide* (1802) noted that 'it is perhaps owing . . . to the very superior accommodation which they afford, as well as the civility and attention of the masters and seamen who navigate them, that Margate stands so highly distinguished in the list of watering places'. Evidence, however, of the volume of traffic carried is sparse. The maximum number of passengers which could be carried at any one time went up from 60–70 in 1763 to about 100 by 1789. It was calculated in 1792 that 'the vessels bring and carry during the bathing season to and from London 18,000 passengers'.[14] The *Morning Post and Gazetteer* of 28 August 1799 reported that 'a single hoy, which arrived on Sunday at Margate, from town, brought 100 passengers', while the *Observer* of 24 August 1800 revealed that 'seven hoys last week conveyed to Margate 1,342 persons'.

Travelling by hoy was very much cheaper than travelling by coach, and the low fares of the hoys had important social consequences for Margate. In 1789 it was noted that 'the chief of the company which come by the hoys are, as you may naturally suppose, of the inferior cast; very few persons in genteel life come by water, without they are recommended by their physicians so to do, to experience sea sickness, which is thought to be very beneficial in some complaints'.[15] *The Times* of 10 September 1803 observed that 'we understand that at Margate the distinctive title of fashionables is given without reserve to all the visitors of that agreeable watering-place who do not arrive there by the hoy'.

The very wealthy despised the vulgarity of the hoys, preferring to travel by public coach or in their own private carriages to Thanet, sending their domestic servants down by the hoy. Coaching was preferred also by ladies of fashion: 'Mrs André was so disgusted with the hoy that she returned to London in the diligence.'[16] The steamboats of the 1820s, having a reputation for comfort and regularity, represented altogether a much more pleasant and convenient way of travelling from London to Thanet than by stage-coach. Every passenger at least had the opportunity of stretching his legs during the seven hours of the voyage, but even so, as late as 1833, 'notwithstanding the safety, expedition, and cheapness with which the steam vessels travel, there are many persons, particularly ladies, who from timidity or choice prefer to travel by coach'.[17] The coaches found it even more difficult to compete with the lower steamboat fares of the 1830s, so that a visitor to Margate could record in 1839: 'I have not heard of one person, in his or her right senses, who has lately made an overland trip to Margate . . . apart from the driver and guard of the royal mail.'[18] Compared to the hoys the coaches had run to a specific time schedule, the time taken in going from London to Margate being cut from thirteen hours in 1804 to eleven hours by 1815. The journey times of the hoys were erratic, the passage in 1770 being 'sometimes made in 8 or 10 hours, and at other times in 2 or 3 days, just as the wind and the tide happen to be for or against it'. When Catherine Hutton visited Margate in May 1780, she travelled down in 9 hours 40 minutes, while the return journey took thirty-six hours.

The introduction of steamboats to Margate coincided with the end of the Napoleonic wars, and from the outset they greatly augmented the traffic to Thanet and increased the prosperity of Margate in particular. It was reckoned in 1817 that owing to steam packets some 5,000 extra passengers had come to the resort. The number of steamboats on the London to Margate run increased to five in 1819, to eight in 1826 and to ten in 1829. Six different companies competed for the Margate passenger traffic in 1836 and 1841.

The Thanet Itinerary or Steam Yacht Companion assessed the immediate impact of steam vessels by 1819 in these words:

> The benefits arising from the noble invention of steam vessels are nowhere more sensibly felt than in the Isle of Thanet. Perhaps it would be no very great exaggeration to assert that the number of visitors has increased in nearly a double proportion, since the establishment of steam packets rendered the voyage from London at once expeditious, safe, pleasant, and certain. . . . The sailing hoys have been known to be 72 hours in going from London to Margate. . . . A steam vessel might actually make nine voyages, while the sailing packets are making one! Such is the great improvement that has lately been introduced into the mode of conveyance between London and Margate.

During the steamboat era there was a notable expansion of traffic, as the evidence given to the Select Committee on Ramsgate and Margate Harbours in 1850 shows.

	Total passengers	Average p.a.
1812/13–1819/20	191,849	23,981
1820/1–1829/30	532,249	53,225
1830/1–1839/40	854,462	85,446
1840/1–1849/50	875,160	87,516

These figures represent the numbers arriving at and departing from Margate pier. This traffic more than quadrupled between 1817 and 1835. The record total was reached in 1835–6 when 105,625 passengers arrived at or departed from Margate, a figure which is all the more significant when it is recalled that the total population of England and Wales was about 15 million at this date. There were ups and downs in the numbers carried annually. The average numbers carried per annum during the 1830s were 60 per cent up on the 1820s. Passenger traffic reached a maximum between 1840–1 and 1846–7, when the steamboats carried 640,804 passengers, or 91,541 annually, which was a further 7 per cent up on the figures for the 1830s.

Greater speeds were achieved by the Margate steamboats after 1815. By the mid-1820s the journey had been reduced from between nine and twelve hours to less than seven hours. The *Maidstone Journal or Kentish Advertiser* of 31 May 1825 was able to report on a voyage from Margate in six and a half hours at 14 m.p.h: 'Sojourners to this asylum of health and pleasure may well call this flying by steam.' Steamboats originate a day excursions, and such a reduction of time on the single journey enabled steamboat day excursions to take place to Margate before the end of the 1820s.

By 1830 the fact of a quicker journey by water was stated thus: 'A journey to Margate, which thirty years ago might have occupied a whole week only in going and returning, may now be performed in a sunny afternoon; and before the week is elapsed, the whole of Margate may have been explored, and the traveller safe back to his own London residence.'[19] The quickest passage ever achieved by 1831 took 5 hours and 17 minutes, and by 1846 this had been further reduced to 4¾ hours.

The Margate steamboats of the 1830s had also acquired a reputation for comfort and luxury, which was described thus in 1831:

Those persons who have not been accustomed to steam vessels will, doubtless, be astonished at the accommodations which they will find on board; the cabins being fitted up in the most elegant manner, and with every possible attention to comfort. The company are provided with draughts, chess boards, etc., and an excellent band of music, and when the weather permits, they often join in the dance, for which the clean and spacious decks of these vessels are peculiarly adapted. It would be an act of injustice towards the stewards were we not to notice their great activity and civility, and the excellence of the refreshments provided. The dinner, which consists of joints, boiled and roasted, of the very best quality, all vegetables that are in season, and pastry, wines, dessert, etc., is served up in a style both pleasing and surprising, when the limited size of the kitchen is considered. . . . There is always a female attendant on board to wait upon the ladies.[20]

High fares were charged at first by the steam vessels, the lowest being 12s. compared with 5s. in 1815 on the hoys. A tendency for fares to decline commenced during the 1820s, so that the average fares during 1824–9 were some 20 per cent lower than in 1819–20. The decline continued to an average of 4s. during the 1830s and 1840s, but there were considerable fluctuations in fares and competition among the steamboat companies was intense. The years 1835–6 witnessed very low fares. *The Dover Telegraph and Cinque Ports General Advertiser* reported on 27 June 1835 that some of the steam vessels were charging only 2s. per person from London to Margate, out of which the proprietors had to pay 15d. pier duty for each individual embarking and landing. They received therefore only 9d. for themselves from each passenger, and supposing the distance from Margate by sea to be 90 miles, this amounted to only 1d. for every 10 miles for travelling. This was only one tenth as much as the 1d. per mile that found its way into the coffers of the parliamentary trains after 1844. (The Regulation of Railways Act, 1844, better known as the Cheap Trains Act, stipulated that all railways had to run at least one train daily charging a minimum fare of 1d. per mile third class.) *The Times* of 24 May 1836 advertised the General Steam Navigation Company's regular summer fares, except that 'on those days the unjustifiable opposition is continued on this Station the fares with be 2s. or 1s. 6d.' This 'unjustifiable opposition' arose on occasions from interlopers intervening to undercut the normal fares. A minimum fare of 1s. 6d. was 6d. under the hoy fare of 1757. Seasons of low fares occurred also in 1839 and 1841.

VI. THE HOLIDAYMAKERS

The demand for holidays came initially from the aristocracy, the clergy and a few among the professional and mercantile classes. In 1787, for instance, Lord George Herbert, later 11th earl of Pembroke, chose Margate as the place most likely to be beneficial to his wife's health, and accordingly rented a house there for two weeks in September at a cost of 10 guineas.[21] Henrietta countess of Bessborough was in Margate in 1798, returning to London in September in the duke of Manchester's yacht.[22] The *Morning Post and Gazetteer* reported on 9 September 1799 that 'Lady Ann and Captain Hudson remain at Margate during the remainder of the month. Lady Glencairn is there for health only'. The *Morning Chronicle* of 4 September 1801 noted 'that the Duke of Manchester is in the neighbourhood of Margate, sporting his elegant pleasure boat'. *The Times* of 31 August 1802 reported as follows on that season: 'Margate is now full in every part. Many fashionables are there; among whom are the Marchioness of Bath and her three daughters, the Ladies Thynne. Mr Littledale, the Dutch Banker, and family are expected, and the Duke and Duchess of St Albans to-morrow.' Lord Broughton paid a visit to Margate in July 1820,[23] and the duke of Devonshire in 1827, both of whom came down and returned to London by the steamboats.

While the aristocracy and gentry were noticed as individual visitors of distinction, a cross-section of society was represented among Margate visitors well before 1800. There are some surprisingly early references to visitors outside the ranks of the nobility and gentry. The cheapness of communications by sea facilitated the development of Margate as a middle- and lower-class resort. When George Keate undertook a journey to Margate in the 1770s, he remarked: 'Here are to be met with many plain, unrefined characters, intermingled with the more polished crowd. The frequent imports and exports of the hoys constantly maintain the inequality. . . . The decent tradesman slips from town for his half-crown, and strolls up and down the Parade, as much at his ease as he treads his own shop.'[24] It was observed in 1778 that 'people also of the middle and inferior classes may have recourse to the benefits of this place by the cheapness of a sea voyage; as hoys and yachts are continually passing between this place and London for the conveyance of goods and passengers at a very cheap rate'.[25]

The social divisions within the company were commented upon by contemporaries. Joseph Farington met in August 1804 in Broadstairs 'Miss Green and Mrs Meyer (the musician) and Miss Meyer, who came yesterday to Broadstairs, not liking Ramsgate or Margate, the latter Mrs Meyer said, is London – Cheapside, Wapping'.[26] In a poem of 1805, entitled 'A Trip to Margate', William Robinson shows how varied the visitors were. They included, apart from a few members of the nobility, many male and female citizens, solicitors, lawyers, surgeons, doctors, undertakers, barbers, tailors, slopsellers, butchers, bakers, tea-dealers. The company at Margate, in short, was 'compos'd of every trade, and each degree'.

Increasing wealth among the middle classes and tradesmen during the first half of the nineteenth century produced greater demands for holidaymaking. By the 1820s the aristocracy were to be found in Margate late in the season, as *The Times* reported on 28 September 1824:

Margate has become unpopular with the fashionable world, but continues more or less the summer retreat of the 'London citizens'. The introduction of steamboats has given the whole coast of Kent, the Isle of Thanet in particular, a prodigious lift; but the visitors to Margate are composed of the inhabitants of eastern London during the early part of the season almost entirely. The company at present are far more select and respectable than they have hitherto been; some of the most opulent merchants, East India Directors, and bankers, are now here; and a few who may be denominated a portion of the fashionable world. Sir Gilbert Heathcote has engaged Captain Cotton's House, in the neighbourhood of Margate, for one month at the high rate of 200 gns., the Captain himself having gone to the Highlands to shoot grouse.

Descriptions such as 'people of the first distinction', 'the genteel' and 'the vulgar' were used to describe in very general terms the company at Margate. Moving forward in time to 1845, to the year before the South Eastern Railway linked Margate to London, Mrs Elizabeth Stone, in her book *Chronicles of Fashion*, noted of the two main Thanet towns: 'Thirty years ago Margate and Ramsgate were crowded in the season by those who now would not be seen but at Brighton, and perhaps will not continue to go there long. It requires marvellous courage now to confess any interest in places so utterly discarded by fashion as are Margate and Ramsgate. They are still crowded, but by decidedly unfashionable people.' Mrs Stone was confirmed in her impressions by other comments dating from the 1840s and 1850s.[27]

'Vulgarity' was a term often applied to mid-nineteenth-century holidaymakers, but its precise meaning varied over time and according

Occupations of Margate visitors, 1841

Independent	352
Servants or governesses	89
Tradespeople	70
Merchants, dealers, factors	25
Professional, other than legal	16
Legal profession	11
Engineers or mechanics	10
Manufacturers or makers	7
Clerks	7
Armed services	5
Farming	5
Church	4
Total	601

to class. Some light on the social trends of holidaymaking emerges from the 1841 census, which was taken in June and lists the occupations of about 600 visitors to Margate.[28]

The social trends of holidaymaking in Margate as revealed by the 1841 census returns suggest that the middle classes were strongly entrenched in this particular resort. Aristocratic and titled visitors in the old category of nobility, gentry and clergy were few in number, though gentry, no doubt, were well represented among the 352 visitors of independent means. This is the hardest category to break down. Independent means could include an unearned income from inherited wealth, or from urban or agricultural rents and/or investments. Industrialisation, the growth of towns, and the construction of canals, railways, harbours and public utilities, particularly gas and waterworks undertakings, greatly widened the opportunities of middle-class investment income.

Titled visitors numbered no more than three, and the church and farming were also noticeably well down the list. Of the 352 visitors of independent means, no fewer than 222, or 63 per cent, were women, some of whom had left husbands behind in London. There is no means of knowing the occupational title which was appropriate to a married woman of independent means, but it may be presumed to have been gentry, middle class, professional or commercial in the vast majority of cases.

The remaining 130 male visitors of independent means, a proportion of whom were elderly or retired, compares therefore with 70 tradespeople, 32 merchants or manufacturers and 27 drawn from the professions. The third major occupational group coming after people of independent means and servants and governesses comprised tradespeople. Tradespeople, merchants, dealers, factors, the professions, engineers, mechanics, manufacturers and clerks, numbering 146, exceeded in total the 130 male visitors of independent means. The professions, including the church and armed services, were outnumbered by tradespeople by about two to one. The 89 servants and governesses were brought down to supervise the domestic arrangements of lodgings and one can only surmise as to whether the change of air and scenery contributed to their health and well-being. Since for no other resort did the 1841 census enumerate so many visitors, no valid comparison with other places is possible.

Nineteenth-century England may have remained an aristocratic country,[29] but confronted by the commercial and industrial changes of the period, the aristocracy was unable to retain its dominance in the resorts and spas of England when faced with the growing economic strength of the middle classes. Margate had become by 1841 one of the holiday resorts of an extensive and diverse middle class. Already by about 1830 something approaching £36,000 every week, or £286,500 over the eight peak weeks of July and August, poured into Margate from the expenditure of about 15,000 resident holidaymakers. This build-up of holidaymaking in Margate since the 1730s had been accompanied by the foundation and growth of specifically holiday industries, apart from long-distance transport. In the intervening period up to 1840 capital was put into a vast array of amusements and an extension of accommodation, particularly in the form of lodging-houses. A recent historical account of the seaside holiday has summarised the direct multiplier effects of holiday expenditure very neatly as follows: 'Half a dozen visitors make a pleasant change. Half a hundred visitors are an event. A thousand visitors mean hotels, extra shops, wider streets.' [30]

Press reports of busy seasons were numerous during the period covered by this essay. The *Morning Herald and Daily Advertiser* noted of Margate on 23 August 1781 that 'as to lodging, we are stowed of a night as thick as well-packed figs in a grocer's cask'. The *Morning Post and Gazeteer* of 24 August 1799 remarked that 'there has been many a wrinkled brow in the City, since Margate was reported so crowded as to oblige the visitors to lie three in a bed.' *The Times* reported twice on the effects of a busy season during September 1804. On 10 September it remarked: 'The visitors to Margate have certainly no reason to be reproached for want of liberality in their expenses while here. . . . A hoy came in loaded this morning. Between comers and goers, we will strike a considerable balance in favour of our population, and still more in favour of our innkeepers and boarding houses, our billiard tables, and bathing machines.'

On 13 September *The Times* reported:

We are now getting in a most plenteous harvest. Ship and coach loads of Cockneys are arriving every day so that we are fuller than we have been all this season, which is one of the fullest we have ever known. Our lodging houses can with difficulty muster an extra bed for a new visitor; and all the provisions in our market are bought up early in the morning by the inn and boarding house keepers; our libraries are filled with people. . . . Our bathing machines are all in a state of constant requisition; and it should be added our doctors find the number of their patients considerably on the increase.

The *General Evening Post* noticed in July 1795 how even the humble profession of shoe-cleaning benefited from the expenditure incurred in holidaymaking, for 'there is, we are told, a man at Margate exercising the profession of a shoe-black who contrives every season to lay up somewhat more than £100! ! !' This interesting phenomenon obviously caught the paper's fancy, for a few days later it remarked that 'this may literally be said to be picking money out of the dirt.'

In the rush to make money out of visitors at the seaside it would have been surprising had there not arisen complaints of extortion at watering-places, a good instance of which *The Times* reported on 1 October 1800:

> Much has been said of the exorbitant charges at watering-places. . . . Families leave their comfortable and sumptuous habitations, both in town and country, to get to the seaside, and content themselves with any hole they can be thrust into in expectation of amusement. . . . The tradesmen, who are generally few in number, charge an unreasonable profit, and in a very few years they make large fortunes, retire from their shops, and turn builders, and every year proves that they let their houses dearer. Yet though fishing villages rise into towns in the season, not a house or apartment is to be got. After an exorbitant charge is made for house-rent, where families do not bring an establishment, a cook, who keeps the house, makes her curtsey, and plays into the tradesmen's hands. . . .

Extortion extended beyond lodgings to coal for cooking, to stabling, and to servants' attendance. Moreover, 'To be genteel, all the libraries must be subscribed to. If you look into the assembly rooms, the books are open to subscribe for the rooms, for the master of the ceremonies, for the clergyman, for the music.' Finally, 'The physician, without attending to the pocket, is sure, when his art fails to cure his patient, to order him to Harrogate, Scarborough, Tunbridge Wells, and the bathing places.'

VII. CONCLUSION

This essay has been concerned to emphasise the origins and importance of pre-railway Margate as a seaside resort. By 1840 the holiday function had progressed considerably in this one town compared with 1730, yet as a steamboat resort in the post-Napoleonic period Margate was neither alone nor unique. In Kent alone, important, though lesser rivals existed in Ramsgate, Broadstairs, Dover, Herne Bay and Gravesend.

6. Early Victorian Coventry: Education in an Industrial Community, 1830-1851

W. B. STEPHENS

THE relationship between industrialisation and social life is of particular significance to the student of urban history, and indeed to those interested in urbanisation and industrialisation generally. It has recently been shown [1] that during the period of the classical Industrial Revolution in Lancashire the effect of the advent of factory life was to depress the opportunities for working-class education. In the factory towns of the north of England existing educational establishments were insufficient to cater for the children of the immigrant workers, while at the same time the textile factories, with their demand for child labour and the inadequacy of parental wages, discouraged school attendance. The result was an urban educational problem which was first tackled piecemeal by the adoption of part-time education through Sunday schools, factory schools, Mechanics' Institutes and the like.

The evidence from Lancashire suggests that up to 1840 the education of the child worker in the textile factories was less well provided for than it had been under the domestic system, and in the Lancashire handloom-weaving areas there was still in times of good business a greater tendency to send children to school than there was in the new urban centres. Only gradually, as living standards rose and Factory Acts limited child labour, did an expanded system of day-school instruction, largely through the voluntary and private schools, emerge in the factory districts. In particular it is evident that the educational clauses of the Factory Act of 1833, and more particularly the Act of 1844, had a beneficial effect on the extent of working-class education in the cotton and woollen districts. [2]

Not all industrial centres, however, were factory towns devoted to the production of cotton and woollen goods, and the influence of industrialisation and economic growth on education facilities in other urban communities is still in need of investigation. Coventry, which is here taken as a case study, was an industrial centre which differed very considerably from the textile towns of Lancashire and Yorkshire. An old industrial city, important for textile production even in the Middle Ages, Coventry experienced population and industrial expansion like other Midland and northern towns in the eighteenth and nineteenth centuries, the number of townsmen doubling between 1801 and 1851. Yet its industry continued to be organised very largely on a domestic basis, and it did not become a typical factory town until the cycle and motor industries made it so in recent times. Indeed it was only in the 1830s, at the very end af the period of classical Industrial Revolution, that any factories began to appear in the city's silk-ribbon industry, its staple trade.

The first steam factory was built in the town in 1831 but immediately burnt down by angry domestic weavers, and, as will be detailed below, orthodox textile factories remained unimportant in Coventry throughout the period under review. Between 1830 and 1860 'cottage factories', in which individual weavers continued to work in their own homes but had steam power communally supplied, appeared in Coventry, but even this development was secondary to parallel changes in the pattern of domestic ribbon production which continued on a large scale.

Change in the organisation of this domestic industry was reflected in alterations in the social structure of the city. In place of the few merchant capitalists (locally called 'manufacturers') controlling in the eighteenth century large numbers of wretchedly poor domestic workers (known as 'undertakers') and their apprentices, there emerged in the early nineteenth century a broader-based class structure. By 1838 the old 'manufacturers' had been replaced by a large class of small industrial capitalists, also known as 'manufacturers' but with more justification, varying in importance from those employing 100 or so looms down to some seventy men each employing 10 looms or fewer. Those weavers employed directly by the new manufacturers were relatively unskilled men known as 'second-hand journeymen', and their social status and living conditions were indistinguishable from the small number of factory workers in the town. The domestic weavers who worked independently on their own looms, but also supplied the 'manufacturers', were 'first-hand journeymen', and their standing was considerably higher, merging with that of the smaller 'manufacturers'. They too employed 'second-hand' assistants.

Almost all Coventry weavers worked Dutch Jacquard 'engine' looms, which were not powered but were capable of producing several ribbons at once. They were not therefore to be classed with the wretched 'single-hand' weavers (producing on traditional looms a single width of ribbon at a time) who occupied the smaller Midland towns and the country districts around Coventry itself, and whose lot was akin to that of the handloom weavers of Lancashire.

Coventry had found, for the time, a compromise between the twilight existence of the handloom districts proper and the booming degradation of the factory towns. It is significant too that despite the demoralising uncertainty of the life of the city's second-hand journeymen, Coventry's industrial society (like, for example, that of Leicester and Birmingham) was as a whole distinctly less divided than that of the Lancashire cotton towns. There were few great mill-owners, and the first-hand journeymen could aspire with some hope to become master manufacturers. More important, the first-hand journeymen outnumbered the second-hand men and did not represent a working-class élite in the numerical sense. In 1838, for example, eight out of every nine looms in the city were worked in the homes of first-hand men. There was little unrest among the second-hand journeymen, for they in their turn looked forward to first-hand status and were quite likely to achieve it: the average age of the second-hand man was lower than that of the first-hand man and to a certain extent advancement came with experience. Indeed, if there was an artisan élite in the city it was to be found in Coventry's second industry, watchmaking. But this also was not a factory industry, and there is little evidence of social friction between watchmakers and weavers.

Coventry's Industrial Revolution was thus achieved without factories and without the social disintegration associated with them. Indeed in 1835 there were only 25 power looms in use in the textile factories in the whole of Warwickshire (Cheshire had 22,913; Lancashire, 62,684; Yorkshire, 7,809) and only five silk factories in the county (Cheshire, 88; Lancashire, 23; Staffordshire, 11; Derbyshire, 15). Some of these factories were in Coventry, but by 1851 there were still only six large steam factories and six small ones in the city. Even in 1859, when there were fifteen large factories, the number of looms worked in cottage factories was equally great, and the predominance of outdoor weaving was still sufficiently strong to prevent further extension of the factory system.

With this background it becomes interesting to examine how far the difference in Coventry's industrial experience *vis-à-vis* the factory towns was reflected in the problem attached to education in this period.

Did the absence of juvenile factory work and the dominance of domestic manufacture of a comparatively successful kind result in a higher attendance at day schools, and a greater parental demand for schooling, as the suggested pattern in Lancashire might lead one to expect? The answer appears to be in the negative, and there does not seem to be any obvious relationship between domestic industry and full-time day schooling or any great demand for education facilities. In Coventry, as in the factory towns, child labour was common and part-time education rather than attendance at day school was the rule. There is no evidence that a higher proportion of children received education in Coventry than in the Lancashire towns, nor that the quality of schooling was any better. Indeed, as the nineteenth century progressed into the period under review, the situation at Coventry may well have been inferior compared with many factory towns. The Factory Acts and the factory inspectors did at least ensure, particularly from 1836, that there was some compulsory education of factory children. To this extent the child labourers of the cotton–woollen complexes had education forced upon them, whereas Coventry children, often employed by their own relatives, were less well catered for. Even the few in factories in the town did not benefit from government legislation, for the silk industry was exempted from the Factory Acts.

At the beginning of Victoria's reign very large numbers of children were employed in the Coventry domestic ribbon industry. Many first-hand journeymen and women working their own looms relied on their own families for labour. In 1838, of 6,796 working members of such families, 2,587 were children under the age of fourteen; of these, 716 boys and 750 girls were under seven. Of 1,520 second-hand workers employed by first-hand men, 435 were under fourteen, of whom 303 were less than seven years old. Those employed in factories numbered only 965, of whom 392 were under fourteen and 249 under seven. It is quite evident that the largest group of children of school age in employment comprised those outside the factories and in particular those whose parents formed the most prosperous group of textile workers. An official investigation undertaken in 1833, when the city's population was some 27,000, found 34 schools in Coventry. Of these, 19 were day schools (including 3 for infants), 11 were Sunday schools, 3 were 'Sunday and day' schools and one a 'boarding school'. The infant schools claimed 300 pupils. Children at the other day schools and day pupils at the 'Sunday and day' schools together numbered 1,022; the boarding school had 35 boys and girls – a total of 1,357 children. In addition the Sunday

schools catered for another 2,124 children some of whom were doubtless also included in the ordinary day-school totals. At the very most
3,480 children were receiving some kind of schooling; that is, 1 in 7·7
of the total population. Those at day school, however, represented only
1 in 20. In 1821 about a quarter of Coventry's population had been
between the ages of five and fifteen; in 1851 one-fifth. At the same
ratio there would have been between 5,400 and 6,750 children of school
age in the city in 1833. If the 3,480 children recorded were all those at
school, they represented between 52 and 64 per cent of the city's school-
age population. It is unlikely, however, that all schools in the city were
covered by the return. In particular, small private schools for middle-
class children were probably omitted. The number of children attending
these, however, was certainly small, and anyway the 3,480 was undoubtedly an exaggerated total.

A more reliable survey was undertaken in 1838 by Joseph Fletcher,
the assistant commissioner reporting to the Handloom Weavers' Commission, and a man with considerable interest in education, later
becoming secretary to the Children's Employment Commission and a
government inspector of schools. He was a founder member of the Royal
Statistical Society and his investigation at Coventry was minute. He
found that there were in the city 15 public day schools (with 1,118
pupils), 78 private and dame schools (1,629) and 18 Sunday schools
(1,346 pupils excluding those also attending day schools). In addition
there was the Free Grammar School, and 20–30 private schools catering for the 'middle and upper classes' the number of whose pupils
cannot be ascertained. The total of 4,093 children recorded amounts,
however, to about 1 in 7·6 of the total population (approximately 31,000
in 1841) at some sort of school, and 1 in 11·3 at day school. The apparent improvement over 1833 is, however, probably due to the inadequacy of the earlier return. Only two public day schools (Thomas Street
Infants' School and Westwood School) were in existence in 1838 which
had not been there in 1833, while one (Holy Trinity National Girls'
School) had been closed in 1836. If there was improvement, measured
in this way, it lay in the expansion of Sunday and private schools.

The total number of children in 1838 recorded as attending one sort
of school or another amounted to about two-thirds of Coventry children
between the ages of two and fourteen. The fact, however, that many of
these attended only Sunday school is reflected in other contemporary
estimates that 'Coventry has not school-room for much above one-third'
of its children. It is clear too that the proportion of children at day

school, public or private, differed from district to district within the city. Estimates from teachers and those responsible for schools as to the number of children not in attendance at school in their own neighbourhoods varied considerably: 'probably one-eighth', 'one-fifth perhaps', 'one-third only go occasionally, one-tenth not at all', 'half nearly'. Many, however, reported between one-quarter and one-fifth not at school. The officers of Vicar Lane Sunday School suggested that about half the children under eight attended, but few older children 'are able to attend other than Sunday schools', and this may well have been a general pattern.

It must be admitted that child employment in domestic industry was not entirely to blame. Not all children who did not attend school were at work: one private-school teacher reported 'nearly half are always on the streets . . . it is astonishing to see what numbers there are playing about'. It is also evident that in times of bad trade some children were withdrawn to save school pence, not because there was employment for them. Nevertheless even in 1838 there was a considerable amount of child labour in Coventry, and this accounted for many who never attended school, and more particularly for those who left school after only a brief acquaintance with study.

In 1847, admittedly a year of depression for the ribbon trade, it was estimated that 4,000 Coventry children did not attend any school at all, and that those who did were irregular in their attendance. At the 1851 census there were some 8,000 children of school age in the city, so that the 1847 estimate would suggest no great improvement, if any, over 1838. On the other hand about a dozen new public day schools were founded between 1838 and 1851. These included four infants' schools, the National schools at St John's, St Michael's and St Peter's, and two British schools (St Nicholas Place and Little Heath, the latter originally a Sunday school).

By 1851, when the population was about 37,000, there were 58 day schools (41 private, 17 public) in the city, and 20 Sunday schools. Total attendance on census day was 2,403 in the day schools and 2,950 in the Sunday schools, although the actual numbers of pupils on the books were 2,805 for day schools (1 in 12·9 of the population) and 3,830 for Sunday schools (1 in 9·5 of the population). At all events between two-thirds and three-quarters of those between five and fifteen (as opposed to the alleged half in 1847) were getting some sort of education. Yet this was not much better than in 1838. Indeed the proportion of children at day school (1 in 11·3 of the population in 1838) had declined. This would suggest that the foundation of new schools had hardly kept up with the increase of population. A report on educational facilities between 1834 and 1852 in Manchester and Salford came to the conclusion that there too school attendance had not kept pace with population growth.[3] At Leeds, however, the proportion of children at day school rose from 1 in 12 of the population in 1839 to 1 in 7·9 in 1851,[4] and the extent of education in Coventry measured in this way did not compare favourably with most factory towns in Lancashire and even less with those in Yorkshire. Table 1, based on the 1851 educational census, illustrates this.

Table 1

Urban centre	Attendance at day school in 1851
COVENTRY	1 child per 12·9 of population
Lancashire	
Blackburn	10·9
Bolton	10·2
Liverpool	8·6
Manchester	11·6
Oldham	13·1
Preston	9·1
Salford	12·2
Warrington	8·4
Wigan	8·5
Yorkshire	
Bradford	10·8
Doncaster	9·2
Halifax	7·7
Hull	8·3
Leeds	7·9
Sheffield	8·7
Wakefield	7·3

It will be seen that only at Oldham was there a worse state of affairs, and even Manchester and Salford were marginally better off. Other industrial towns also had better ratios than Coventry; in the Midlands, Birmingham (11·0), Derby (7·8), Leicester (9·5), Northampton (7·8), Nottingham (9·7), Stockport (12·3), Wolverhampton (12·0); in the north-east, Newcastle upon Tyne (9·7), Sunderland (9·9). Towns in the south with roughly the same population as Coventry were Devonport (7·4), Exeter (6·8) and Southampton (6·4). Portsmouth, with twice Coventry's population, had a ratio of 1 in 7·6, and Bristol, with 100,000 more people than Coventry, 1 in 7·7. The average for England and Wales as a whole was 1 in 8·4.

If we examine attendance at Sunday school, Coventry had one pupil for every 9·5 of its population. This was a better proportion than several of the other large towns mentioned above, including Birmingham (10·4), Liverpool (17·1), Exeter (15·5), Hull (10·1), Leicester (12·8), Newcastle upon Tyne (14·1), Portsmouth (15·6) and Southampton (10·1), but these figures to a certain extent must reflect the better day-school facilities in these towns. Taking school attendance at both day and Sunday school together, only three of any of the towns so far mentioned were worse off than Coventry. These were Liverpool, Newcastle upon Tyne and Portsmouth, the last two of which were only marginally inferior to Coventry. The average for England and Wales was 1 in 7·5.

Yet despite periods of depression in the late 1830s and early 1840s and in 1847, by the mid-century Coventry's working population was comparatively prosperous. The city had a near-monopoly in the fancy brand of silk-ribbon production, and the small manufacturers and first-hand journeymen were particularly well off for working men; the watchmakers were even more so. Coventry's apparently deficient educational record thus cannot be attributed to its being the centre of domestic industry depressed by the competition of the textile factory towns. Coventry's great crisis came with foreign competition after the period under review.

There seems every reason to believe that the bulk of Coventry's working population were quite satisfied with existing educational facilities. They were neither socially nor economically depressed, nor was there evidence of any great political motivation for change. In the late 1830s a group of young socialist weavers was active in the town and was sufficiently strong to cause a split in the Mechanics' Institute. Despite this, at least until the 1850s any great dissension between social classes was absent from Coventry. There was a wide parliamentary franchise, social mobility was feasible, and militant Owenism and Chartism, so strong in Lancashire factory towns, obtained little foothold in Coventry. The independent nature of the watchmakers was a further moderating influence. The very absence of feelings of political and social deprivation may indeed have contributed to a lack of interest in education. In addition the stimulus to educational provision given by the Factory Acts was absent. It is significant that in Lancashire factory education was worst promoted in the smaller firms,[5] where conditions approximated more to domestic industry.

To evaluate education in Coventry at this time, it is, however, necessary to look further than the sort of 'statistics' so far examined. Equally important was the nature of education and its quality. The types of school in existence at Coventry did not differ from those available in most towns: endowed public schools (often called charity schools), private schools, Sunday schools, and public unendowed day schools, including infants' schools and often connected with churches or chapels. These last were the 'voluntary schools', so important in English educational history. Though it is, strictly speaking, difficult to measure such a subjective term as 'quality', the examination of certain aspects of the education provided by these schools can give some indication of the extent to which some offered a better education than others. Relevant considerations in this context are the ages of children, the length of time spent at school, the subjects studied, the methods of instruction, the availability of books and apparatus, the qualifications of the teachers, the attitude of teachers and parents to the nature of the schools' work, and the orderliness or otherwise of the atmosphere in which learning was pursued.

In the first place it is clear that the numbers or percentages of children in, say, the age range 5–15, at school at any one time, are not the same as the number or proportion of the townsfolk who at some time in their life received some schooling. The figures discussed above, taken with the fact that many children attended school for only a few years, may thus suggest that a larger percentage of the population than is immediately obvious received some basic education. The obverse is that such brief instruction may have resulted in superficial learning, soon forgotten.

In the public day schools of Coventry in 1838, of the 1,515 children whose age and sex is ascertainable, 950 were over seven years of age, and of these 653 were boys.

At the endowed or charity schools all the children were over seven; indeed at most of these schools pupils did not enter until they were ten or eleven years old. Of the ten other public day schools in the city and its suburbs four were specifically called infants' schools, though in fact the distinction between these and other schools was not rigid. Exactly half of the 80 pupils at Far Gosford Street Infant School in 1838, for example, were over seven; while of the 249 pupils of Union Street National School, which was not an 'infant school', 130 were under seven. Generally, however, children over eight or nine were not catered for by the infant schools.

For private schools such information is generally lacking, but of the 730 pupils (392 boys) at such schools for whom information is available, 425 were under seven. For nearly 2,500 children at school in the town in 1838 ages are not known, but it is clear that most of the private schools, including 'dame' schools, catered for infants and very young children.

No exact figures are ascertainable of the ages of children at Sunday schools, but the majority were certainly over seven. At Holy Trinity School, for example, 100 were over seven and 54 under that age in 1838; at Hill Field Independent School the numbers were 140 and 40, and these ratios were fairly typical of other city Sunday schools. This suggests that the pattern of education often tended to be attendance at day schools until the age of seven or a little older, followed by part-time instruction at Sunday schools. Investigation of the length of time spent at school corroborates this suggestion. At the unendowed public day schools attendance varied from one to five years but generally appears to have been about two to three years. At private and dame schools the period was from a few weeks to four years, but was often one or two years. For many, attendance at such establishments was ephemeral. As one private-school owner explained, it was 'sometimes a week, sometimes a month, sometimes a year or two'. They were clearly used as baby-minding shops, or at best preparatory institutions before attendance at public infant or day schools. One modest proprietress admitted that her pupils were with her 'one year, perhaps, until they are taken away to be sent to those more able to teach them'; and another, less indulgent, remarked that 'infant schools rob us, so few remain long'. At the Sunday schools, however, attendance often continued over many years, even as long as eleven, many Sunday-school teachers claiming that their pupils entered at five or seven and remained until sixteen.

Only at the six endowed public schools (the charity schools) was there attendance at day school until what today would be regarded as a normal school-leaving age. There, children entered at ten or eleven and usually stayed for three years. At the Blue Coat Charity School for Girls some remained for up to five years. It is not surprising, therefore, that it was in some of these schools that working-class children in Coventry were able to obtain the most superior instruction. This was particularly so of the boys' schools, which required basic literacy before entry and claimed that none left unable to read and write well. The two girls' schools conformed more to the traditional conception of charity-school education, aiming mainly at training for domestic service. Both taught sewing and knitting, and the Blue Coat School offered in addition only reading, but no writing, 'the six eldest girls being taken into the mistress's house for the last year to fit them for household servants'. Bridget Southern's Charity School for Girls, however, taught spelling, reading and arithmetic as well, though it was admitted that about 25 per cent of the pupils were unable to read or write well when they left. All the boys' charity schools, however, taught the three R's. Baker, Billing, and Crow's School offered also history and geography to older boys, and drawing, music and geometry to 'those who showed talent for it'. Bablake School, where education was sufficiently good to attract 54 fee-paying day pupils in addition to the 40 charity boys, taught grammar, book-keeping and mensuration. At Fairfax's Charity School reading occupied ten hours a week, writing five, arithmetic ten, spelling fourteen and geography two hours.

The unendowed public day schools confined their instruction very largely to religious education and the three R's, with sewing and knitting for girls. Occasionally, however, other subjects were taught: the Lancasterian Boys' School hopefully claimed to provide 'any other branch of education they [the pupils] may be fit to acquire', and an infant school in the Butts taught natural history and geography. The school day at these schools generally lasted six hours. At St John's National School the mornings were devoted to reading, spelling and needlework. The Sherbourne House Infant School, which had 30 of its 120 pupils over seven, devoted one hour a day to reading, one hour to tables and mental arithmetic, twenty minutes to spelling, half an hour each to scripture, natural history and writing, and two hours a week to grammar, geography and geometry.

The Sunday schools, where many children received instruction over the longest period of their childhood, taught only scripture, church catechism and reading. Generally the hours of attendance were from two and a half to four hours. Only three of these schools taught writing, though one felt obliged to defend itself on that count: 'writing is not taught, because the teachers being dependent upon their labour for subsistence . . . could not without abridging their labour, and consequently their income (which is now far too small), go . . . on the week-day night to teach it'. Stoke Independent Sunday School, however, did provide one and a half hours' writing instruction on two evenings in the week. In only one Coventry Sunday school was arithmetic taught in 1838.

In the private and dame schools those which catered exclusively for infants at best concentrated on reading, writing and sewing, though the claim of many may well be exaggerated. Smacking of honesty, however, is the admission of one Coventry dame that her aim was to 'keep them out of harm's way; and a little reading'. Similarly another, asked what she taught, replied: 'Why to be still, and read as well as I can.' Those taking older children added arithmetic and knitting. One evening private school was an exception, catering for 30 working-class pupils aged from eight to sixteen, and teaching them arithmetic, book-keeping, geography and grammar.

Teaching methods also give some idea of the quality of education. In the unendowed public schools and the larger Sunday schools varieties of the monitorial system, whereby older pupils were used to instruct younger, were in use. The church schools used the National or Bell's system, and the Nonconformist and independent schools the so-called Lancasterian or British system. There was little difference: both sought to enable one teacher to instruct large numbers of pupils indirectly through older children (monitors) who passed on the lessons learned directly from the master or mistress. Some of the infant schools, however, claimed to use the methods advocated by Samuel Wilderspin. These to a certain extent eschewed the mechanical aspects of the monitorial method in favour of learning by experience and through the use of specially devised apparatus, though it is alleged that in practice Wilderspin's 'plan' often degenerated into the drudgery of rote-learned catechisms of questions and answers.[6]

In the voluntary schools in particular, however, the monitorial system became well established. A government inspector of schools reported in 1846 that in the Midland counties generally, 'with few exceptions, the children are taught by each other'. The land and buildings of the Coventry Central School (closed 1853) were presented on the condition that Bell's system should be used. In 1847–8 circulating monitors were teaching at St John's and St Peter's and there is evidence that they were still in use in the early 1860s, although by then pupil-teachers were replacing the monitors.

In the 1830s, however, only in the charity schools was there any clear evidence of a determined effort to preserve direct teaching by master or mistress. At Bablake School it was reported with some smugness that 'the master is not confined to any particular system; he adopts those plans which he considers best calculated to accelerate the improvement of his pupils. They are not taught upon Bell's or Lancaster's system.' At

Fairfax's and Bridget Southern's, however, the monitorial system was used for reading.

The superior instruction in the boys' charity schools is also evidenced by the fact that only in these, where there were older children and a variety of subjects taught, was there any variety of textbooks – in grammar, natural history, geography, history and so on. At these schools and at the unendowed day schools Mrs Trimmer's *Abridgements of the Bible* was a commonly used work. At the latter schools, however, there was little variety. Bibles, testaments, scriptures and catechisms predominated, as well as school books especially produced or sponsored by the National Society. Indeed the society at this time required church schools in union with it to use only books from the catalogue of the Society for the Promotion of Christian Knowledge, and these were then entirely religious and moral in content. Even in the mid-1840s St John's and St Peter's had no secular reading books.

At the Sunday schools reading matter was predictably almost entirely scriptural in nature. The infant and dame schools similarly favoured scriptural works which, including the Bible, were the chief readers for older children. Young pupils had 'penny readings', 'very easy readings', spelling books and alphabets. One school in Salutation Row, perhaps more honest than others, claimed to have no books worth naming, while another admitted that the children used any they were pleased to bring.

Of equipment there was little. The better charity and public day schools had maps and globes; others, nothing – except some infant schools. The Well Street Infant School possessed geometrical and transparent frames; Sherbourne House Infant School had 'frames with balls; a box of miscellaneous objects and large blackboard'; and Far Gosford Street Infant School pictures and books – all for use in Wilderspin's 'plan'. Three of the charity schools had libraries, the emphasis again being on religious works, especially those produced by the Religious Tract Society and the S.P.C.K. Only one of the other public day schools possessed a library – Sherbourne House Infant School, where 'the amusing books are read most'. About a quarter of Coventry Sunday schools, however, claimed to have libraries, largely but not entirely religious and moral in content. There is no evidence that working-class private and dame schools possessed any equipment or libraries.

Discipline was most severe where education appeared best – in the often maligned charity schools (see below, p. 178). There the main punishments were the cane, extra tasks and detentions. Corporal punishment at Fairfax's School was not confined to cases of misbehaviour but applied for non-performance of work too, and at Catherine Bayley's School it was said that 'sometimes the cane is absolutely necessary; that depends upon inability or wilful inattention'. At the other public day schools physical punishment was also employed: at the National School for Boys and Girls a 'tap on the hand occasionally', at St John's National Girls' School 'a tap on the hand or so'. Corporal correction was the only form of punishment used at Far Gosford Street Infant School, 'but as little and light as possible'. It seems likely, however, that such claims for moderation made by schools and teachers played down the actual use of severe punishment, corporal or otherwise. There is sufficient evidence, especially for church schools, that punishment was severe, even vicious. At Bayley's School the practice of dressing those who misbehaved in church in a yellow jacket as a badge of disgrace dated from 1817 and lasted into the 1840s. At the church day schools corporal punishment was used regularly at this time, and in 1856 the master of Stoke School was twice warned for excessive flogging of children and threatened with dismissal. In the 1860s, following the introduction of 'payment by results', another Stoke teacher administered frequent beatings, such as 'six stripes for non-attendance in the morning' and a caning 'for making blots in his copy book'.

At the Sunday schools there was much less punishment, most claiming that corporal correction was never used; at some it was forbidden. At Whitefriars' Lane Sunday School for All Denominations bad behaviour was said to be met with 'good advice and kind reproof'. At Wesleyan schools, however, there was 'sometimes the stick'. Information on private schools is lacking.

Rewards in the charity schools included library tickets, books and money; at the day schools it was mainly the gift of religious books published by the S.P.C.K. and, at times, clothing. At Sunday schools money and books were given.

The quality of teachers must have been affected partly by the emoluments or profits of office. Here again the charity schools were the best off, with salaries varying between £25 and £63 a year plus free accommodation and heating. The mistress of the Blue Coat School received a salary of £35 a year plus 5 per cent profit from work done by the girls. The allowance of 8s. a week for each girl for board (125 in 1838) perhaps afforded some further profit.

In the unendowed day schools emoluments varied considerably. The master and his wife at the Central National School received £70 with a house, but in the other schools of this type rewards were much smaller. At the Lancasterian Boys' School the salary was £20 a year, out of which rent had to be found; at the Lancasterian Girls' School the mistress received £16 plus school pence. A salary of about £20 a year was provided at St John's National Girls' School, and at the Roman Catholic school in Hill Street. In two infant schools a free house and weekly pence for the children were the sole perquisites.

At private and dame schools the income of the proprietors derived entirely from fees, which ranged from 3d. to 8d. a week per child, according to the age and the subjects taught. The pittances which resulted can hardly have attracted many teachers of high calibre. Mrs Price's school at Spon End, for example, brought her in 3s. 3d. a week. Mr and Mrs Marsh, with a large school of 40 pupils in Union Street, the Butts, made 10s. a week. The best off were Mr and Mrs Holland of Jordan Well who had 110 day pupils paying 3d. and 6d. a week, and 30 'evening scholars' paying 3d. This school was one of the few private schools for the working classes which provided an education perhaps approaching the level of the public unendowed day schools. Most private establishments were kept by much less able persons; the dame schools, in particular, were in Coventry, as elsewhere, the last resort of the unfortunate, or those unfit for other occupation. They were commonly housed in low confined kitchens, up narrow courts and dirty alleys. At Foleshill one dame worked a loom, did her washing, looked after her own family of seven and kept school in one tiny room. Another, kept by a 'failed coal-higgler' in his kitchen, had 50 children.

Instruction in the Sunday schools was given free of charge by unpaid teachers with an undoubted desire to promote at least spiritual welfare. Many of these persons were, however, themselves barely literate, a fact which led Fletcher in 1838 to regard the Sunday school in Coventry as 'an institution of discipline rather than instruction'.

The most obvious clue to quality is in the level of attainment of pupils on leaving school. Here we rely on evidence provided by the schools themselves, which if anything tended to exaggerate their achievements. In 1838 schools were asked to state how many pupils left school before they could read fluently or write. We have noted that Bridget Southern's Charity School for Girls admitted that a quarter of the pupils left deficient in this way. At the other charity schools, however, it was claimed that no pupils left like this, except at the Blue Coat Charity School for Girls, where writing was not taught. The charity schools were of course schools for older children, and Baker, Billing, and Crow's School pointed out that no children were admitted who could not read and write.

The attainments of the voluntary (unendowed public day) schools were not so high. The majority of children left the infant schools, perhaps understandably, unable to read and write well. But the other day schools were suspiciously evasive in their answers to the enquiry. Most, however, admitted that some of their pupils left school without acquiring any reasonable standard in reading or writing.

The Sunday schools were not asked about writing, since few taught it. Most claimed that many or all of their children learned to read. At High Field Chapel Independent School it was said that 'most can read well, and many write well', and at Holy Trinity and St John's Sunday schools it was alleged that only a few left unable to read. Some schools, however, admitted only a limited success. West Orchard Independent School, for example, reported 'we have many leave school before they have the ability to read well'. The proprietors of the Unitarian Sunday School bitterly admitted that many pupils left illiterate: 'the parents think they confer a favour on the conductors of the school to which they send their children, and hence often remove them, from caprice, from disappointed expectations of charity, etc.'. The private schools, again largely concerned with the youngest children, generally agreed that most left unable to read or write well.

On the whole elementary education in Coventry was very defective in this period. Fletcher reckoned that whatever the actual figures (see above, p. 165, the proportion of Coventry children to the urban population receiving *adequate* education was only about 1 in 24. The report of the Select Committee on the Education of the Poorer Classes, also reporting in 1838, suggested a similar proportion for a group of large towns.[7] Fletcher believed that the vast majority of those attending private day and dame schools in 1838 in Coventry 'are not receiving any instruction worthy of the name'. Nine years later Joseph Squires, headmaster of one of the best infant schools in the town, Sherbourne House, attested that only 90 of the 1,590 children (less than 6 per cent) he had taught there had attended regularly enough to proceed to an elementary school.

Indeed, just as the quantity of education had not kept pace with population, so there is little evidence of any very great improvement in quality in the years immediately following 1838. Parliamentary grants for education increased in the late 1840s, when they became available for maintenance as well as new building, and in the 1850s. Only by the 1860s, however, did even most church schools in Coventry have a single qualified teacher each. Government inspection, which accompanied government money, revealed that even the education of those Coventry children who did attend day school still left much to be desired. An inspector visiting the boys' department of St John's National School in 1847 noted that standards of both reading and arithmetic were defective. In arithmetic the pupils had got no further than very simple addition. No boy was able to write correctly in figures '4,050'. There were no secular reading books – indeed no reading book at all belonging to the school. The first class allegedly used the New Testament as a reader, yet half the children in the school were still learning letters and monosyllables and the others had advanced only to easy narrative. Of the 60 children in the school all but 17 had had no instruction in writing at all, while the 17 were merely at the stage of copying letters. Religious instruction, despite the New Testament, was 'very defective', discipline poor and the noise great. There was no regular class teaching and the teacher still had only circulating monitors to help him. The master himself, who was said to 'make what he can of the school', was untrained, unpaid, and deficient in skill. The girls' department of the school was no better. One untrained mistress taught 70–80 girls in six classes with the aid of monitors, and was not unnaturally overwhelmed with her work. As with the boys there was a great deal of noise and there were no secular reading books, and though the reading of the first class in the Gospels was 'tolerable', 49 of the girls were still unable to read letters and monosyllables. So far as writing was concerned, only 13 were even at the stage of copying letters, and arithmetic was confined to elementary addition.

By the standards of the day both departments of St John's were unsatisfactory. Such a picture of a National School in the late 1840s, eight or nine years after its foundation, does not say much for what was, after all, one of the types of school providing the best sort of education available to most working-class children in the city. It must be noted that many of the children at the time of the inspection described were under seven years of age, suggesting that many Coventry children were still leaving school at an age before they were able to absorb much learning.

There was only marginal improvement at St John's by the early 1850s. In 1851 an untrained master still struggled with 100 boys in six classes with the aid of monitors, and the school was very crowded. In

1853 there were at last enough books, but not enough blackboards, and the teaching of reading and writing was only moderate, and of arithmetic imperfect. There was no playground and the ventilation was bad, the furniture unsuitable and the organisation bad, though the master was said to work hard.

Two other church schools, founded in the 1840s, by then provided a better education, but only one considerably so. St Michael's National School (founded 1848)was said by 1853 to be managed well, and it offered geography, history, grammar, needlework and singing, besides the 3 R's. But if there was any great improvement in the quality of public education in Coventry in these years it was in the boys' department of St Peter's National School (founded 1844). Soon after its opening its pupils were considered remarkably well taught. Its early curriculum included, as well as the fundamentals, geography, etymology, singing and, from 1852, science, allegedly with good success. Inspectors in the 1850s found it highly satisfactory and remarked that organisation and discipline were good, despite the poverty of the district. Indeed, unlike other Coventry schools St Peter's boys' department was above the average for the Midland counties in reading instruction, 1 boy in 5 being able to read the scriptures with ease, compared with 1 in 7.3 for the area as a whole This exceptional position was maintained after the period under review. In 1866 the school was placed seventh out of 52 boys' schools in the Midland area. The number of children involved was, however, comparatively small: in 1852 the average attendance was 120, these being taught in five classes by a master, an apprentice and a monitor. The following year, however, the apprentices and monitors were replaced by four pupil-teachers.

The foregoing analysis would suggest that the education provided at the four boys' charity schools was the best available for working-class children. Indeed Fletcher found these schools to be a standard similar to that of schools for the middle classes. To a certain extent the charity schools provided 'secondary' education for the more ambitious of the lower classes. In 1832-3, for example, 24 of the pupils who left the Central National School did so to pass on to charity schools. Joseph Gutteridge, a local worthy born in 1816, the son of a workman, was sent to a dame school at five and then to a charity school until he was thirteen or fourteen. This verdict on Coventry charity schools conflicts with the textbook picture of the charity school as a spent force by the late eighteenth century, concerned only with religious indoctrination and occupied mainly with the practical training of future servants and workmen, eschewing all but the merest rudiments of academic instruction and being superseded by the Sunday and voluntary schools.[8]

Of the public unendowed schools the best in the 1830s were without doubt the infant schools, which Fletcher found 'not behind those in other places' and which, despite their shortcoming, were more enlightened and efficient than day schools for older children. With the exception of St Peter's in the late 1840s and the 1850s and possibly St Michael's, these left much to be desired. Yet they were certainly superior to many of the private schools. In even the best of these a little reading and spelling was all that was acquired, though in some pupils did 'read pretty well . . . with uncouth pronunciation'. Many were merely 'subscription nurseries of the very poorest description', 'out of the way' schools. Instruction in the Sunday schools, which the Handloom Weavers' Commission found to 'afford all the instruction to which the greater portion attending them can attain', was mainly religious in intent, reading only being considered important in order to facilitate acquaintance with the scriptures. Not only was day-school attendance at a lower level than in the factory towns, but also there is no evidence to suggest that the quality of education in Coventry was any better.

Moreover the suggested experience of Lancashire, where worthy handloom weavers were deprived of education by the factories yet still thirsted for it, is not applicable to Coventry. There appears to have been as little desire for education among the prosperous weavers of Coventry as among the less fortunate single-hand weavers of the surrounding districts. Indeed there may be some truth in a hypothesis which supposes that factory life with its attendant interest in politics gave a greater spur to the attainment of education than the 'sufficient unto the day' mentality of domestic labour in Coventry. It is true that the few single-hand weavers in the town were both too poor and too depraved (as the *Reports from Assistant Handloom Weavers' Commissioners* indicate) to seek education even in good times, and the second-hand men were also unlikely to be able to afford continuous education for their children. They were said never to save a farthing although earning good wages, and at best to 'expect nothing from a school but the hasty instruction of mere infants in the art of reading, so that they may have their uninterrupted services in throwing, filling, nursing, etc.'.

The first-hand men, the most numerous working group, were certainly able in most years to afford elementary education. Yet demand from them for schooling was distinctly apathetic. Of Coventry working men, only the watchmakers showed any great wish to educate their children, often keeping them at school up to fourteen years of age. Watchmakers' sons and daughters were to be found in the private and public day schools and charity schools in a proportion in excess of their numbers in the city. When the Children's Employment Commission took evidence from Coventry children in the early 1840s it found that all the young watchmakers interviewed could read and write and had tended to stay at school until their early teens, leaving to take up three-year apprenticeships. None of the silk-winding children could sign their names and only one could read, despite attendance at Sunday school. The more revealing advantage of a higher educational facility in the more skilled trade of watchmaking no doubt partly explains the differences in parental attitudes.

A questionnaire to teachers and school proprietors in 1838 about the views of parents on schooling provided differing answers. Some said that most were anxious to have their children educated, others that parents were very indifferent. On the whole, however, it was clear that many children were kept away 'more through carelessness and indifference than any actual pressure of want'. At some schools attendance actually increased in times of bad trade, despite the existence of fees, because children could then be spared from work. This does not suggest great poverty. Very young children were sent to all the types of school which would receive them, less for schooling than to keep them out of the way. Fletcher found this the main reason for the popularity of infant schooling in the city.

Nor is there much to suggest that there was any great increase in the demand of the Coventry working class for education in the period under review. It is true that in 1851 it was said of St John's School that children were constantly rejected from inability to take them, but since most were infants this does not mean very much. What advance in educational facilities there was came as a result of an increase in middle-class energy more than anything else, though even this in Coventry must not be exaggerated. In the later 1840s the vicar of St Michael's felt that 'the interest taken in the education of the working classes is not great; it has hitherto been deplorably chilling'.

Such middle-class support as existed was actuated largely by religious and moral rather than purely educational motives. The charity schools were of course financed from endowments and connected very much with the established church. Between 1811 and 1870, 16 of 23 schools founded in Coventry were directly sponsored by religious sects. When Holy Trinity School was founded in 1853 it was described as a 'nursery for God's children', and in the same year the objectives of St Michael's National School put first 'the evidences, doctrines, and duties of Christianity'. The Sunday-school movement in Coventry had been philanthropic and moral rather than purely religious in its eighteenth-century origins, but by the 1830s it was clearly mainly religious, though most of the schools were still non-denominational.

Many of the church public day schools in Coventry received financial aid through the Worcester Diocesan Board, the National Society and local religious societies, as well as from parliamentary grants. Coventry was regarded, like many other urban centres, as a place where proselytizing and mission work was very needful. In 1851, out of a population of 36,208, only 6,827 attended a place of worship on the morning of census Sunday, 1,827 in the afternoon and 5,892 in the evening. (Figures include Sunday-school children.) [9]

Apart from purely religious sources, much money for elementary education in Coventry came from private individuals, particularly from gentry and aristocrats from the neighbouring countryside who gave sites for schools and financial assistance. Sherbourne House Infant School was founded and maintained by Joseph Cash, the Quaker industrialist, and Far Gosford Street Infant School by Charles Bray, the local newspaper proprietor and friend of George Eliot.

Yet while philanthropic and religious motives may have been responsible for much of the education provided in the city, it is possible that differences between Nonconformists and churchmen over state-aided schooling may have been an influence retarding educational advance in Coventry in this period. In 1847 Vicar Lane British School, for example, returned a £200 grant as a protest against the Education Bill of that year, which was felt to favour the Anglicans.

Religious difficulties also hindered the development of adult education in the city. A Mechanics' Institute was founded in 1828 but it split over religious-political differences in the 1830s, a rival Anglican institute being founded by some dissidents. The lack of provision for adult education, however, is yet another example of apathy among Coventry workers towards education. By 1849 the Mechanics' Institute was largely attended by middle-class students. This was a tendency in adult education not confined to Coventry, yet in the factory towns of the north and Midlands a much greater desire for adult education was evident than in Coventry. There had been a few adult schools in the city in the early years of the century, but by 1851 there were no evening adult schools in Coventry. This compared with 4 in neighbouring

Birmingham (324 students), 9 at Macclesfield (191), 6 at Congleton (91), 18 at Manchester (810) and 47 at Stockport (925). The examples of Congleton and Macclesfield are specially interesting since both places, like Coventry, were silk-manufacturing towns. Coventry also had no literary or scientific institutes at this time, though a government school of design, founded in 1843, had 153 pupils in 1849.

In most cities the great spur to adult education came from the substantial professional and factory-owning middle class. Coventry in the nineteenth century, as in the twentieth, lacked a substantial upper class, for 'gentry' preferred the more salubrious atmosphere of Warwick and Leamington.[10] The middle class too was not large, consisting of the most substantial ribbon manufacturers, together with a small number of professional men. This state of affairs may also account for the fact that middle-class education in Coventry as well as working-class schooling was very deficient.

In 1838 there were some 20–30 superior private schools devoted to the education of the middle classes in Coventry. A directory of 1830 lists 18 such schools, 6 of them boarding schools. The descriptions give an indication of their nature: 'ladies seminary', 'gentlemen's academy', 'ladies' school', 'boarding academy' and so on. In 1850 White's *Directory of Warwickshire* listed some 23 such schools, again including 6 boarding establishments. These schools offered elementary as well as secondary education, but about most it is difficult to obtain any information.

More is known about the Free Grammar School which provided education not entirely confined to the middle class. In the 1830s, however, it was in a state of decay. The headmaster, also rector of St John's, had been appointed in 1779, and in 1833 he was eighty-two years old. Under his rule the size of the school had gradually diminished from some 40–60 pupils in the late eighteenth century to an average of 10 in the years immediately up to 1827. From 1802 the head had left his duties to an usher who by the late 1820s had only one pupil to teach. The Charity Commissioners found only one boy in 1833, and consequently encouraged reorganisation. In the autumn of 1833, 70 boys were recruited from Coventry elementary schools. They paid 2s. 6d. a quarter for incidental expenses but received their education free because they were sons of Coventry freemen. (The freemen were a large and popular group in the city.) The school thus became a sort of 'higher elementary' school, but instruction was nevertheless ineffectively provided by the usher and his son, and a new head was appointed in 1834.

By 1857 the school had 57 boys, and by 1866, when the Endowed Schools Commissioners investigated it, it had clearly resurrected itself, partly by expanding its middle-class intake. Then there were 54 boys, of whom 34 were freemen's sons receiving virtually free instruction. The rest were fee-payers, the fees being either 6 guineas a year in the 'commercial' department or 10 guineas in the 'classical' department. The classical instruction was clearly considered the more important, however, and 'commercial' boys received only a half-hearted 'business' training, comprising extra arithmetic, French or history. Few working-class freemen's sons advanced to the fifth or sixth forms, being deterred by the cost of books, so that the upper forms were largely the preserve of the middle-class children.

None of the children's fathers were 'artisans or labourers'. On the other hand, less than 10 per cent came into the categories 'independent, professional or mercantile', the rest being rated as 'farmers, shop-keepers'. Essentially the Free Grammar School was a school for the lower middle classes. Indeed Coventry was still as poorly off for good secondary-school education as it was for elementary schools. Many of the professional classes and even the better-off tradesmen sent their sons to boarding schools outside the town. If they could not do this, they patronised superior private schools in the city. About 40 tradesmen's sons even attended Bablake Charity School, as private pupils at £4 a year: an indication on the one hand of the reputation of the commercial education provided there, and on the other of the inability of the Grammar School to meet local needs.

The general picture of education in Coventry between 1830 and 1850 is not a very encouraging one. Not only were educational facilities inferior to those in many other industrial cities, but the desire for improvement was not particularly strong among the domestic textile workers. The types of school and their characteristics do not greatly differ from the national pattern, but there is every reason to believe that the interplay between the peculiar social structure of Coventry and the outlook of its inhabitants affected the quality and extent of educational provision. Detailed investigation of other industrial towns is needed before a general picture of education in industrial communities in the early Victorian period can emerge, and it is hoped that this study may encourage others interested in local society and in educational history to pursue similar local studies.

7. The Old Centre of Croydon: Victorian Decay and Redevelopment

R. C. W. COX

SOME Victorian towns, like Middlesbrough, Crewe and Barrow-in-Furness, were new; others developed from older and smaller settlements that had grown up around church and market place. As these long-established places expanded, their well-to-do inhabitants moved out and settled in healthier, more select localities. The properties they vacated were then occupied by poorer people who lived there in conditions of ever-increasing overcrowding.

This situation led to demands for improvement – a word, as Professor Asa Briggs has reminded us, that can be fittingly applied as a label to a whole age. But improvement was much easier to talk about than to implement, a fact illustrated by the account that follows. It relates to Croydon, but it might equally well have been about Newark, or Exeter, or any one of a substantial number of towns where the old commercial centres had fallen into decay as the wealthy tradesmen moved out to the new genteel suburbs.[1]

In Croydon that centre was only two acres in extent. It was also, quite literally, on the doorstep of the town hall and served as a constant reproach not only to those who transacted business in the town but also to the local magistrates and to members of the local Board of Health. Yet its clearance came only after a struggle lasting over half a century. The story of the improvement of Croydon's market area is one of indifference and apathy, of greed and selfishness, of benevolence and faith. It can no doubt be paralleled elsewhere. But much remains to be done to discover in detail what happened in other towns and, perhaps more important, to compare the motives, methods, achievements and failures of those Victorians who sought improvement in different urban centres about the country.

In the introduction to *Victorian Cities*, Professor Briggs stressed the importance to the urban historian of two things: a familiarity with the concepts used by sociologists about urban growth and change; and secondly, an appreciation of the urban landscape. If the context in which he was writing had been different he would doubtless have gone on to lay emphasis on two further requirements: the need to seek out and analyse the contents of a mass of primary source material that in many cases will have lain untouched since it was compiled; and also the necessity of relating the body of information so obtained to the situation in other places.

The principal primary material for the essay that follows is housed in Croydon Public Library. It includes the detailed manuscript minutes of the local Improvement Commissioners, of the Sanitary Committee of the local Board of Health, of the High Street Improvement Scheme, and of the High Street Special Committee. These volumes concern themselves with the minutiae, while the broader picture is provided by the more generalised minutes of the local Board of Health and the printed reports of that body. The principal secondary sources are the files of microfilm of the local newspapers which extend over more than a hundred years: the particularly influential and still existing *Croydon Advertiser* which, in the nineteenth century, unfailingly supported the Liberal cause; the *Croydon Guardian*, which gave comfort and encouragement to the Tories; the rather second-rate, middle-of-the-road *Croydon Chronicle*; and the impoverished-looking *Norwood News*, all of which are now defunct.

G. O. Cowley's 'Sussex Market Towns 1550–1750' (London M.A. thesis, 1964) is a work that exemplifies, for another part of the Home Counties, the earlier gradual encroachment of buildings on to the open market area. But although contemporary Victorian observers like Croydon's own John Ollis Pelton sometimes described most fully the later decay of the properties, many of the recent spate of books and papers on individual Victorian towns have merely recorded the dereliction and the subsequent improvement without investigating it in any depth. An exception to this is the article on Glasgow by C. M. Allan, published in 1965 in the *Economic History Review*.[2]

A good starting-point for anyone contemplating a comparative study would be the list of theses on British urban history published in the December 1965 number of the *Urban History Newsletter*. The list contains a reminder of the early work of, for example, Dr. W. H. Chaloner and Prof. Roy Church on Crewe and Nottingham respectively. It also names studies of many other urban areas that have not subsequently received such detailed treatment. Later editions of the *News-*

letter provide a running list of research in progress. The publication constitutes a valuable weapon in the armoury of the student of the Victorian town.

I. THE CROYDON SCENE

Croydon is a London borough, only 10 miles from Charing Cross. But it has a long history as a market centre, due partly to its being for a thousand years a seat of successive archbishops of Canterbury and partly also to its position on a fertile, well-watered site at the foot of the North Downs dip slope.

By 1801 its population was well over 5,000, more than that of any other nearby place. The Brighton coaches stopped there; a horse-drawn railway and a canal were built to connect it with the Thames; in 1837 Croydon became one of the first places south of the river to be linked to London by steam train; and shortly afterwards it had lines to Brighton and Dover as well.

It was also one of the first fifteen places in the country to have a local Board of Health. Heathland, fields and gentlemen's estates were rapidly built over as the population grew from 20,000 in the middle of the century to over 130,000 by 1901.

Yet despite its importance as a communications centre and despite its proximity to London, Croydon remained very self-contained. It was largely Croydon men who bought the building plots, who financed the house construction, who regarded the rents from their newly erected cottages as their security, and who as they grew in wealth exercised considerable influence in the government of the town. Almost invariably the same people were the purchasers of land for building, the directors of local public utilities, finance or investment companies and building societies, the patrons of local charities, the principal supporters of projects to improve the town, the justices of the peace, and the men prominent in the local chapels and in the debates of the local Board of Health, the School Board and, later, the town Council which was incorporated in 1883. For most of the nineteenth century the typical man of power in Croydon was the successful local tradesman, Liberal in politics, Nonconformist in religion, modestly housed behind or above his shop, humanitarian in outlook, and with a zealous pride in and loyalty to the town. But increasingly as the century wore on his supremacy was challenged by the equally successful commuter, not uncommonly Conservative and Anglican, living in comfort and perhaps in some splendour on the expensive Park Hill estate, disdainful of the *petit bourgeois* attitude of the man in trade, and vociferously critical of any improvements to the town that might increase the rate burden and, incidentally, the shopkeeper's profit.

This conflict was at its fiercest over the nineteenth-century decay and redevelopment of the town's market area; and a study of that conflict highlights the very real difficulties, social, legal, political and financial, that beset any attempts at Victorian town improvement.

II. THE GROWTH AND DECLINE OF THE MARKET AREA

Professor W. G. Hoskins has drawn attention to the fact that the medieval market place was often triangular in shape, and that what had initially been an open space might gradually become built over with permanent stalls and then shops. Croydon appears to be no exception to this; and the three sides of its original market area remain to this day as Crown Hill, Surrey Street and High Street.

At Croydon corn and meat appear to have been the most important commodities sold in the market, certainly in the late eighteenth century. There was also a butter-market house and a fish market, the latter being served by carriers on their way to London from the coast. By the beginning of the nineteenth century, however, both the butter-market house and also the main market house, which had come to be known as the town hall and was used as a courthouse, were ruinous. They were then rebuilt out of money obtained from the sale of land apportioned to the town by an Enclosure Act of 1801. The new butter-market house had one floor at High Street level where dairy produce, eggs and chickens were displayed by higglers from other parts of the county, and a lower floor, at ground level at the rear of the building, the whole market triangle being on a steep slope down from the High Street, where meat, bacon and cheese were sold.

It was on Saturdays that the market was most active, with, according to one eye-witness, many farmers driving into the town in their light carts and gigs, accompanied by wives and daughters bent on making purchases at the more fashionable drapers' shops. Apart from the quality trade in the High Street, there were also numerous stalls set up inside the market triangle, in Market Street, Middle Row and King Street. It is clear that in the 1820s there must still have been very little regular trading with the metropolis, and one writer relates that the inhabitants so confined their dealings to the town and credit was so commonplace that one might go from end to end of the High Street without being able to obtain change for a sovereign.

But by the 1870s things were different. The railways had altered the pattern of commerce and shops had supplanted the public market. One victim of this change was the butter-market house, which the local Board of Health considered converting into a fire station but then leased instead to the *Croydon Chronicle*. It seems that the sale of stock was still flourishing, there being complaints about the nuisance and obstruction caused on Saturdays by horse-dealers trotting their animals up and down the street to show their paces; but the corn market was in decline. Even those who came to market spent less time in the town than previously, one resident lamenting that formerly 'market folk dined at the various inns where substantial dinners or ordinaries were prepared. Now the few that attend the markets come by rail in the middle of the day and return home . . . to tea'. When the Royal Commission on Market Rights and Tolls sent a representative to the town in 1888, his attempts to interest the corporation in the establishment of a covered public market were ignored, not only because the proposition was commercially unattractive but because the majority of established shopkeepers were opposed to it. By 1914 only a small open Saturday market remained, and that was confined to Surrey Street. This is now held every weekday but trade is almost exclusively in fruit and vegetables.

Thus, after a period of medieval growth, and despite the building of new premises in the early nineteenth century, the high Victorian era showed a marked diminution in Croydon's market trade, and the complete disappearance of many of the activities that had formerly taken place there. But the shops and houses that had earlier been built over much of the ground still remained.

Once the market area was completely developed, the road pattern was such that its base, on the north, was represented by the steep slope of Crown Hill; the eastern side by the High Street; and, down the slope, the western side by Surrey Street (see Fig. 13). Two other roads led away from Crown Hill in the direction of the triangle's southern apex: Market Street, approximately parallel with High Street, and Middle Row, roughly parallel with Surrey Street. They converged just short of the apex.

Across the triangle, and down the slope, from east to west, there were parallel alleys linking High Street with Surrey Street. These, from north to south, from base to apex of the triangle, were Bell Hill,

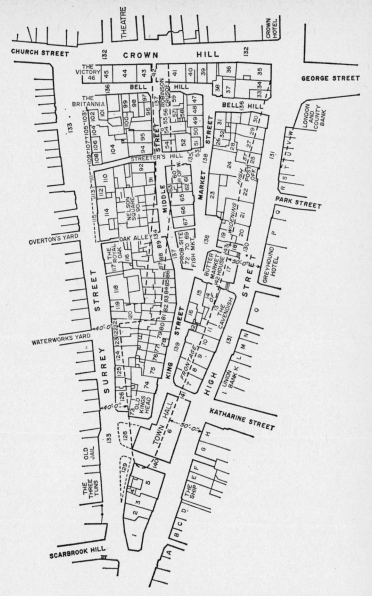

FIG. 13 MAP OF CENTRAL CROYDON IN 1888
From J. O. Pelton, *Relics of Old Croydon*, 1891

Streeter's Hill, Oak Alley and King Street. The roads were very narrow, and even the High Street was, in one part, only 25 ft wide.

The fullest account of the locality is that of John Ollis Pelton, a local historian who knew it well, for his family had a shop in the High Street. He described the area in great detail at the time of its final demolition at the end of the century. From what he says, it is apparent that many of the properties were substantial ones and had been the homes of prosperous tradesmen but that they had become much neglected. The decline was noted too by many other observers and was attributed variously to the narrowness and steepness of the streets, the age of the property, the smallness of each plot, the changing pattern of retail trading, the effects of the railway, and the constant and rapid growth of Croydon. Precisely when the decay had begun, it is impossible to say. Descriptions of its extent and speed are coloured by the personal attitude and motives of the informant, who might be concerned particularly with sanitary or moral reform, or estate values, or the virtue of philanthropy, or even in one case the presence of Italian organ-grinders. Any proposal to widen the High Street was vigorously opposed by shopkeepers elsewhere in the town, and the possible removal of the town hall was equally opposed by the High Street tradesmen. Those who demanded wholesale demolition on the grounds of the appallingly insanitary state of the houses found that some of the most ardent supporters for demolition, happening to be members of the Board of Health's Sanitary Committee, were claiming that although for other reasons the locality should certainly be redeveloped, the state of health there – thanks to the efficiency of the Board – was quite exceptionally good. So a really accurate picture of the state of the market area is hard to come by. But there is one way in which the condition of the area, and its deterioration, can be fairly measured. This is by examining and comparing the census returns for the years 1851 and 1861.

When this is done, it becomes apparent that even by the latter date the economic and physical deterioration of the market area did not extend outwards to the roads constituting its boundaries. Narrow and congested they might be, but the shops were still of a kind to attract a considerable part of their clientele from elsewhere in the town. But by 1851 both Market Street, where Ruskin's aunt had earlier kept a baker's shop, and King Street had a mixture of shop properties and of working-class households not involved directly in local trade. There were also one or two beershops which housed casual lodgers. In Middle Row and its adjacent alleys the transition from trade to working-class poverty, and from shop to lodging-house, had gone much farther. Of the 97 men of employable age in Middle Row and its courts, 54 were labourers; of the 206 inhabitants, 19 were Irish. One lodging-house contained thirty people. The details can be filled in by reference to an 1849 government report on the locality. This described, for instance, eleven houses without water supply and sharing one broken-down privy; a two-roomed house occupied by a family of nine, the parents and baby sleeping in one room and the other six sons and daughters, aged between ten and twenty-seven, sleeping in the second; and a family of seven occupying two sub-ground rooms each 8 ft 6 in by 9 ft, 'with three filthy privies within about 18 ft of the door and windows'.[3]

By 1861 things were worse. The number of people living inside the market area had increased from 449 to 590; and in Market Street and Middle Row there were on average more than eleven people to a house, or about twenty-four in the case of lodging-houses. In one decade the total number of such places had increased from under a quarter to nearly half of the properties in four of the streets. The lodger population had grown proportionately.

Who were these lodgers? The census returns do not indicate whether they were resident or vagrant, but other evidence strongly supports the latter idea. In 1861 over 15 per cent of them were under the age of fifteen, a higher proportion than there was of people over fifty. In the decade there had been a substantial increase in the percentage of female lodgers and a diminution in the previous preponderance of unemployed craftsmen and unskilled labourers; and it is clear from other evidence, both earlier and later in date, that many of the women were prostitutes.[4] Yet despite the evidence that these people were drifting homelessly, about 14 per cent of the lodgers were in fact natives of the town and about half of them had been born at places within thirty miles of Croydon.

III. THE LODGERS AND THE LODGING-HOUSES

These lodging-houses were partly the cause, and partly the result, of a decaying physical environment which is illustrated by the frequent criticism of inadequate water supply and poor drainage in the locality.

It is true that the report of a house-to-house enquiry, following on a fever epidemic in the winter of 1852–3, suggested that the recently completed works of the new local Board of Health had effected a great improvement.[5] One householder in King Street commented: 'No obstruction – no smell – beautiful water – very wicked to say it's the water that has caused the fever. Well worth the rate. Don't grudge the money. Hope to gracious they won't take it away. Very bad smells before the works.' But such recorded comments (and one cannot be sure to what extent they were quoted verbatim) may perhaps represent something of a 'whitewashing' exercise. There is a lot of evidence that the situation after 1852 was not all that it should have been, and a leading article in 1862 in the *Croydon Chronicle* described Middle Row, which by then was a term being used generally for the inner part of the market area, as 'a small edition of the lowest part of Whitechapel; or, to speak more correctly, a cross between Rosemary Lane and Seven Dials'.[6]

The inhabitants themselves did not help the situation. A stoppage in a main drain in Middle Row was reported as having been caused by an old shirt, and residents there ignored the dustcart and then threw their refuse in the street after it had gone. Furthermore a passage leading from Crown Hill to Middle Row was used as a public urinal, and a member of the local Board, who lived opposite, complained that he had to keep down the blinds in his house to avoid the frequent scenes of indecency. Conditions were made worse by the fact that some of the houses were derelict, and the local Board of Health's only remedy seems to have been to order the owners of such properties to board up the fronts.

There was frequently, in official comment, a remarkable air of complacency about the locality. This reached its height perhaps in an 1884 report of the Poor Dwellings Committee. It said that there were no unhealthy areas in the town and that such legislation as the Artisans' and Labourers' Dwellings Acts of 1875 and 1879, providing for compulsory purchase and demolition, were inapplicable. It asserted that the lodging-houses of Middle Row were 'well looked after and described by the police as a credit to the town'. The report later suggested optimistically that a conspicuous example of the operation of private enterprise in bettering conditions by closing dilapidated poor dwellings was that of four tenements in Middle Row that had been closed by the landlord and had subsequently changed hands 'in prospect of further improvements'.

One wonders why the two police constables, Smith and McSweeny, who gave evidence to the committee, made highly condemnatory remarks of other parts of the town yet chose to praise Middle Row. Were they on the defensive because of criticisms of lack of police vigilance? In that case, surely, they would have tended to exaggerate, rather than play down, the evil insanitary conditions, the existence of which would strengthen any argument about the difficulties of adequate police supervision. It seems much more likely that the evidence was put into their mouths by the members of the committee: perhaps through civic pride, perhaps to diminish criticism of a new (and, in the minds of many, extravagant) corporation, perhaps because they hoped to benefit from the operation of private enterprise in effecting improvements.

The best description of the local lodging-houses appeared in the *Croydon Advertiser* in 1888.[7] The writer claimed he had spent from Saturday morning until Sunday night there, except for an interval for refreshment at midday on Sunday. He stressed the inadequacy of the accommodation and went on to suggest that 'the greatest danger in the system of common lodging-houses is the commonness itself. Here are people herded together in the kitchen, young and old, saints and sinners. The immediate consequence is indiscriminate love matches and a system of wholesale depravity.' One local magistrate, Alderman Edridge, who was not averse to using his position as chairman of the bench to make public pronouncements, frequently expressed concern about the corrupting influence of the houses. He commented, for instance, when he gave Eliza Cuthbert, 'a woman of ill-fame at Day's lodging-house', seven days' hard labour for indecent conduct, that while unfortunate people like the prisoner must have lodgings, 'a number of people are travelling about the country . . . respectable though poor, and it is very undesirable they should be associated in these lodging-houses with disreputable persons'.

One group of people in several of the houses were not disreputable and were also rather unusual. The local directories for the early 1890s show several Middle Row householders as having Italian names; and the reason is given in an article, published in the *Croydon Advertiser*, entitled 'Italian Organ Grinders and How They Live'.[8] It falls neatly into two parts, the first explaining factually that pianos and organs were manufactured in London by Italian firms, some of which let out to their nationals as many as a hundred at a time at between 7s. 6d. and 10s. per week. About every six months the instruments were changed for others having the popular new tunes. If in need of repair, 'an intelligent Italian' would come from London, usually on a Sunday so that the hirer lost no time, and the person renting the instrument had to find the other's board. The article went on to describe the frugality and thriftiness of these organ-grinders and how they invested their money in the

Post Office Savings Bank until they had sufficient to send back to Italy, or until they themselves returned home comparatively rich men. Unfortunately, and surprisingly since the *Croydon Advertiser* was a very liberal paper, the article then lapsed into a frenzy of xenophobia, concluding: 'Poor crippled Englishmen that are not able to work ought to be getting the living that the sponging Italians are now doing.'

But of course Italian lodgers and Italian lodging-house keepers were a comparative rarity in Middle Row. With the big increase in the number of lodging-houses in the 1870s and 1880s, two Englishmen, William Huggett and Charles Day, had built up a near-monopoly of ownership.

Huggett seems to have been over forty when he took his first lodging-house in the market area, having previously been a labourer, a marine-store dealer and a bricklayer. In the census of 1861 he had five premises occupied by 78 lodgers, including labourers, travellers, garden women, hawkers, a journeyman sailmaker, a miner, a pugilist, a journeyman bellows-maker, two sailors, an army pensioner and seven German musicians of both sexes. He was in frequent and increasing conflict with the local Board of Health, and in 1875 there were at one time fifteen summonses against him, for such offences as failing to display the lodging-house regulations, failing to keep the seat, floor and walls of the water-closets clean, failing to wash and sweep the floors and wash the walls of the rooms, and failing to keep blankets and rugs clean. He was represented in court by his somewhat aggressive wife, Sarah, but was fined a total of £4 10s., plus £5 1s. costs, with three weeks to pay – hardly a large sum, since he was probably collecting well over £1 a night in rent.

After his death Sarah assumed control and finally fell foul of the Board in 1879 over her premises at Nelson Square, off Middle Row. She had there failed to comply with various notices served on her and she complained in court that the Board required so much done that they might just as well shut up the Square, a remark which drew from Edridge, on the bench, the comment that perhaps it would be as well if they did. She went on to assert that she had done all that was required of her except the building of water-closets and the fitting of windows at the back of the premises where there had been none. There were, she claimed, no cleaner houses than hers in all Croydon. The case was adjourned while two magistrates visited the houses, and one of them on his return said that the lower rooms had no flooring bar an admixture of mud and filth and that the best thing to do would be to burn down

the premises. Mrs Huggett was ordered to repair the houses within
fourteen days if they were not to be closed down. She did not do so; and
they were then boarded up and left untenanted and derelict until the
whole area was finally cleared thirteen years later. Very soon Sarah
Huggett vacated the remainder of her properties as well.

As she did so, another more nearly complete monopoly of the lodging-
houses in the market area was developing, in the hands of Charles Day.
He took over an existing house in King Street in 1879 and applied for
its registration, submitting three letters of testimony as to his respectability. The application was approved. He then gradually added to his
empire until, by the time he died in 1892, he controlled twenty of the
twenty-eight lodging-houses in the locality, including all twelve in King
Street where, before his advent, there had been only a very few. He also
had lodging-houses at Kingston upon Thames.

As criticism of conditions in the market area increased, Day became
the subject of veiled attacks by the local newspapers, as in a leading
article in the *Croydon Chronicle* in 1888, which described his houses as
a human moral piggery that, for low depravity, either Newcastle or
Manchester might match, but certainly could not surpass.[9] He apparently became a well-known figure in the neighbourhood and all the local
newspapers described his funeral, at the age of fifty-two, in considerable
detail. They added various asides suggesting that 'Uncle' Day, as they
called him, had become something of a police informer. He was unable
to sign his name; but, unlike his predecessor Huggett, he was a man
of some wealth at the time of his death.

Probably all the lodging-house keepers had some reputation for
working hand in glove with the police; and there is certainly plenty of
evidence, in the columns of the local press, of crime in the market area.
This ranged from two attempts by a mother and daughter to burn down
their beerhouse in Middle Row, the premises being insured by two companies, to the theft from the town's police station of its clock, which was
recovered next day at a Middle Row baker's shop.

The commonest criminal activities were drunkenness, theft, assault
and prostitution. Drunkenness and minor brawls were especially commonplace. But the claim by contemporaries that, had it not been for
Middle Row, the local magistrates would have been virtually unoccupied
is incorrect. Analysis of the place of residence of all defendants named
in the *Croydon Advertiser* as appearing in the local police courts during
1871 shows that, out of 261 cases, only 17 involved people definitely
living in the market area.

IV. FIRST ATTEMPTS AT AMELIORATION

Beyond doubt, then, the market area by mid-century was in a state of moral and physical decay. The buildings were dilapidated; there was overcrowding, lack of proper sanitation, drunkenness, crime, violence and immorality; casual visitors formed a high proportion of the population; and all this existed within a few yards of the town hall. There was general agreement that some remedy was needed. But what should it be?

C. M. Allan, in a study of urban redevelopment in Glasgow, found that there were five successive ways in which decay there was tackled in the nineteenth century.[10] There was, firstly, reliance upon *laissez-faire*; secondly, attempts were made through the medium of philanthropic bodies; thirdly, by a rigid enforcement of public health legislation; fourthly, by municipal purchase and demolition followed by private-enterprise redevelopment; and lastly, by the municipality undertaking all the processes, including rebuilding. That same order was followed in the case of the Croydon market area, though the work was completed there at the fourth stage, so that municipal rebuilding never entered into consideration.

The earliest method, that of leaving redevelopment to what Allan described as 'the workings of the market', was based, he suggested, on the fallacy that obsolete buildings would show a diminishing return until, eventually, demolition and rebuilding would be found profitable. But as the houses decayed, the middle classes vacated them and let them at high rents to people who were prepared to put up with intense overcrowding to spread the real burden of cost. The landlord then had no incentive to rebuild, for the poor could not afford to pay more than they were already being charged.

When Sarah Huggett's slums in Nelson Square were closed down by order of the local Board of Health they changed hands, so the Poor Dwellings Committee told the council, 'in prospect of further improvements'. But, as has been said already, they remained derelict and untenanted for the next thirteen years, and if *laissez-faire* offered little incentive to the redevelopment of individual properties, it offered even less to more widespread improvement. Wider streets would have meant less land for remunerative buildings; and in any case fragmentation of ownership made such replanning quite out of the question.

With the failure of the market forces to improve the urban scene, the middle-class conscience became disturbed. The result was the com-

mencement in 1841 of a movement to finance the building of suitable
workers' dwellings. Many of the bodies thus created were a great success,
and usually managed to make a modest profit; but not so the one in
Croydon.

This was the Croydon Labourers' Dwellings Improvement Society
Ltd, which was registered in 1866, offered 500 shares of £10 each, and
looked for a minimum return of 4 per cent on capital.[11] Its seven founder
members, all resident in the town, were John Grantham, the inventor
of one of the first steam tramcars; Thomas Edridge, shipowner, magistrate and a prominent local Conservative; Samuel Woods, a stockbroker
who was concerned in the London Society for Promoting Christianity
Amongst the Jews; George May, a merchant, and Frederick Ditmas,
a retired major in the Royal Engineers, both of whom were local superintendents of the Croydon branch of the London City Mission; Alfred
Cowdell, a solicitor, a Liberal and treasurer of the Croydon Sunday
School Union; and Frederick West, also a solicitor, and honorary
secretary of the Paper Makers' Provident Society. These men comprised
the first committee, together with a draper, a brewer, a merchant and
two gentlemen. None of them was a member of the local Board of
Health.

Typically, the society's prospectus described the low physical and
moral condition of the poor as being due especially to the absence of
good housing at moderate rents. As a consequence, they said, all efforts
to improve their conditions or to introduce them to 'the saving truths of
religion' were frustrated. But to build improved cottages on new sites
would leave the existing slums untouched; the aim, therefore, was to
start by erecting, in the heart of the worst area, lodgings at moderate
rents 'with every accessory for light, cleanliness, ventilation, and moral
control'. The articles of association stipulated that the committee could
set apart a portion of the buildings 'for moral and Christian instruction,
free from denominational distinctions'.

It is evident that the main supporters of the society, while well known
locally and in many cases active in the town's philanthropic life, were
only exceptionally involved in local government and politics. Of twenty-
three known members, at least ten were Anglicans, two were Quakers
(one of them was Horniman, the tea merchant) and one a Congregation-
alist. There is no reason to believe that the religious affiliations of the
others, if known, would upset the apparent predominance of Church of
England membership.

The society got off to a bad start. Despite the employment of a most experienced architect from London and Grantham's pleadings that the society had been especially attentive in matters of ventilation, light and cleanliness, the local Board of Health shortly rejected an application to build in the market area, since there was not quite the amount of space at the back of the buildings required by the by-laws. The society accordingly abandoned its proposal and purchased instead a ninety-five-year lease on land on the edge of the town, where it subsequently had the Shaftesbury Buildings erected at a cost of £5,200. But despite all the good intentions, expectations were not fulfilled and the society soon went into voluntary liquidation. Its rent for one unfurnished room was 1s. 6d., for two 2s. 6d., and for sets of three or more 3s. 6d., compared with 4s. 8d. per week paid by a couple living in a lodging-house. But the very poor could not afford the society's rents with sufficient regularity, were unable to make the necessary capital investment in goods and chattels, and were sometimes excluded or given notice to quit on grounds of turpitude. However, as Allan has said, the importance of the housing societies lies in the fact that they brought the problem of slums and of renewal to public attention.

But that was not in itself sufficient. Allan has pointed out that a third possible stimulus to redevelopment might be through the intervention of the local authority in the enforcement of the public health Acts, which forced private landlords to improve or demolish their worst properties. The 1851 Common Lodging Houses Act permitted the inspection and regulation of those places; and the Artisans' and Labourers' Dwellings Act of 1868 empowered local authorities to order private landlords to improve or demolish insanitary buildings. There is evidence that in the 1870s and thereafter increasing pressure was being brought to bear on landlords in the market area of Croydon to improve their properties, but the powers were purely permissive and were not exercised with unrestrained enthusiasm. In any event improvement by legislation was necessarily piecemeal. The only people with the administrative machinery and the financial resources to clear an entire slum area, such as this part of Croydon, were the local authorities. Even for them the work might take many years to reach fruition.

V. UNSUCCESSFUL EFFORTS AT LOCAL GOVERNMENT INTERVENTION

It was the state of the High Street, along one side of the triangular market area, that later became the focal point of interest in the struggle for improvement. One of the local Board of Health's members, a Dr Carpenter, drew attention in 1861 to the detrimental effect on business of the street's narrowness. Ladies, he said, objected to visiting shops there because of the danger of their carriages being scratched or damaged by passing vehicles. Throughout his lengthy public life in Croydon Dr Carpenter was an indefatigable campaigner on behalf of working-class housing, and when he returned to the subject of the High Street three years later, he linked his aim of widening it to 50 ft with a proposal to sweep away Middle Row. He was careful to point out that increasing the value of the town centre would also increase the value of property in more distant parts of the parish. In saying this, he was giving an early indication that one of the many sources of future opposition to redevelopment of the market area would be the residents, and especially the shopkeepers, living elsewhere in the town. Improvements, it was claimed, were borne by all the ratepayers but would benefit only the people in the immediate vicinity.

With only one dissentient the local Board set up, in the same year (1864), a committee to obtain improvement powers; but when the question of the expenditure of money to obtain those powers came before the Board, enthusiasm evaporated and only the chairman's casting vote gave a favourable majority. As a result Carpenter withdrew his proposal.

For the next few years the matter was hardly discussed at all by the local Board, and only occasionally in the columns of the press, although the question was asked in the *Croydon Chronicle*: 'Is there no Haussmann to widen High Street and erect a market with a *Maison de Ville* on top of it?' [12] Following on the 1875 Artisans' and Labourers' Dwellings Improvement Act, many towns started the systematic purchase of property, using where necessary compulsory powers; but when the Croydon Board had earlier discussed the Bill there had been general agreement that it would not be workable in Croydon, and so its members continued to discuss, without reaching any conclusion, the limited question of bettering the High Street, rather than the much wider one of slum clearance. Even for that the Board appeared to have lost much of its earlier crusading enthusiasm, despite mounting criticism from the local newspapers, one of which commented: 'It would be difficult, if perhaps we except Gravesend, to find the High Street of an important town so exceptionally disagreeable.' [13]

However, in March 1883 the local Board went out of existence and incorporation took place. Eighteen months later a High Street Improvement Committee was appointed and, with one exception, the local newspapers welcomed the revival of the proposal for demolition. That exception was the *Croydon Guardian*, which suggested that only a few individuals would benefit, that with the nearness of London and the intensive competition among traders no one would be able to afford the increased rentals on new shop property, and that only if the scheme could be carried out without increasing the rates – perhaps by purchasing the Croydon Gas Company and utilising its profits – should it be accepted.

The committee soon faced a barrage of criticism. Its chairman, Councillor Hinton, a wholesale provision merchant and Strict and Particular Baptist, who had described Middle Row as a gigantic upas tree, presented a precipitate report only six weeks after his committee had been appointed. Dissatisfaction with the document was such that the council readily accepted an amendment proposing that plans and estimates should be invited with prizes for the best three schemes. The resultant competition attracted twenty-five entries and the first prize of £100 was awarded to J. M. Brydon, who was responsible at about the same time for Chelsea Town Hall, and later for the new government offices on the far side of Parliament Square from Westminster Abbey.

In the meantime the Improvement Committee had been reconstituted so as to exclude three grocers (including Councillor Hinton) and a draper, all of whom had properties in the High Street and therefore a vested interest in the whole matter; but it was made quite clear, when the awards were announced, that there was no commitment to implement the prize-winning or any other scheme. Indeed when an appointed firm of estate agents produced their calculation that the cost of demolishing all the properties and compensating the owners in the entire area would amount to £182,000, the newly constituted committee was sent away to produce a less expensive alternative. This it did, mainly by abandoning any demolition proposals for Surrey Street, and so reducing the estimated cost to £62,865, on which the interest and sinking fund would amount to about £2,580 per annum. The committee further recommended that the Water Committee should be asked to say whether the current charge for water might be relied on to produce a profit of that order.

Croydon was rapidly developing at that time on its north-eastern side, with a mixture of working- and middle-class housing at South Norwood and some particularly affluent estates further north still, at

Upper Norwood in the vicinity of the Crystal Palace. Not unnaturally the ratepayers there had little general enthusiasm for improvements in the town centre, but with the proposal that the scheme should be financed out of the Croydon water profits, instead of out of the rates, the Norwood newspapers joined with almost all those of the town centre in welcoming the revised plan. Upper Norwood and much of South Norwood too were supplied by the Lambeth Water Company, so that residents there would not be financing the scheme even indirectly.

The overtly Conservative *Croydon Guardian*, however, maintained its opposition; and one of its correspondents, a City solicitor who lived on the Park Hill estate, indicated another reason why well-to-do commuters were against improvement. It is clear from his letter that the wealthy businessman who worked in town saw Croydon as a kind of sylvan retreat; not only was he unenthusiastic about having to pay additional rates to benefit those who remained in the place all day, but he was positively against any destruction of what he saw as the town's quaint charm. The growing influence of such people was referred to later by the *Croydon Advertiser* when it spoke, wistfully, of the earlier Liberal ascendancy in the town which had diminished as the place had become 'a huge dormitory for the merchants and other City men whose votes as Conservatives in London have been repeated in Croydon'.[14]

But even if the proposal that the cost of improvement should be met out of the water profits was acceptable to the people of Norwood, it was still to bring about the downfall of the scheme. The Water Committee's natural objections to the idea were overridden by the council. But during the autumn of 1886 debate on the subject became increasingly lengthy and acrimonious ('animated' is the euphemism used by one local paper), and finally the whole project was abandoned when a councillor who favoured improvement moved, late at night, that provision of the necessary money out of the water rate should be deleted from the report. His reason was a rather special one: he wished that the surplus on the water rate should be used for a quite different purpose, his own pet project of softening the town's water. After debate, his amendment was carried by 23 votes to 15, some of the members of the council having already left for home. The mayor then put the adoption of the Improvement Committee's report as amended, and not a hand was held up in its favour.

In its next edition, with a bitterness that was quite uncharacteristic, a *Croydon Advertiser* editorial commented: 'We cannot conceive how businessmen, of ordinary mental capacity and of reasonable public

spirit, could have brought about so disgraceful and depressing a decision.'[15] So ended many years of fruitless argument and successful
obstruction. The slums remained, their decay doubtless hastened by
the uncertainty that had for so long hung over their future.

VI. THE SUCCESSFUL TOWN COUNCIL SCHEME

The following summer the *Croydon Chronicle* suggested that the council no longer had any sincere or determined intention of grappling with
the problem; but events were shortly to prove the comment incorrect.

The revival of interest was led by a Croydon hatter and tailor,
Alderman Francis Coldwells, who had taken no particular part in
earlier debate. Although never honoured subsequently by the town,
probably because of his marginal association with the Liberator Building Society frauds, the final success of the improvement scheme was
due in large measure to Coldwells.

He had been born at Stoke Newington in 1832 and had attended the
British School there. He became steward to a Croydon landowner and
then went into partnership with a tailor in the town. During his period
as chairman of the final High Street Special Committee after 1888 there
was frequent reference to his negotiating skill and to his ability as an
orator; and in the 1892 parliamentary election, as a Home Rule candi-
date, he won Lambeth North from the Conservatives, on a platform of
reform of London's water supply and markets, and enlarged powers
for the London County Council. Then came the Liberator crash, at
which time he was a newly appointed director of the Building Securities
Company, one of the speculative enterprises of Jabez Spencer Balfour,
the town's charter mayor. Coldwells's total profit appears to have been
only £36; but his public career was finished. He did not contest the
next general election and he resigned his aldermanic seat; but by then
the final improvement scheme was almost complete and its physical
results remain virtually unchanged to this day, long after his name has
been forgotten in the town.

His proposal, submitted to the council in June 1888, was that a
committee should report on the possibility of improving the roads
forming the three sides of the market area – High Street, Surrey Street
and Crown Hill – and of abolishing Middle Row, Market Street and
King Street, without having to buy all the properties affected and
afterwards resell the sites. The attractiveness of the idea was that it
opened up the possibility of a substantial improvement without either

raiding the water profits or incurring considerable indebtedness. It represented the widespread extension of a principle that had recently been used in connection with a single property on the other side of the High Street, where much of the cost of purchase for road widening had been offset by an 'equitable arrangement' with the occupiers, who retained the site and were compensated for setting back the frontage of their new premises. It was an idea that had to be modified subsequently, but it formed a good starting-point for discussion.

Coldwells had considered the constitution of the committee with great care. He favoured a small one with no *ex officio* members, not even the mayor, with no one interested in any property likely to be affected (a contrast with Hinton's earlier committee), nor even with any lawyer or solicitor who was likely to be employed by an owner of property in his own interest. Coldwells even went so far as to oppose the appointment to the committee of anyone living outside the area but who was in the same business as a trader likely to be affected by the scheme.

The High Street Special Committee's first report was adopted unanimously by the council; but one of its proposals, that the High Street should be widened to 50 ft, was criticised on the grounds that if that were done the town hall would be left jutting out into the middle of the road. It quickly became apparent that this was a serious handicap in persuading High Street shopkeepers to co-operate; and yet to rebuild the town hall on the new building line, even only to its existing inadequate size, would occupy a valuable High Street frontage of 180 ft. The fact that the improvement could not reasonably be carried out without the demolition of the existing town hall probably explains why in Croydon, unlike Leicester for example, there was no clear-cut division between those who wanted improvement only to the extent necessary for public health and those who wanted it to embrace such embellishments as a new town hall, the widening of the High Street and the provision of recreation grounds.

Providentially the Brighton Railway Company had a terminus, called Croydon Central, at the rear of the properties on the other side of the High Street, and although the station had seemed ideally placed and a street had been built specially to give access to it, both the building and the line linking it with the main line near East Croydon had been an embarrassment to the company and were little used by the travelling public.

Negotiations were accordingly entered into between the committee and the company; but the agreement that emerged was both complex and controversial. Between the decaying Central station and the main London to Brighton line lay the Fairfield, across which the branch line had been built. The field had earlier been sold to the railway company who had fenced it in and extracted its gravel, leaving only a diagonal path running across it which gave easy and quick access to the town centre from the affluent Park Hill estate. The company made the sale of the Central station site conditional upon the closure of the footpath; and a majority of the council was prepared to accept this since it answered the otherwise insoluble problem of the town hall, and hence of the whole project. But the Park Hill residents, who, it will be remembered, were against the improvement scheme anyway, were not unnaturally incensed.

In the meantime the committee was hard at work. It was rapidly becoming obvious that although voluntary arrangements were possible in many instances, in others it would be necessary to obtain compulsory powers, apparently because of the considerable doubt that existed in many people's minds as to whether even at this stage the council was really determined to carry out the project. But before many more weeks had elapsed a plan was published in the local newspapers showing the full details of the scheme (see Fig. 14, p. 211 below); and estimates suggested that the cost of purchasing the scheduled properties would be about £146,000, which would be offset by £66,000 on capitalised rents of new building sites. By negotiation the gap of £80,000 might be reduced to £50,000, on which the charge for principal and interest would amount to about £2,000 per annum for sixty years; and £442 of this £2,000 would be met by additional rating revenue from the new properties, leaving only about £1,550 to be provided. That sum, suggested the committee, could readily be found by using the water profits, or increasing the general rate, or levying a special rate, or making a charge on the financial relief that might be expected to flow from the Local Government Act; but no decision need be made on the point until the actual cost was known accurately.

The committee thus avoided the pitfall into which its predecessor had tumbled; but it was still possible for the scheme to founder. In November 1889 the council gave notice of its intention to apply to Parliament for powers of compulsory purchase, but the expense of promoting any Bill in Parliament could not be incurred until the burgesses had been consulted, and at that time any individual could demand a poll. At the public meeting Alderman Coldwells described the scheme and the way it would benefit not only the town centre but the people elsewhere in the borough. Subsequent discussion, however, largely revolved around the loss of the Fairfield footpath; despite which, when the count was taken, only one person voted against the expense of promoting the Bill. But that one man, Henry Bremner, a writer of fierce letters to the local newspapers about the corruption of the council, then demanded a poll. He was not supported even by the Park Hill residents who had been so critical of the loss of the footpath. Nevertheless he remained adamant, and at the close of the meeting he had to be escorted to a cab stand by the Town Clerk, a magistrate and half a dozen constables. Between that night and the date of the poll, the committee persuaded the council that the cost of the scheme should be borne as far as was practicable out of the Croydon water charge, thereby winning the timely support of the waverers in the Norwood area. The result of the subsequent poll was: in favour, 10,618; against, 2,722; majority, 7,896. Rather more than 10,000 of the 14,787 burgesses (some of whom had more than one vote) had taken part. From that moment the completion and, so it turned out, the success of the scheme were at long last assured.

VII. MOTIVES FOR SUPPORT AND OPPOSITION

At this distance of time it is of course impossible to decide whether the declared motives of individual supporters and opponents of the various attempts at improvement were genuine.

The project had stemmed above all from complaints about the sanitary, structural and moral conditions of the lodging-houses in Middle Row. It was believed by many that it was really the migrant population that was troublesome, and that this would leave Croydon for other towns once Middle Row was removed.

It has been shown too that the question of improvement was closely linked with the need to widen the High Street. It was very easy of course for opponents of the scheme to attack High Street shopkeepers who supported it, on the grounds that they were doing so for their own gain at the ratepayers' expense. It was equally easy for supporters of the scheme to attack shopkeepers elsewhere in the town who opposed it, on the grounds that they were doing so out of jealousy. But the *Croydon Advertiser* perhaps put those arguments in perspective with the comment that it was the corporation's duty in any event to provide proper trading facilities.[16] It was unfortunate, however, that until the formation of the last committee little or no effort was made to exclude from the decision-making not only people who might benefit indirectly but even those whose property was involved.

The state of trade, so often the reason for doing or not doing things in Victorian times, was cited both by opponents and by supporters of the scheme, the latter anticipating both direct improvement in the building trade and also increased prosperity throughout the town. Other opponents, as was said earlier, were against the sacrifice of the Fairfield path to the railway company, wished to retain the town's rural charm, were unwilling to allow the water profits to be used, or were un-enthusiastic for a possibly substantial burden to be put on the rates. Linked with all this were doubts as to whether improvement in one part of the borough should be financed by people elsewhere. Finally, among the supporters, there was fear: fear of the reservoirs of disease, crime and vice that the worst slums tended to be, and the feeling that such areas, especially when alongside the town hall, were an affront to civic dignity.

So much for the motives of the individual; but Croydon, in the second half of the nineteenth century, was acquiring a sense of collective responsibility as well. Unfortunately it is not possible to discover the political and religious affiliation of all the members of the council who took part in the later discussions on the scheme; moreover they did not in every instance vote consistently.

But certain distinct trends do emerge. The figures, while not statistically reliable, give the general impression that the Liberals were likely to favour improvement whether they traded in the town or commuted; the Conservatives, however, were likely to be against improvement unless they traded in the town. Of thirteen aldermen and councillors who can be identified as supporting the project, at least nine were Liberals and only two (both traders) were certainly Conservatives. It has been noted that the Liberal local newspapers favoured the successive schemes; the Conservative paper was bitterly opposed to them.

There were moreover nineteen members of the council interested in the improvement whose religious connections can be identified. Four were Baptists, three of them at least, all wealthy men, attending Spurgeon's Tabernacle at West Croydon; two others were Congregationalists; one was a Quaker; and one was a Methodist. Of these eight nonconformists, six at least favoured improvement, and the other two are not known to have been against it; all but two of them are known to have been Liberals. Of the nine known Anglicans, three commuters (two Conservatives and a Liberal) attended churches that were Evangelical. The Liberal favoured improvement, and at least one of the other two was against it. One Liberal who favoured the scheme was connected with a Tractarian church.

It would seem from this necessarily slight analysis that support for the improvement came especially from Liberal tradesmen, who might be Nonconformist or at either end of the Anglican spectrum. Nonconformists tended to be Liberal in any case, in Croydon as in most towns at this date. Opposition, on the other hand, came especially from those Conservatives who were commuters; and such Conservatives were not uncommonly Anglicans.

VIII. IMPLEMENTATION OF THE CROYDON IMPROVEMENT ACT

The Croydon Improvement Act received the Royal Assent in July 1890. It provided for the street improvements; the demolition and sale of the sites of the town hall and butter-market house; and the right of the corporation to purchase land compulsorily and then to lease, sell or exchange it. The council was empowered to borrow £125,000 for street improvements and for the erection of a new town hall; and it could, if it thought it desirable, issue stock.

The corporation went to considerable lengths to be fair to the dispossessed. Where agreement was not reached informally, notice to treat was served but recourse was had to arbitration in only five instances; and in those cases the claimants finished up with, on average, £629 less than they had demanded, whereas the council had to pay out an average of only £48 more than its initial offer and only £18 more than its final offer. Further proof of the council's fairness is shown in the fact that in all the cases which did not reach the arbitration stage and where the relevant figures are known, the average discrepancy between the original council offer and the finally agreed figure was only £28. The committee also showed an awareness of the need to cause as little inconvenience as possible to traders. Wherever possible it deferred taking possession until the occupier's tenancy had expired and until he had found either permanent or temporary alternative accommodation.

When the Act had been passed, the 143 properties and pieces of land involved, including those in the High Street, were held freehold by as many as eighty different people or bodies. Two of the most substantial owners were the Ecclesiastical Commissioners and the corporation. Almost exactly three-quarters of the inhabitants of the market area, apart from the High Street, were temporary residents and this was a blessing for the nearby streets, since it meant that those displaced did not move into them and reduce their value. There is accordingly no evidence of subsequent overcrowding or of property deterioration in the neighbouring locality arising from the implementation of the scheme.

122 permanent residents also were living in the area scheduled for demolition, excluding the High Street, but there were at the same time sixty-five houses elsewhere in the town let at weekly rents and vacant, twenty-seven of them being in Wilford Road, another slum area a mile or more away. There were also ninety-nine vacant rooms, twenty-two of them at the Labourers' Dwellings. It seemed to the council, therefore, that this available accommodation, bearing in mind the temporary nature of so much of the residence, was more than sufficient; but the Local Government Board took a contrary view, insisting on accommodation being provided for at least 150 people, and suggesting the erection of a municipal lodging-house to take 100 and cottages for the remainder. Accordingly ten cottages, each housing about five people and costing £250, were built on land at the rear of the new town hall site, and when nearly complete their tenancies were advertised by bills posted in the market area. The rents were 9s. 6d. to 10s. per week. All the cottages were occupied within a few months.

The committee at first considered that the required lodging-house should be provided by private enterprise; but it was obviously ridiculous to clear the market area and then to allow the land to be used again for the same purpose as before. There were also fears that what had been a localised problem might spread. Therefore, goaded on by the Local Government Board, the committee had second thoughts, and plans were drawn up for a municipal lodging-house for 66 men and 34 women. This was subsequently erected on the Mitcham side of the town at a cost of £6,000. It was difficult to find suitable superintendents and several of the early ones had to be dismissed for insubordination, absconding with the takings, or drunkenness. It was soon found, moreover, that the men's side was full almost every night and the women's side almost empty, doubtless because the ladies who had been counted in the market lodging-houses found it impossible to ply their trade under municipal protection. Eventually the Local Government Board was persuaded to allow the house to be rearranged with weekly men lodgers on one side and nightly men lodgers on the other.

Demolition of property began in June 1893. The derelict houses in Nelson Square were sold by auction together with adjoining properties in Middle Row for a total of £24 10s. The town hall later fetched £55, the clock previously having been sold for 8s. and then displayed at Louis Tussaud's exhibition in Birmingham.

Removals brought about by the demolition included the town hall, the post office and the corn market. The land that had been bought from the railway company was adequate not only for a new town hall but also for a new police station as well; while part of the railway cutting was adapted as a particularly beautiful public garden. The town hall was designed by Charles Henman, Jr, and it incorporated police courts and a free library. But the Postmaster-General, having decided that the post office should be rebuilt in the High Street rather than near the new town hall, bought land there from the corporation for that purpose. As regards the corn trade, despite the decline of the markets over the years, the council was persuaded to provide accommodation in the new town hall for stands that could be removed at the end of market day. The resultant corn exchange, clearly so designated but virtually unknown to Croydonians, still remains. It is now incorporated in the public library.

Apart from such ancillary activities as the planning and erection of the municipal lodging-houses and cottages, the committee, once it had completed negotiations for the purchase of the condemned property, had to attend particularly to the resale and redevelopment of the sites. Some shopkeepers wished to return, but many plots were available to newcomers. In both cases the committee had the responsibility of negotiating the best prices it could for ensuring that the buildings were an improvement on the old ones, and that those on the High Street frontage would contribute to the town's new-found dignity. Parliament refused a Bill giving the corporation power to retain the ground rents in perpetuity, but agreed to their being held for ten years from the dates of the various leases, for which purpose the corporation borrowed £70,000 from the Local Government Board, since it foresaw that appreciation in value would more than pay the interest on the loan. Building in the area was not permitted until the plans and specifications had been approved; the sale of intoxicants was not to be allowed, and neither were activities of a 'noisome or offensive' nature. There was a ban too on projecting and sky signs.

The council had little difficulty in disposing of the High Street land. One firm of drapers, Grant Brothers, also bought land at the rear, in a new Middle Street, and obtained permission to connect the two sites with an enclosed bridge forming part of its shop. Generally, however, the new Middle Street was a planning error. It had been designed to run southwards between High Street and Surrey Street but with a right-angle bend westwards into Surrey Street so as to avoid shortening the depths of the valuable frontages at the southern end of the High Street. However, it failed to give Surrey Street the kind of outlet it had previously enjoyed to the High Street, so that the new road became simply a backwater, and so it remains today.

The sudden isolation of Surrey Street from the mainstream of the town's trading activity came as a shock to shopkeepers there. They and the council had failed to appreciate, when examining the published plans, that the local customers would be forced to move away and that there would be no direct contact in future with shoppers in the improved High Street. When the Surrey Street traders did react, the council were reluctant to sacrifice valuable High Street land for a linking road and saw the steepness of the slope as a handicap to a more modest access. Even the expressed fear that by its isolation Surrey Street might become another Middle Row failed to produce a positive scheme from the council. Time was running out, for the High Street frontages were rapidly being disposed of; but at the eleventh hour three men (two of them councillors) who had business interests in Surrey Street bought a plot on the High Street and persuaded the council to let them build an arcade of six shops, at right-angles to the main road, leading to a light iron bridge spanning Middle Street and then on to steps descending into Surrey Street.

Chronologically this arcade represented the last major part of a municipal improvement scheme that had been made necessary because of the failure of private enterprise; yet ironically the arcade itself was a minor triumph of private enterprise, made necessary because of the failure of municipal planning.

IX. THE BALANCE-SHEET

By the improvement scheme Croydon had gained much: the total disappearance of Middle Row, a wider High Street, a new town hall, a new police station, municipal cottages, a municipal lodging-house, the Town Hall Gardens; and above all a new civic dignity.

It remains only to consider one further question that had given the council and the ratepayers so much anxiety. What had been the cost?

The answer is given in the final statement of accounts of the Special

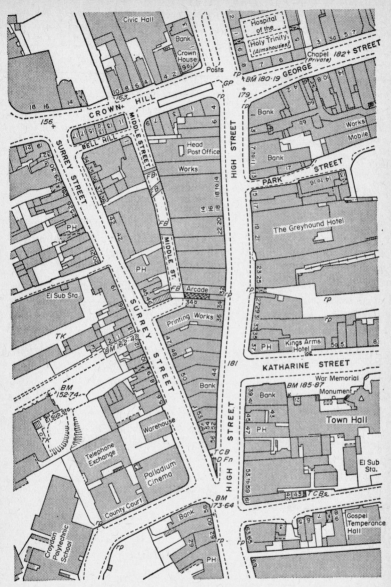

FIG. 14 MAP OF CENTRAL CROYDON IN THE 1950S
Composite map based on Ordnance Surveys of 1954 and 1961.
Scale 1 : 1250

Committee. It shows that the total expenditure had amounted to just over £173,000, but that against this could be offset nearly £124,000, representing money received from the sale of sites and the estimated value of property and ground rents in hand. The eventual net cost would thus be about £50,000, as against an original estimate of £90,000. The committee had indeed done its work well. The townscape it then created remains almost unchanged to this day (see Fig. 14).

Despite the opponents of improvement and despite the fears of some of the supporters of improvement, the heart of the town had been renewed. Croydon had ended its period of existence as a market centre and as the principal doss-house on the London to Brighton Road. Henceforward it would be chiefly significant as a prosperous retail shopping centre, with the resident poor living in side streets well away from the new town Hall and the growing departmental stores. *Laissez-faire*, philanthropy and the rigid enforcement of the public health Acts had failed; whereas the corporation, once it found the right leader, albeit a man of little education, had succeeded.

In retrospect it was a good thing that it had found the right leader. For the closing stages of the improvement scheme coincided with the long-term imprisonment for fraud of the first and third mayors of the town. This was a blow to civic dignity and to the confidence and pride the burgesses had in the integrity of their new corporation. The situation was aggravated too by the fact that many Croydonians had lost their hard-earned savings in the collapse of their charter mayor's bogus financial empire. It therefore seems unlikely that in the years that remained before the First World War any corporation improvement scheme, necessarily involving trust in the integrity of the councillors, would have received any support at all from the vast majority of people in the town. In that event another thirty or more years might well have been added to the sixty or so that the improvement had required to reach fruition. Without doubt the town owes more to Francis Coldwells than even his contemporaries realised.

8. Town and Country in Victorian Leicestershire: The Role of the Village Carrier

ALAN EVERITT

I. INTRODUCTORY

WHEN W. H. Hudson wrote *A Shepherd's Life*, the story of a Wiltshire shepherd in the late nineteenth century, he included in it an unforgettable description of Salisbury, the capital city of Salisbury Plain. 'To the dwellers on the Plain,' he said,

> Salisbury itself is an exceedingly important place – the most important in the world. . . . For Salisbury is the capital of the Plain, the head and heart of all those villages, too many to count, scattered far and wide over the surrounding country. . . . To set out betimes and overtake the early carriers' carts on the road, each with its little cargo of packages and women with baskets and an old man or two, to recognise acquaintances among those who sit in front, and as I go on overtaking and passing carriers and the half-gipsy, little 'general dealer' in his dirty, ramshackle, little cart drawn by a rough fast-trotting pony, all of us intent on business and pleasure, bound for Salisbury – the great market and emporium and place of all delights for all the great Plain . . . the mere sight of it exhilarates like wine. The numbers – the people and the animals! The carriers' carts drawn up in rows on rows – carriers from a hundred little villages on the Bourne, the Avon, the Wylye, the Nadder, the Ebble, and from all over the Plain, each bringing its little contingent.[1]

Hudson's account of Salisbury and its carriers might be paralleled from descriptions of many other English towns at this period. Readers of Somerset Maugham's *Cakes and Ale*, for instance, may remember how Willie Ashenden's first bicycle was brought to him from Canterbury by the village carrier of Whitstable. (The two places are disguised as Tercanbury and Blackstable in the story.) The passage is clearly autobiographical – Maugham was born in 1874 and educated in Kent – and is of considerable interest. For anything that could not be acquired in the few ordinary shops of Whitstable – butchers, bakers and the like – the local village folk were entirely dependent upon the weekly carrier's services to Canterbury, the principal shopping centre of east Kent.

In west Kent much the same function was performed by Maidstone. Its role is described in another literary work, the *Memoirs of a Fox-Hunting Man*, by Maugham's contemporary Siegfried Sassoon:

> I seldom spoke to anyone while I was out for my walks, but now and again I would meet John Homeward, the carrier, on his way back from the county town where he went three days a week. . . . Homeward had been making his foot-pace journeys with his hooded van and nodding horse ever since I could remember, and he seemed an essential feature of the ten miles across the weald [from Brenchley to Maidstone]. . . . All the year round, whether there was snow on the ground or blossom on the fruit trees, the carrier's van crawled across the valley with its cargo of utilities. . . . His burly figure and kindly bearded face must have gone up and down that hill about five thousand times before he retired to prosper with a small public-house.[2]

In Westmorland the town of Kendal formed the economic capital of the region, and the carrier's role in the economy of the dales was described by a country parson of the time:

> One of the great institutions of the valley was the country carrier. With his slowly rolling cart and old horse, he was an all-important individual, and performed a multitudinous number of offices. It was perhaps because he could neither read nor write that he had such a marvellous memory, and this was essential to his compound trade. He made journeys twice a week to Greytown [Kendal], and upon these occasions carried commissions from nearly everyone in the dale. These ranged from strings of beads to sacks of flour, and from pins to new gowns. There was nothing which might be required that the carrier could not bring, and with his many-sided character he had a marvellous power of pleasing everybody. In many cases the carrier brought the whole of the groceries for the year, and a hundred things besides. It mattered not of how great a number of items his individual orders consisted; he always rendered a faithful and accurate account upon his return.[3]

The carriers' carts and country people streaming into towns like Salisbury and Kendal on market days were indeed as characteristic a feature of Victorian England as the industrial cities and slums. Yet this aspect of urban history is one that is now largely forgotten. Most counties had at least one town like Salisbury or Kendal, the capital and emporium of a hundred villages or several hundred scattered farms and cottages, the centre of the local universe. And the vital link between this traffic of town and county was the country carrier. Without his services, week in week out, summer and winter, no village in Victorian England could have long survived, and the wealth of the county capitals themselves – Salisbury or Leicester, for instance, Canterbury or York – would have been seriously depleted. Yet the village carrier has never received much attention from English historians. His story and the part he played in bringing town and country together have never been written.

For the present essay a single county has been selected, Leicestershire, and more particularly the local carriers of two towns within that county: Leicester, the capital of the shire, and Melton Mowbray, perhaps the busiest market town after Leicester.* For comparative purposes a certain amount of evidence from Northamptonshire has also been included. The period selected is the 1880s, a time when carriers were probably as numerous and influential in local economic life as they had ever been. This was not quite the last generation of village carriers; for in some areas at least they continued to expand in numbers until the First World War. After the war, however, with the development of motor-bus services in rural areas, the decline of the carrier was rapid. And in a sense his passing marked the end of an epoch in both urban and rural history.

The origins of the country carrier in England, as a regular feature of provincial life, cannot be precisely dated. Packmen and pedlars were no doubt a common sight on the medieval roads of England; they were certainly common enough between the major towns by the middle of the Tudor period; but it may not have been until towards the end of the sixteenth century, when so many local economic changes took their rise, that a complete network of regular carriers' routes around these major towns came into existence. By the year 1637, when the first 'directory' of these services was published – John Taylor's *Carriers' Cosmography* – it is clear that London at least was already linked by carriers' wagon with every part of the kingdom. One of the ultimate factors in

---

* For Leicester carriers' routes *c.* 1884, see Fig. 15, p. 236 below, with the accompanying numbered key.

this development, so far as London was concerned, was the dramatic expansion of the metropolitan population, and the extension of its hinterland for food supplies and raw materials. The parallel growth of provincial towns did not generally begin until rather later, of course, and in some parts of the provinces the development of carriers' services on a comparable scale to those of London may not have taken place until after the Restoration.

Whenever they began, it is not really until the nineteenth century that it becomes possible to track down the carriers' services of most country towns with any completeness. With the spate of trade directories during that century, an excellent and easily accessible source becomes available for reconstructing the pattern of carriers' routes and services around every town of any size in the kingdom. In no earlier century is it possible to discover the local 'catchment area' of so many provincial towns with the same precision. The reconstruction of these urban hinterlands provides an important field for local historians to explore, and it is one which hitherto has been surprisingly little worked.

Closely associated with the extension of carrying services, between the seventeenth century and the nineteenth, was the growth of the larger market towns of England. In virtually every county the smaller towns tended to lose ground to the larger as shopping and marketing centres between 1600 and 1900. Little by little the larger towns gradually absorbed their trade and annexed their hinterland. In Leicestershire, for example, where there had been at least thirty markets in the early fourteenth century, each probably with its own distinct area, there were by the 1670s only thirteen, and by the 1880s no more than seven. Slowly but surely places like Leicester, Loughborough and Melton Mowbray absorbed virtually all the market and shopping traffic of the county, attracting in away from the smaller centres like Billesdon, Hallaton and Bottesford, once busy little markets in their own right.

By the late nineteenth century one of the most obvious features distinguishing the English market town from the rural village was the possession of a network of carriers' services to the surrounding area. Judged by this criterion (there are obviously others that might apply), in Leicestershire and other counties the distinction between town and village was clearly defined. From C. N. Wright's *Commercial and General Directory of Leicester and Fifteen Miles Round*, published in 1884, it is evident that only six places in the area were centres of carriers' routes: Melton Mowbray, Hinckley, Loughborough, Lutterworth, Market Harborough and Leicester itself. To these we must add Ashby de la Zouch, which was outside Wright's fifteen-mile limit, to complete the county total of seven towns.

Lutterworth, smallest of the seven, was linked every market day and on certain other weekdays by regular carriers' services with at least 30 surrounding villages. The market area of Hinckley also comprised 30 or more villages, and was more populous than Lutterworth's, since many of these places were semi-industrialised communities by this date. The Market Harborough area comprised at least 36 villages; that of Loughborough 38; that of Melton Mowbray 60; and that of Leicester itself at least 220. Old towns like Castle Donington and Market Bosworth, by contrast, evidently no longer existed as centres of carriers' routes in late Victorian Leicestershire. They still had a number of shops, of course, and probably some of their shopkeepers ran delivery services to neighbouring villages; but they had ceased to be genuine regional centres of trade and shopping. They had lost their hinterland to Loughborough, Hinckley and Leicester, and in a sense they were now little more than large villages themselves. Every week their carriers set out for the surrounding market towns, just as they did from neighbouring villages. The seven Victorian market towns of Leicestershire, on the other hand, had managed to survive all the vicissitudes of seven hundred years of history. Since then they have continued to expand, moreover, and with the addition now of Coalville they still remain the only considerable shopping centres in the county.

It is sometimes assumed that it was the coming of the railways that brought about the decline of the rural carrier. The country roads of Victorian England are often represented as deserted and grass-grown tracks. But a distinction needs to be drawn between local and long-distance road traffic. Certainly a good deal of the latter was killed off with remarkable celerity by the railways. Within a few years of the establishment of rail connections to towns like Newark and Market Harborough, the old long-distance coach and carrying trade from which they had derived so much benefit during preceding centuries was extinct. Many of the great coaching inns of England were either forced to close down, or else sank to a very prosaic level of hospitality, from which, alas, most of them have never recovered since. But local traffic on the roads was certainly not brought to an end by the railways. It could not have been, if only because most rural communities had no railway station. In the country districts of counties like Kent and Leicestershire perhaps only one village in eight or nine possessed rail communications; in a county like Dorset or Westmorland it was no doubt fewer. A recent study of Victorian Newark has shown that, far from declining with the coming of the railway, local carriers rapidly increased in numbers and considerably extended the market area of the town during Queen Victoria's reign.[4] In a sense the railway helped to increase their prosperity, because of the growing need for road connections between outlying villages and the new railhead.

With rail connections, moreover, market towns like Newark and Leicester acquired fresh advantages as shopping centres, since many new sources of supply – of foodstuffs, raw materials and manufactured goods – were readily opened up to them. So far as Leicester is concerned there can be little doubt that the establishment of rail connections and the remarkable proliferation of carriers' services into the town were among the main reasons for its overwhelming preponderance among the Victorian market towns of the county. By the 1880s there were more carriers' routes centred on the county capital than on all the other towns in the shire put together. They were particularly numerous along the roads to the north and west of Leicester, serving the many semi-industrial villages of this area. Nearly ninety routes entered the town along these four main westerly roads, from the direction of Hinckley, Coventry, Coalville and Loughborough. From the more rural parts of the shire, to the south and east of Leicester, a further sixty routes entered the town by way of the principal roads, from Welford, Harborough, Uppingham and Melton Mowbray. Another twenty or so routes entering Leicester by minor roads, such as Evington Lane, brought the total number to 170.

What precisely were the functions of the village carrier in Victorian England? Briefly, as the quotations from W. H. Hudson and others have indicated, they were twofold. First, he provided a kind of primitive country bus, often a mere cart, conveying the village folk, especially women and children, to the local town on market day for the family shopping. Secondly, they themselves acted as shopping 'agents', purchasing goods ordered by villagers who did not wish to visit the town themselves, or were unable to do so, and also bringing back any goods due to be delivered in the village. Their purchases for the villagers were as varied as those of the bus-driver-cum-carrier in remote areas of the Scottish Highlands today, the last true descendant of the species: everything, in short, from fish and frying pans to bread and bicycles, all stowed away in the back of the vehicle. Recently, in Leicestershire, a carrier's notebook dating from the end of Queen Victoria's reign has come to light, in the remote little village of Walton-by-Kimcote, about

14 miles from Leicester. Roughly written, mostly in indelible pencil, it lists, week by week, the purchases the carrier made in Leicester on market days, and the names of the villagers who had ordered them. The variety was endless. It included, for example, wallpaper, varnish, gripe-water, clogs, Indian corn, lamp oil, toothache pencils, knitting wool, lung tonic, teapots, Scotch oatmeal, football bladders, garden plants, thermometers, cups and saucers, mittens, lanterns, lamp-glasses, serge jackets, sheep netting, joints of meat, mob caps and tea. A third important function of the village carrier, which was not mentioned by Hudson, was supplying the town shops with farm produce.

II. LEICESTER

Leicester has always been the principal town of Leicestershire, and until the nineteenth century it was the only incorporated borough. Situated in the centre of a county of 514,000 acres – about half the size of Kent or Somerset and a third that of Lincolnshire or Devon – it focuses on itself nearly all the main roads of the county and most of its economic and cultural life. Nowadays more than half the 770,000 inhabitants of the shire live in the built-up area of Leicester, if the population of adjoining townships like Wigston and Oadby, physically no longer distinct from it, is added to that of the city itself. In the 1880s much of the Leicestershire countryside was more populous than it is today, and the predominance of Leicester in terms of population was not quite so striking. Nevertheless, with nearly 130,000 inhabitants, it contained 40 per cent of the people of the county and was nine times as large as the second town, Loughborough, with a population of 14,600, or twenty-two times as large as Melton Mowbray, with barely 6,000.

In these respects, though not unique, Leicester and Leicestershire contrasted strikingly with counties like Lincolnshire, Somerset and Kent, where there were no very large towns at this time (except for the part of Bristol in Somerset), but instead a considerable number of moderate-sized places. In Kent there is still no borough with as many as 90,000 inhabitants, though the county is twice as large and more than twice as populous as Leicestershire. In the 1880s no Kentish town contained more than 30,000 inhabitants, though there were fourteen or fifteen with a population of between 10,000 and 30,000. As a consequence, shopping and marketing were more dispersed in Kent than in Leicestershire, and the Midland county was notably more dominated by its county town.

Leicester is still the shopping centre for its shire in a way that no single town in a county like Kent can ever be. The size of the city's shopping hinterland, nowadays comprising nearly the whole county or about 400,000 acres and more than half a million people, is one of the main reasons why Leicester has retained, and continually expands, its great retail market. The market is still held every Wednesday, Friday and Saturday, and with more than 400 stalls each day it is said to be the largest in Britain. In recent years it has extended itself also to Monday and Tuesday in addition to the three traditional market days. Few people in the county ever think of visiting the surrounding conurbations of Nottingham, Derby, Rugby, Coventry or Northampton for their purchases. They still go shopping in the medieval market place of the county town, shaped like a vast horseshoe, where their forebears have been buying and selling for more than seven hundred years.

The following account of Leicester and its carriers is based principally on C. N. Wright's *Commercial and General Directory of Leicester and Fifteen Miles Round*, published in 1884. It may be pointed out in passing that it is a mistake to suppose that the important themes of English urban history can be written only from relatively inaccessible manuscript sources: there is still a vast amount waiting to be discovered in readily available printed records like directories and newspapers, though like any other historical source these need care in interpretation. The district covered by Wright comprises most of Leicestershire except for a small area around Ashby de la Zouch in the north-west and the countryside beyond Melton Mowbray, in the direction of Grantham. Amongst the information given in the directory are what purport to be complete lists of country carriers to and from each market town, with the days and times when they operated, their destinations, and the 'stations' – in Leicestershire almost invariably inns – from which they set out. This kind of information was commonly provided by the directories of the time, and was no local peculiarity of Leicestershire, of course. For a list of directories before 1856 the reader should consult J. E. Norton's *Guide to the National and Provincial Directories of England and Wales excluding London, published before 1856*, issued by the Royal Historical Society (1950). For subsequent directories the first obvious place to search is one's borough or county library. In the present writer's experience the later nineteenth-century directories usually appear to give fuller details of carriers' services than the earlier. It may also be added that, where they have survived, local railway timetables of the period, produced by country printers, often provided information about village carriers. As a rule, however, these are not nearly so readily available as directories.

One cannot necessarily assume that the list of carriers given in directories is exhaustive. So far as Wright's *Leicestershire* is concerned the present writer believes it is reasonably complete for Leicester and other market towns in the county. There is no certain means of checking this conviction; but whether or not Wright's lists are entirely comprehensive, it is unlikely that the market areas they indicate would be much altered by the discovery of additional names. Wright certainly includes a very large number of carriers, altogether about 400 for the county as a whole.

So far as Leicester is concerned, the entries for each town and village in the county have been searched for the present study, as a cross-check, in addition to that for the county town itself. There are not many discrepancies between village and city entries, except in the spelling of surnames; but the former add a further 18 carriers' names to the 187 listed under the county town. (In some counties the discrepancy appears to be much greater.) There are no entries in Wright's *Directory* for villages beyond his fifteen-mile limit; but the carriers of these villages are in fact mentioned, either under Leicester or under other market towns. From these it is evident that many places beyond the fifteen miles were linked by carrier with the county town. By carefully analysing all the carriers on separate slips or cards (a tedious but relatively simple task), and sorting the slips in various ways, it is possible to reconstruct the extent of the market area of Leicester and other towns in the county with some precision. It is also possible to work out the population of each market area, the routes the carriers took, the inns from which they set out, the days on which they operated, and the extent to which the Leicester area overlapped that of secondary markets in the county. Something at least may be discovered, moreover, about where the carriers lived and who they were, though on the latter topic information is unfortunately scanty and difficult to track down.

Altogether there were about 250 parishes in Victorian Leicestershire, and approximately 350 villages. From at least 220 of these 350 there were direct carriers' services into the county town. There were also many places with indirect connections to Leicester; for another 100 villages were linked by carrier with the subsidiary towns of Melton, Loughborough, Harborough, Hinckley and Lutterworth, from which services also operated into the county town. The village of Stoke Golding, for example, near the south-western boundary of the county, had no direct communication with Leicester; but it was linked by carrier four days a week with Hinckley, whence there were at least nine weekly services into Leicester as well as connections by rail. To what extent indirect routes like these were utilised by country people there is no means of ascertaining, however, so that this essay confines itself to the area linked with Leicester direct. This area covered more than 345,000 acres altogether, extending in a radius of 15–20 miles on all sides of the town, and comprising a population of nearly 160,000 inhabitants in 1881. Not all these people can in any regular sense have been dependent on weekly shopping facilities in Leicester. Many of them lived in market towns like Melton and populous villages like Burbage and Barrow-on-Soar, with shops of their own at this time. If we exclude all these larger places, we are left with a wholly rural population in the Leicester hinterland of more than 90,000 people. Quite clearly these 90,000 potential customers must have been of considerable importance to Leicester shopkeepers. There must in addition have been some thousands of people from the larger villages and market towns of the county who at least occasionally visited the Leicester shops for their more specialised purchases. With the 90,000 rural inhabitants and the 130,000 inhabitants of Leicester itself, the weekly shopping population of the county town must have amounted, potentially at any rate, to something like a quarter of a million people. It may possibly have been rather larger, for country people who came in by train are not included in these figures.

The hinterland of Leicester must not of course be envisaged as wholly isolated from those of other towns in the area. There was in fact a considerable overlap between them. Of the 220 villages within the Leicester area, 94 were also linked by carrier with the smaller market centres of the county: 26 with Loughborough, 20 with Hinckley, 17 each with Lutterworth and Melton, and 14 with Market Harborough. Frequently it was the same village carrier who operated services to both county town and subsidiary market. John Eyrl of Thrussington, for example, operated services to Melton on Tuesday and Leicester on Wednesday and Saturday. John Forman of Stapleton visited Hinckley on Monday and Leicester on Wednesday and Saturday.

While there is no means of telling the proportion of village trade accruing to each urban centre, it seems clear that on the whole Leicester was much the dominant partner. Of the 30 villages in the Hinckley area, for example, 20 were also connected by carrier with Leicester, and apparently none with any other Leicestershire town. Of the 38 in the Loughborough area, 26 were linked also with Leicester, and again none with any other town in the shire. Much the same circumstances obtained in the Harborough and Lutterworth districts, though here a number of villages were also connected with Northampton. Of all the five subsidiary towns Melton was the most independent of Leicester: of the 60 settlements in its hinterland 43 appear to have had no direct connection at all with the county town. These facts indicate that Leicester not only had its own independent hinterland but, as one would expect with so large a town, it had succeeded in poaching on its neighbours' territories and attracting a certain amount of their trade. For anything at all unusual in Leicestershire you usually had to visit the county town (as you still do today) rather than your local market. It offered a far wider range of shops and services, and quite three-quarters of the villages in the shire were situated within 15–20 miles of it.

The weekly 'shopping population' of Leicester was in fact certainly much larger than that of any other town in the area, and was probably exceptional among Victorian county towns generally. It would be interesting, however, to have comparative figures for other places. It would also be interesting to trace the effect of this very large shopping population upon the development of Leicester's retail trade, and the fortunes of its many trading dynasties. In the history of provincial towns these subjects are still much neglected, yet at the time they were obviously of immediate importance to many thousands of provincial people.

So far as the 'shopping population' of the neighbouring county of Northampton is concerned, a number of interesting contrasts and parallels with Leicestershire may be traced.[5] Northamptonshire was almost as much dominated by its county town as Leicestershire. Though Northampton was itself less than half the size of its sister capital (61,000 inhabitants in 1891), it was more than four times the size of any other town in the county. Its hinterland comprised nearly 200 villages and covered an area not far short of that of Leicester's, or almost 300,000 acres. The population of the Northampton hinterland was a good deal smaller than Leicester's, amounting to 150,000 in all, but the strictly rural element in this figure (81,000) came near to that of Leicester (90,000). In relation to the size of the town, the country shopper was in fact a good deal more important to Northampton retailers than to those of Leicester. Of the eight other market towns in Northamptonshire, only Wellingborough, Kettering, Peterborough and Daventry came anywhere near the towns of Leicestershire in the extent and population of their hinterland. Towcester, Oundle, Thrapston and Brackley were only of very local importance, serving as markets for fewer than twenty villages each, while the old towns of Rothwell and Higham Ferrers had ceased to act as regional shopping centres on even the smallest scale. They still had shops; but these apparently catered only for their own inhabitants and those of immediately neighbouring villages, though probably some of the shops ran their own delivery services. The only connections of Higham and Rothwell by carrier were with Wellingborough, Kettering and Market Harborough. Higham was still a borough, with its own mayor and corporation, and at the beginning of the nineteenth century it still held three markets a week; but by Queen Victoria's reign its markets had been discontinued, though a single weekly market was revived, for a time at least, in 1888.

In both Northamptonshire and Leicestershire the market area of the county town extended only a little way beyond the borders of the shire. Both places were county capitals in a very real economic sense, as well as in a social, political and administrative one. Of Northampton's 180 or so dependent villages, fewer than twenty were situated beyond the county, and these for the most part only just across the Buckinghamshire boundary, six or seven miles to the south-east. Of the 200 or so country villages represented in Leicester every week, fewer than a dozen were situated beyond the bounds of the county itself: one each in Derbyshire and Northamptonshire, two each in Warwickshire and Nottinghamshire, and four in Rutland; and these only just across the borders of the shire. Except for the parts of the county to the east of Melton and west of Coalville, the market area of Leicester virtually coincided with the area of the county. The insularity of Leicester's connections will probably come as no surprise to Leicestershire people; but it may well seem curious to outsiders. For a town which is only 20 or 30 miles from four other conurbations – Coventry, Derby, Nottingham and Northampton – Leicester is still comparatively isolated, and the county remains remarkably introverted in its interests. (Many Leicestershire people still read no other newspaper than the *Leicester Mercury*.) In Queen Victoria's reign there were evidently good economic and geographical reasons for the insularity of the town. The network of carriers' routes centred upon Leicester at once indicated and accentuated the local preoccupations of the shire.

Some Leicestershire villages were of course much better served by carriers than others. For more than half the 220 villages around Leicester (118) there were at least four weekly carriers' services into town. There were more than 70 places with six or more weekly services, and 10 places with at least fifteen. As might be expected, it was the comparatively populous industrial or semi-suburban villages to the west and north of Leicester that had the most frequent services. From Anstey, for example, a village four miles north-west of Leicester with a considerable shoe industry and nearly 1,300 inhabitants, there were at least two services every day and twenty altogether each week. From Birstall (487 inhabitants), about the same distance to the north, there were eighteen each week; from Mountsorrel (3,927 inhabitants), the centre of the county's important quarrying industry, fifteen; from Earl Shilton, an industrial village (shoes and hosiery) near Hinckley, with 2,252 inhabitants, thirteen; and from Wigston Magna, another hosiery village, with 4,299 inhabitants, twenty-three – the largest number from any village in the county. From many small agricultural villages on the other hand, like Dadlington (170 inhabitants), Cranoe (106) and Thorpe Satchville (169), there were no more than two or three services into Leicester each week. Fewer than thirty villages had only a single weekly service. Most of these were small, remote parishes with fewer than 300 inhabitants, like Blaston, Cold Overton and Slawston; and the majority were in the predominantly agricultural east or south of the county. Seven or eight, however, were relatively populous villages like Somerby, Hallaton and Lubenham, for which Leicester was only a secondary market and Melton or Harborough the usual shopping centre.

Altogether the 204 country carriers operating in the Leicester region ran 461 services every week into the county town. Some of these carriers served only a single village, particularly if it was a populous one. John Bindley, for example, operated only between Leicester and Great Glen, a village between Leicester and Harborough with nearly 900 inhabitants at this date. John Ward and John Wright operated only between Leicester and Wigston Magna, and William Edwards between Leicester and Syston (2,470 inhabitants). The great majority of carriers, however, worked a regular route and called at two or three villages or occasionally as many as seven or eight before reaching Leicester. Altogether the 204 carriers of the Leicester area operated 170 distinct and independent routes in the county.

Some of these carriers must have set out very early in the morning. Mr Jeffcott, for example, who seems to have started from Thringstone, called at Greenhill, Coalville, Bardon, Shaw Lane, Copt Oak and Markfield – a group of villages to the north-west of Leicester – before arriving at the Anchor Inn in Halford Street – a journey of at least fifteen miles. Samuel Lovitt of Loughborough operated a route based on as many as ten villages in the Loughborough area. These were so scattered that he can hardly have visited all of them in person. In all probability he operated two or three subsidiary services, one calling at Long Whatton, Kegworth and Shardlow, and others at Walton-on-the-Wolds, Hoton, Rempstone and Willoughby-on-the-Wolds. These must have met in Loughborough and continued together to Leicester, calling at Quorndon, Mountsorrel and Birstall before reaching the Champion Inn in Humberstonegate, from which they returned at 5 p.m. Samuel Lovitt was unusual among Leicestershire carriers in operating on more than a local scale: he also ran a Loughborough furniture-removal business. Most carriers almost certainly worked their route themselves and probably called personally with their carts at all the villages they served. Billesdon, Skeffington, Tugby, Keythorpe, Goadby, East Norton and Loddington, for example – a group of villages between Leicester and Uppingham – were all served by John Bryan, who lived at Tugby. Littlethorpe, Broughton Astley, Frolesworth, Leire, Dunton Bassett, Ashby Parva and Bitteswell, a group to the south of the town, were served by Mr King of Lutterworth. Many of the 170 carriers' routes in fact extended over 15 or 20 miles of countryside before reaching their destination in Leicester early in the morning on market day. For a map of this elaborate network of routes centred on Leicester, the reader is referred to p. 236 below.

If all the 'calls' which all the Leicester carriers made during the week at all the villages on their routes are added together, what is the total? Altogether they made nearly 1,100 'calls' every week. In other words there were on average five services a week to Leicester from each of the 220 villages in the area: a figure which, one imagines, compares favourably with the number of rural bus services from some of these places today. The great majority of 'calls', more than 960 in all, were made on the two principal market days, Wednesday (382 calls) and Saturday (480). For some reason – possibly because the usual pay-day was on Saturday – the third ancient market day of Leicester, Friday, now as busy as either of the others, was of little importance to country people in the 1880s. Only 35 villages had any connection with Leicester on Friday, not many more than on Tuesday and Thursday and actually fewer than on Monday (59).

The fact that most of these services operated only on market days suggests that they had come into being to bring goods and people into market. They were the villagers' lifeline for many of their weekly necessities and almost all their luxuries. It must have been a remarkable sight, at sunset on a Saturday evening in autumn, to watch these scores of country carriers leaving the town, on the eight or nine main roads out of Leicester to north and south, east and west. One or two of them began to leave by three o'clock, and between four and five nearly 200 took their departure. By five barely half a dozen remained; for many had long journeys to make, by rough country roads, with only a horse to draw them, and darkness rapidly closing in.

Nearly all the Leicester carriers operated from one of the inns of the town. There was only one important carriers' station that was not an inn, namely Chapel Yard in Gallowtreegate. In some towns the association of carriers with inns was not so universal a practice as in Leicester. In Northampton about a third of the carriers operated from street sites like the Woodhill and yards like Reeve's Yard, and not from local inns. As a general rule, however, inns were the obvious places to furnish carriers with the facilities they required, whether to put up their carts, bait their horses, collect goods for delivery, pick up passengers and parcels or gather the news. There were more than 450 inns and public houses in Leicester at this time, or one to every 270 or so inhabitants. The number may seem surprising but was in fact proportionately less (if Wright's lists are complete) than in other Leicestershire towns. There was one to every 210 inhabitants in Hinckley and Loughborough at this date, one to 170 in Melton, and one to 110 in Market Harborough.

Only a small number of the Leicester inns, of course, became noted as carriers' stations. Of the 455 listed in Wright's *Directory*, 43 were carriers' inns, all of them in the centre of the town. Thirteen of these were situated on the old north–south route through the town, along Highcross Street, Southgates, Oxford Street and the Welford Road. Seven were situated on the alternative north–south route, in Churchgate, Gallowtreegate and Granby Street; another seven on the main east–west route in High Street and Humberstonegate; and four on the north-easterly road, in the Haymarket and Belgravegate. The rest were mostly dotted about in ones and twos in the minor streets of central Leicester, such as Halford Street, Pocklington's Walk and Loseby Lane.

It might be thought that certain inns would become associated with the country carriers of a particular area of the county. Such an association was not uncommon but it was not the invariable rule. From the Fox in Humberstonegate, for example, there were services to Withcote, Brooke and Uppingham to the east of Leicester; Barrow on Soar and

Wymeswold to the north; Desford and Market Bosworth to the west; and Earl Shilton and Hinckley to the south-west. Where a village was served by more than one carrier, moreover, its services were usually based on different inns. The four carriers of Bruntingthorpe ran from the Rutland and Derby Arms in Millstone Lane, the Town Arms in Pocklington's Walk, the White Lion in Cank Street and the White Swan in the Market Place.

On market days, with rows of carts drawn up outside them or lodged in their yards, the forty-three carriers' inns of Leicester must have formed a notable feature of its life. They were dominated by nine or ten hostelries at the top of the hierarchy. Busiest of all was the Fox, strategically sited in Humberstonegate, the widest street in the town, where there was ample space for parking and turning. At least fifteen carriers based themselves on the Fox, running twenty-six services to forty-six villages in the county. Nearly as important was the Anchor in Halford Street, whence thirteen carriers operated twenty-seven services to thirty-eight villages. Another busy inn was the Saracen's Head, at the corner of the Market Place and Hotel Street, which was the focal point of eleven country carriers and thirty-four services. From each of seven other inns in the town more than a dozen services operated: the Blue Boar, the Crown and Thistle, the Globe, the Golden Lion, the Town Arms, the White Swan and the Woodmen's Arms.

The services based on these ten principal inns alone accounted for about half the carrying trade of the town. A number of them, like the Blue Boar and the Saracen's Head, were among the most ancient of Leicester hostelries. Several were of medieval origin. By and large they were of moderate size, among neither the largest nor the smallest inns of the town. The latter must have lacked the facilities the carrier required; the former doubtless thought the village trade beneath their notice. From the Bell Hotel, for example, the principal hostelry in Humberstonegate, only a single service operated, and from its neighbour the Stag and Peasant none at all. Few of the carriers' inns were sited near the main railway station of Leicester; nearly all of them, however, were within five minutes' walk of the Market Place – the forum not only of retail trade but of the news and views of the county.

Of the Leicestershire carriers' families information is tantalisingly meagre. One would like to know something of a man like the wonderfully named Shadrach Warner, whose service ran from Glooston and Cranoe to the Crystal Palace in Humberstonegate; or of the three redoubtable matrons, Mrs Cave, Mrs Ward and Mrs Warner, the only women carriers in the county. (It is a curious fact that in some districts, such as Herefordshire, women carriers seem to have been much more numerous.) Of these figures, however, we know nothing save their names and routes; but a few general facts about carriers' families stand out. Virtually all were of country origin, and often, like Frederick William Palmer of Walton, whose notebook has been quoted, they were younger members of local village families. It is doubtful if any of them lived in Leiester. For more than 150 carriers Wright's *Directory* gives the place of residence, either under Leicester or under the village entries. In every ascertainable case they lived in one of the villages on their route, often, as one might expect, in the last or penultimate one. John Butlin, for example, whose route probably began at Bruntingthorpe and passed through Walton, Kimcote, Claybrooke, Frolesworth and Broughton Astley before reaching Leicester, lived at Walton. John Coulson, whose route covered Illston-on-the-Hill, King's Norton, the Strettons, Stoughton and Evington, lived at Illston. Enoch Curtis, who called at Wysall, Wymeswold, Walton-on-the-Wolds and Barrow-on-Soar, lived at Wymeswold. It is possible that some of the carriers for whom Wright gives no place of residence, under either Leicester or the villages, were in fact Leicester townsmen; but few or none of them can be definitely identified in the lists of Leicester tradesmen in the directory. More probably the omission was merely due to Wright's carelessness in classifying some of his information or to ignorance of exactly where they lived. For obvious reasons it would have been difficult to operate a route unless it ended at the carrier's home village, or at any rate close to it.

What little is known of the carriers' families suggests that most of them were small, self-employed men, with little capital, running their own cart or wagon, and deriving their livelihood from a single country route. There were evidently a few exceptions to this generalisation, however. The firm of Samuel Lovitt of Loughborough has already been mentioned. As well as working a number of country routes around Loughborough and Leicester, Lovitt also ran a considerable furniture-removal business. At Wigston Magna, three men by the name of Wright – John, Charles and Huram – as well as running daily carriers' carts to Leicester also operated a family business in the village as cab proprietors. A number of carriers seem to have run more than one service at the same time from the same inn to different parts of the county, and hence must have employed several carters of their own. William Tillson, for example, ran services from the Hat and Beaver in High

Cross Street both to Sharnford, in the south of the county near the Warwickshire border, and to Groby, Markfield, Thornton and Stanton under Bardon, in the opposite direction.

In some parts of the country, particularly around the smaller towns like Melton Mowbray, it seems clear that the village carrier's occupation was often only a part-time one. Around Leicester, by contrast, there can be little doubt that in most cases it was full-time. For only 43 of the 204 carriers are additional occupations recorded in the directory. This figure is probably an underestimate, it is true, since Victorian directories were necessarily selective in compiling lists of local inhabitants. It is unlikely to be seriously misleading, however, because Wright clearly made considerable efforts to be comprehensive so far as *tradesmen's* occupations were concerned. Moreover, since in this area most carriers ran services on several days a week, either to Leicester alone or to Leicester and other towns, they cannot generally have had much time to spare for additional occupations.

What were the alternative occupations of the forty-three part-time carriers in the Leicester region? They are not without interest. Twelve of them ran some kind of village shop, usually a general grocery store, like John Kirby's shop at Sapcote, or in a few cases a baker's, fishmonger's or fruiterer's, like William Egginton's at Ibstock. Half a dozen or so ran a local inn or beerhouse, like John Cross of the Wheat Sheaf at Husbands Bosworth or William Reynolds of the Roebuck at Earl Shilton. A similar number ran some other small business for which their carts or wagons came in useful, such as coal-dealing or furniture removal. Another group of part-time carriers were clearly of very humble status and were described simply as gardeners, cottagers or cowkeepers.

All these occupations were such as part-time carriers in any part of the country might have been engaged in. More distinctly local were the Leicestershire carriers whose principal occupation was grazing. These formed the largest single group of the forty-three part-time operators and numbered at least fourteen in the Leicester region. For centuries grazing had been one of the chief occupations of Leicestershire people, as indeed it still is, and Wright's *Directory* in fact lists nearly 2,000 inhabitants described as 'grazier' or 'farmer and grazier'. With 90,000 head of cattle and 300,000 sheep, Leicestershire was for its size one of the most densely stocked counties in England at this period.[6] Many of the graziers listed by Wright came of old Leicestershire farming families, with obviously local names, probably traceable in many cases far back in the county's history. A large number of them were clearly operating on a comparatively small scale, since they were running some additional occupation to that of grazing, such as carpenter, innkeeper or corn-dealer. The fourteen or so graziers in the Leicester region who ran carrying services thus formed a small but significant instance of this kind of dual occupation in the county.

It would be a rewarding enterprise to pursue the history of some of these Leicestershire carrying families further, in the context of their own local community. In many cases they clearly belonged to closely knit village dynasties, with many kinsmen in their own parish and in those near-by. (In this kind of exercise, by the way, it is usually the 'neighbourhood', consisting of several adjacent parishes, that is the significant unit of study, and not the individual village in isolation.) One would like, for instance, to know something of the family history of a typical carrier like Thomas Hubbard of Countesthorpe, who operated a daily service into Leicester, five miles to the north of his home. There were at least five other male members of this family in Countesthorpe, and no doubt there were several women members whose names are not recorded but who would have connected them by marriage with other local dynasties in the area. Of the five, George Hubbard was a general carter, Joseph Henry a grazier and Robert a bag-hosier; the occupation of the fourth member, John Hubbard, is not recorded, but if it was the same as that of John Hubbard junior, who was probably his son, he was a grazier.

To what extent did Leicestershire carriers form a self-conscious community of their own, connected by ties of kinship as well as common interest? Only detailed research into the history of local village families like the Hubbards, among parish records and the like, would settle this question definitively. Probably most of them were not related; but it is interesting to note that several characteristic local surnames crop up again and again. One cannot but suspect that the Joseph Hornbuckle of Whitwick who ran services between Coalville, Thringstone, Whitwick and Loughborough was a kinsman of the Joseph Hornbuckle of Frisby-on-the-Wreake who operated a route from Melton to Frisby and Kirby Bellars. Another well-evidenced local family group was that of the Toones, a thoroughly Leicestershire surname. One of them, Josiah, lived at Queniborough and ran a service to Leicester; another, Joseph, lived at Markfield and operated routes between Coalville and Leicester; while two others, whose Christian names remain unknown, ran services to Earl Shilton and Hinckley to the south-west of Leicester, and to Loughborough to the north.

III. MELTON MOWBRAY

The story of Melton Mowbray repeats in little, more or less, that of Leicester, though the town and its hinterland were of course essentially rural rather than industrial in character. Melton in the 1880s was a market town of nearly 6,000 inhabitants, the chief shopping centre of the north-eastern parts of the county and of neighbouring parishes in Rutland, Lincolnshire and Nottinghamshire. The sixty parishes served by Melton carriers covered more than 105,000 acres, an area nearly one-third the size of that served by the carriers of Leicester, and a good deal larger than that of any other town in the county.

In terms of population the Melton area was not so remarkable. For the most part it was an agricultural region at this time (as it still is), and in many parishes the population was small and declining. Rural industries like framework knitting, which had flourished earlier in the century in such places as Somerby and Wymeswold, appear for the most part to have died out in the area by this date. The large industrial population of west Leicestershire, which brought so much business to the retailers of towns like Loughborough, Hinckley and Leicester itself, had no parallel at this period in the hinterland of Melton Mowbray. Its total population, including that of the town of Melton, amounted to no more than 27,000 or 28,000 inhabitants.

This figure needs to be slightly reduced, moreover, if we are to arrive at a reliable estimate of the regular 'shopping population' of Melton Mowbray. As already remarked, the extent to which the hinterland of the town overlapped that of Leicester was smaller than in the case of other Leicestershire towns; but at least sixteen of Melton's sixty villages also had weekly carriers' services into Leicester. (Some of them also had services to Grantham or Stamford, which are situated 15-20 miles from Melton, to the north-east and south-east.) The total population of these sixteen parishes amounted to about 7,600 inhabitants, and they covered an area of nearly 25,000 acres. Among them were a number of places close to Leicester, like Syston, which must in reality have belonged to the economic orbit of the county town rather than that of Melton. Most of them, like Asfordby, Pickwell and Somerby, were situated nearer to Melton, however, which must have formed their usual shopping centre for anything that could not be obtained in the village. The regular population of Melton Mowbray, potentially speaking, therefore probably amounted to nearly 25,000, while its hinterland, if we exclude the parishes primarily dependent on Leicester, covered somewhere around 100,000 acres. This area, one suspects, was unusually extensive for a country town of fewer than 6,000 inhabitants at this time. But it would be interesting to have comparative figures for towns of similar size and function in other parts of the country at this date, such as Leominster (Herefs.), Ashford (Kent) and Richmond (Yorks.).

In Northamptonshire the only close parallel to Melton Mowbray was Daventry. As already remarked, the hinterland of other country towns in this county was either exceptionally small, like that of Brackley, or semi-industrial, like that of Wellingborough. The market area of Brackley, so far as it was defined by carriers' routes, covered no more than six surrounding villages, and the potential shopping population of both the town and its villages certainly did not exceed 5,400. Though Brackley was an incorporated borough, it was just about as small as a Victorian town could be without becoming a mere village, the dependent settlement of some neighbouring market centre. Wellingborough's hinterland, on the other hand, ostensibly comprised more than forty villages, or an area of 90,000 acres with nearly 50,000 inhabitants. The actual 'shopping population' of Wellingborough, however, is very difficult to work out precisely, since many of these villages also came within the orbit of Northampton, and several were industrial centres like Rushden (7,443 inhabitants) and Irthlingborough (nearly 3,000), with numerous shops and services of their own. Probably a more realistic estimate of the Wellingborough hinterland would set the area at about 50,000 acres and the population (including 15,068 for the town itself) at about 30,000 or a little more.

Daventry, by contrast, was essentially a market town at this date, and it was the principal shopping centre for west Northamptonshire just as Melton was for east Leicestershire. With about 4,000 inhabitants, the town was a little smaller than Melton and its hinterland comprised only thirty villages to Melton's fifty or sixty. Most of these were rather larger and more populous than those in east Leicestershire, however, so that the Daventry area covered nearly 80,000 acres with a total population of approximately 20,000. These figures may be compared with the 100,000 acres of the Melton Mowbray area with its 'shopping population' of approximately 25,000.

The comparative sparseness of the rural population around towns like Melton and Daventry and the relatively modest facilities of such places no doubt largely explain one marked difference between their carrying services and those of Leicester. From more than half the Melton villages (33 out of 60) there was only one weekly service into Melton, and from only six were there more than three. In the Leicester area, by contrast, nearly seven villages in eight had more than one weekly service and more than half (118 out of 220) had at least four. As a consequence, whereas there were nearly 460 weekly carriers' services into Leicester from the 220 villages in the area, there were only 60 from the villages around Melton. This comparatively small number of services was also partly due to the fact that in the smaller town there was only one weekly market day (Tuesday), whereas in Leicester there were three. In both towns four-fifths of all country services ran on market day. As a consequence of the comparative infrequency of carriers' services around Melton, the villages in the area were in a sense more isolated, by and large, than those around Leicester.

The number of carriers in the Melton area was 47 (Leicester: 204) and the number of routes they operated 46 (Leicester: 170). Most of these routes, as one might expect, were shorter than those into Leicester, and many of them served only a single village. Samuel Johnson, for instance, operated only between Melton and Great Dalby, his home village (where he was a grazier), a journey of three miles. Alfred Routen operated only between Melton and his native village of Asfordby (where he was also a grocer and baker), another journey of three miles. Nevertheless some of the Melton carriers' routes extended over nine or ten miles of countryside, if not more. Michael Smith of Wymeswold came ten miles to Melton every Tuesday, as well as visiting Lough-borough on Thursday (five miles) and Nottingham on Saturday (ten or eleven miles). Thomas Tidd of Knossington operated a Melton service on Tuesdays covering the parishes of Newbold, Owston, Knossington, Cold Overton and Pickwell – a journey of at least nine miles – as well as a Saturday service to Leicester, a journey of fifteen.

Of the Melton carriers' inns none compared in scale with the largest of those in Leicester. Altogether there were 13 of them out of 35 licensed premises in the town listed in Wright's *Directory*. All, of course, were in the centre of the little town, eight of them in two of the chief shopping thoroughfares, Sherrard Street and Nottingham Street. The busiest were the Black's Head, the Fox and the Crown. The carriers based on each of these inns made fourteen or fifteen 'calls' per week in the surrounding villages. This is a figure that needs to be compared with seventy or eighty 'calls' a week from each of the three largest inns in Leicester.

The comparatively modest scale of the Melton carrying trade must not obscure the fact that, in relation to the size of the town, it was as important as that of Leicester. In the lives of Melton tradesmen it was in a sense more vital, for to many of them the village trade was not merely a convenience but a necessity. More than three-quarters of the potential 'shopping population' of Melton lived in the countryside, not in the town, so that without the carriers' services many shopkeepers could not have made a living. Some of them – grocers and bakers, for example – probably ran their own conveyances to neighbouring places; but the majority must have been largely dependent on village carriers for their country custom. In the case of Leicester, by contrast, nearly two-thirds of the 'shopping population' of about 250,000 people lived in the built-up area of the borough. They had no need of the country carriers to convey them to the shops; they used instead the city omnibuses, which by the 1880s were already running every few minutes from the centre of Leicester to its principal suburbs.

IV. CONCLUSION

The Victorian market town has not generally received much attention from English historians. Perhaps it is often thought of as a sleepy backwater, an anachronism, outside the mainstream of historical development. The impression is in many ways a false one, though certainly, if we wish to study the past only from the limited standpoint of what it has contributed to the modern world, the Manchesters of the nineteenth century are more important than the Melton Mowbrays. Yet the Victorian world contained both Meltons and Manchesters, and probably at least a third or a half of English people at this time either lived in or were dependent upon provincial market towns. There were then more than 400 of these places, with an average population of perhaps some 10,000 each, and two or three times that number in their rural hinterland. They included, moreover, not only the Meltons and Market Harboroughs of the time, but the Leicesters, the Yorks and the Northamptons. The customs, the activities and the ideas of these places went to shape the minds, for good and ill, of many millions of provincial people. And in these activities the village carriers of Victorian England – probably about 30,000 or 40,000 of them all told – played a humble but essential role. Their memory deserve a salute.

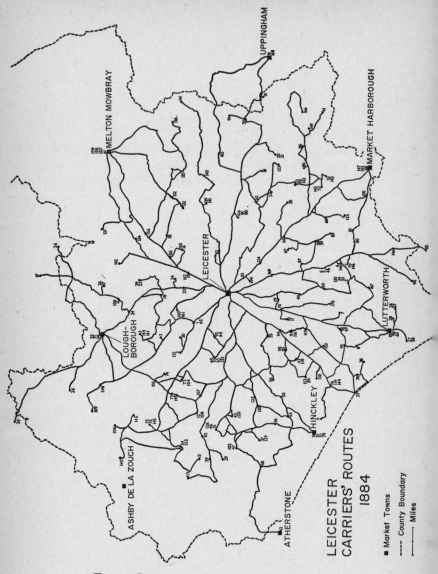

FIG. 15 LEICESTER CARRIERS' ROUTES IN 1884

LEICESTER CARRIERS' ROUTES

The figures on the map on p. 236 refer in most cases to the *terminal points only* on routes from Leicester. Intermediate places served by carrier are indicated by route numbers on the map only where it is evident that the carrier turned off the main route to reach them and then returned to the main route to complete his journey. Thus on route 91, from Leicester to Uppingham, the carrier turned off the main route twice, to reach Launde and Allexton, and then returned to it to complete his journey to Uppingham. All three places are therefore marked, to indicate the route taken, but intermediate stops along the main route (in this case King's Norton, Billesdon, East Norton and Belton) are omitted in order to avoid overcrowding the map. The following is a complete list of routes and villages served.

1. Anstey
2. Anstey, Newtown Linford
3. Anstey, Cropston, Roecliffe, Maplewell, Woodhouse
4. Arnesby
5. Arnesby, Knaptoft, Bruntingthorpe
6. Arnesby, Shearsby
7. Ashby Magna
8. Ashby Parva, Leire
9. Aston Flamville, Burbage
10. Aylestone, Whetstone
11. Aylestone, Blaby, Whetstone
12. Bagworth
13. Bardon-on-the-Hill, Hugglescote, Ibstock, Heather, Odstone
14. Barkby
15. Barlestone
16. Barrow-on-Soar
17. Barrow-on-Soar, Walton-on-the-Wolds, Wymeswold, Wysall
18. Belgrave, Rothley
19. Belgrave, Thurmaston
20. Billesdon, Skeffington, Tugby, Keythorpe, Goadby, East Norton, Loddington
21. Billesdon, Skeffington, Tugby, Goadby
22. Birstall
23. Birstall, Cossington, Sileby
24. Birstall, Wanlip, Mountsorrel, Quorndon
25. Birstall, Rothley, Mountsorrel, Quorndon, Loughborough
26. Birstall, Mountsorrel, Quorndon, Loughborough, Kegworth, Hoton, Rempstone, Willoughby-on-the-Wolds, Walton-on-the-Wolds, Shardlow, Long Whatton
27. Bitteswell, Lutterworth, Cotesbach, Walcote
28. Bitteswell, Lutterworth, Cotesbach, Misterton, Walcote
29. Botcheston, Nailstone, Carlton-by-Bosworth, Barton-in-the-Beans
30. Bradgate
31. Braunstone, Desford, Barlestone, Osbaston, Hinckley
32. Broughton Astley
33. Broughton Astley, Frolesworth, Claybrooke, High Cross, Kimcote, Walton, Bruntingthorpe
34. Bruntingthorpe
35. Burton Overy, Carlton Curlieu
36. Cadeby, Stapleton
37. Cadeby, Sutton Cheney

38. Claybrooke, Ullesthorpe
39. Cossington, Sileby
40. Countesthorpe
41. Cranoe, Medbourne
42. Dadlington, Shenton, Sibson, Atherstone
43. Desford, Croft
44. Desford, Barwell
45. Desford, Newbold Verdon
46. Desford, Newbold Verdon, Barlestone
47. Desford, Cadeby, Market Bosworth
48. Desford, Cadeby, Market Bosworth, Shenton
49. Dunton Bassett
50. Earl Shilton
51. Earl Shilton, Barwell, Hinckley
52. Earl Shilton, Hinckley
53. East Langton, West Langton, Tur Langton, Church Langton, Shangton
54. Ellistown, Ibstock
55. Enderby
56. Enderby, Thurlaston, Normanton Turville
57. Evington, Stoughton, Stretton, King's Norton, Illston-on-the-Hill
58. Evington, Stoughton, Stretton, King's Norton, Galby, Illston-on-the-Hill, Shangton
59. Fleckney
60. Foston, Peatling Magna
61. Gaddesby, Ashby Folville, Twyford, Burrough-on-the-Hill, Melton Mowbray
62. Galby
63. Gilmorton, Lutterworth
64. Glenfield
65. Glenfield, Anstey, Ratby
66. Glen Magna
67. Glen Magna, Wistow, Newton Harcourt
68. Glen Magna, Kibworth,

Smeeton Westerby, Market Harborough
69. Glen Parva
70. Glen Parva, Blaby
71. Groby, Markfield, Loughborough
72. Groby, Markfield
73. Groby, Markfield, Thornton, Stanton-under-Bardon
74. Groby, Markfield, Shaw Lane, Copt Oak, Ulverscroft
75. Groby, Markfield, Shaw Lane, Ellistown, Coalville
76. Groby, Shaw Lane, Hugglescote, Coalville
77. Groby, Ratby
78. High Cross, Wibtoft, Claybrooke
79. Hinckley
80. Houghton
81. Houghton, Billesdon, Rolleston
82. Humberstone
83. Huncote
84. Huncote, Stoney Stanton
85. Husbands Bosworth, Welford
86. Kibworth, Tur Langton, Church Langton, Stonton Wyville, Glooston, Cranoe
87. Kilby
88. Kilby, Fleckney
89. Kilby, Fleckney, Saddington
90. Kilworth
91. King's Norton, Billesdon, East Norton, Launde, Allexton, Belton (Rut.), Uppingham
92. Kirby Muxloe, Glenfield, Ratby
93. Knaptoft
94. Knighton
95. Leire
96. Leire, Frolesworth, Sharnford
97. Littlethorpe
98. Littlethorpe, Broughton Astley, Frolesworth, Leire, Dunton Bassett, Ashby Parva, Bitteswell, Lutterworth

99. Loughborough
100. Lubenham
101. Lutterworth
102. Market Bosworth
103. Market Harborough
104. Markfield
105. Markfield, Copt Oak
106. Markfield, Copt Oak, Shaw Lane, Bardon-on-the-Hill, Coalville, Greenhill, Thringstone
107. Melton Mowbray
108. Mountsorrel, Barrow-on-Soar
109. Mountsorrel, Quorndon, Loughborough, Shepshed, Belton (Leics.)
110. Mowsley.
111. Mowsley, Laughton
112. Nailstone
113. Nailstone, Shackerstone, Newton Burgoland
114. Narborough
115. Narborough, Huncote
116. Narborough, Littlethorpe
117. Narborough, Littlethorpe, Cosby
118. Narborough, Croft
119. Narborough, Sharnford
120. Newbold Verdon
121. Newtown Linford
122. Newtown Unthank, Botcheston, Bagworth, Ibstock
123. Noseley
124. Oadby
125. Oadby, Glen Magna, Kibworth, Smeeton Westerby, Gumley
126. Osbaston, Barleston
127. Peckleton & Roe's Nest
128. Peckleton & Roe's Nest, Kirkby Mallory
129. Peckleton & Roe's Nest, Kirkby Mallory, Sutton Cheney
130. Peatling Magna, Peatling Parva, Bruntingthorpe
131. Queniborough

132. Queniborough, South Croxton, Barsby
133. Ratby
134. Ratcliffe-on-the-Wreake, Thrussington
135. Rearsby, Gaddesby, Ashby Folville, Thorpe Satchville, Twyford
136. Rearsby, Twyford, Burrough-on-the-Hill, Somerby, Pickwell
137. Rearsby, Brooksby, Rotherby, Hoby, Ragdale
138. Sapcote
139. Scraptoft, Keyham, Hungarton
140. Scraptoft, Keyham, Cold Newton, Lowesby
141. Scraptoft, Keyham, Hungarton, Lowesby, Marefield, Owston, Knossington, Cold Overton
142. Seagrave
143. Shangton, Tur Langton, Church Langton, East Langton, West Langton
144. Sharnford
145. Shawell
146. Shearsby, Knaptoft, Husbands Bosworth
147. Shearsby, Mowsley, Laughton, Market Harborough
148. Shepshed
149. Slawston
150. South Croxton, Melton Mowbray
151. Stoneygate
152. Stoney Stanton
153. Sutton-in-the-Elms, Broughton Astley
154. Swithland, Woodhouse
155. Syston
156. Syston, Rearsby
157. Thornton
158. Thornton, Bagworth
159. Thrussington, Asfordby, Melton Mowbray

160. Thurcaston
161. Thurcaston, Cropston,
     Swithland, Woodhouse
162. Thurmaston
163. Thurmaston, Syston, Barkby
164. Thurnby, Bushby, Houghton
165. Tilton, Halstead
166. Tur Langton, Church

     Langton, Glooston, Hallaton,
     Horninghold, Blaston
167. Walton-by-Kimcote
168. Whatborough, Withcote,
     Braunston (Rut.), Brooke,
     Ridlington, Uppingham
169. Wigston Magna
170. Willoughby Waterleys

List of Abbreviations in Bibliography and References

BM	British Museum
CSPD	*Calendar of State Papers, Domestic Series*
HMC	Historical Manuscripts Commission
LAO	Lincolnshire Archives Office
MHLG	Ministry of Housing and Local Government's duplicated lists of buildings of architectural or historic interest
NM	*Northampton Mercury*
PRO	Public Record Office
VCH	*Victoria County History*

Bibliography

I. LATE MEDIEVAL STAMFORD

Manuscript Sources

It has not been possible to provide detailed references for every statement in this paper, but the material has come from many sources. Largely it is based on the unprinted records of the corporation of Stamford at present in the Town Hall. The most valuable of these are the Hall Books, the first of which runs from 1465 to 1637. Most boroughs have such council minute books, often under different titles, some of them starting earlier than at Stamford, others starting later. There are also collections of deeds, a rental and a few other miscellaneous items, most of them common to other borough archives. I am most grateful to the Borough Council for permission to use them and to Mr H. Bedford, Town Clerk, and his staff for every facility to consult them frequently. Other sources come from the records of private estates in the town, preserved in a number of places. For Stamford these include Court Rolls (St Leonard's Priory) and Ministers' Accounts in the Public Record Office (estates of the dukes of York, St Michael's nunnery, etc.); gild accounts in the Bodleian Library (Browne's Hospital) and in the library of Gonville and Caius College, Cambridge (St Katherine's gild); deeds at Magdalen College, Oxford; and accounts for St Leonard's Priory in Durham University Library. Many other sources, such as surveys, transcripts of feet of fines, wills and inventories and the like, have been drawn on, especially in the British Museum, and the diocesan collections in the Lincolnshire Archives Office and the Northamptonshire Record Office. To all these bodies I wish to express my thanks.

Printed Sources

Among the printed sources the most valuable have been the Public Record Office series of Calendars, of Patent, Close and Fine Rolls, of Inquisitions Post Mortem, etc., which contain many incidental references to Stamford, among other places. For instance, the charters of 1462 and 1481 are summarised in *Calendar of Charter Rolls*, vi, 164–7, 253–4. The most valuable local printed source, the only one with original material, is Francis Peck, *Antiquarian Annals of Stamford* (1727).

Local Histories

There are many histories of Stamford, but most of them are purely repetitive. The most useful studies are the essays in A. Rogers (ed.) *The Making of Stamford* (1965). See also A. Rogers, *The Medieval Buildings of Stamford* (1970). R. Butcher's *Survey and Antiquity of Stamford* (various editions after 1646) is valuable only for his account of the town in the seventeenth century.

Other towns

Similar studies to this on other towns are scarce. A good deal of work has been done recently on the greater 'national' boroughs. Thus the volume of VCH *Yorkshire* which deals with the *City of York* (1961), pp. 65–84, is valuable. J. W. F. Hill, *Medieval Lincoln* (1948), pp. 289–303, also surveys the town council, as does B. Wilkinson, *The Borough Council of Exeter in the Reign of Edward III* (1931). G. A. Williams, *Medieval London, from Commune to Capital* (1963), S. Thrupp, *The Merchant Class of Medieval London, 1300–1500* (1948), and R. Bird, *Turbulent London in the Reign of Richard II* (1948), have explored the rich archives of the metropolis. But little has been done on seigneurial towns. M. D. Lobel's account of *Bury St Edmunds* (1935) is one of the fullest explorations. Coventry, Warwick and Leicester have all been treated in recent volumes of the *Victoria County History*. On towns in general, the fullest treatment of government is James Tait, *The Medieval English Borough* (1936). Still useful is S. and B. Webb, *History of Local Government: Manor and Borough* (1924). See also, more generally, F. Rorig, *The Medieval Town* (1967).

2. YORK UNDER THE TUDORS

The printed works consulted for this essay are of two kinds, general and local. The first are works which, whether or not they refer to York, are useful for general economic background. On the regional pattern of agriculture the best introduction is J. Thirsk (ed.) *The Agrarian History of England and Wales*, iv (1967), ch. 1. Studies of particular trades and commodities include N. S. B. Gras, *The Evolution of the English Corn Market* (1926); P. J. Bowden, *The Wool Trade in Tudor and Stuart England* (1962); and L. A. Clarkson, 'The Leather Crafts in Tudor and Stuart England', *Agricultural History Review*, xiv (1966), 25–39. Useful on towns directly involved with overseas trade are G. D. Ramsay, *English Overseas Trade during the Centuries of Emergence* (1957), and T. S. Willan, *Studies in Elizabethan Foreign Trade* (1959). Professor Willan's third chapter, based largely on port books, is the most useful survey of the provincial ports' overseas trade. For internal trade there is little yet except for Alan Everitt's pioneer study of marketing in ch. VIII of *The Agrarian History*, and his survey 'Urban Growth and Inland Trade, 1570–1770: Sources', *Local Historian*, viii (1968–9), 196–204.

The local works include three which are useful for Yorkshire as a whole: H. Heaton, *The Yorkshire Woollen and Worsted Industries* (2nd imp., 1965), still invaluable half a century after its first publication; A. Raistrick and B. Jennings, *A History of Lead Mining in the Pennines* (1965); and B. F. Duckham, *The Yorkshire Ouse* (1967). For further reading on York and Hull, the following are particularly recommended, both in their own right and as models for other places: E. Miller and A. G. Dickens in VCH *Yorkshire: the City of York*, ed. P. M. Tillott (1961), pp. 84–106, 122–32; J. N. Bartlett, 'The Expansion and Decline of York in the Later Middle Ages', *Economic History Review*, 2nd ser., xii (1959–60), 17–33; and R. Davis, *The Trade and Shipping of Hull 1500–1700* (East Yorkshire Local History Soc., 1964). VCH *Yorkshire: The East Riding*, i (1969), concerned wholly with Hull, appeared too recently to be consulted. Mention should also be made of three studies as yet unpublished: J. N. Bartlett, 'Some Aspects of the Economy of York in the Later Middle Ages 1300–1550' (London Ph.D. thesis, 1958); B. M. Wilson, 'The Corporation of York, 1580–1660' (York M.Phil. thesis, 1967); and D. M. Palliser, 'Some Aspects of the Social and Economic History of York in the Sixteenth Century' (Oxford D.Phil. thesis, 1968).

The most valuable published collections of source material on Tudor York are M. Sellers (ed.), *The York Mercers and Merchant Adventurers 1356–1917* (Surtees Soc., cxxix, 1918), containing all the documents bearing on overseas trade among the York merchants' archives; and A. Raine (ed.), *York Civic Records*, 8 vols (Yorks. Arch. Soc. Record Ser., 1939–53), an invaluable selection of corporation minutes between 1476 and 1588, thought not well edited or indexed. The minutes themselves form class B of the York City Archives, which also include other useful material, mostly unpublished, especially the chamberlains' accounts and the city's quarter sessions records. They also comprise the invaluable freemen's registers, which have been published: *Register of the Freemen of the City of York*, ed. F. Collins (Surtees Soc., xcvi and cii, 1897–1900). Information can also be gleaned from the records of the various trade and craft gilds, which are scattered in several archive repositories in York and London. A little material has been extracted from the surviving wills and inventories of citizens, which are nearly all kept by the Borthwick Institute of Historical Research and by the York Minster Library. There are of course also references to York in the archives of other places with which it traded. Most are still unprinted, but useful exceptions include the *Durham Household Book*, ed. J. Raine (Surtees Soc., xviii, 1844), and the Chester corporation records printed in *Child Marriages, Divorces and Ratifications . . .*, ed. F. J. Furnivall (Early English Text Soc., 1st ser., cviii, 1897).

The most valuable records of the central government for this purpose are the customs accounts and port books at the Public Record Office. In the same repository are the records of the courts of Star Chamber, Chancery and Requests, useful for many towns but of only limited value for York, and there and at the British Museum are informative letters to and from the government. This correspondence is usefully calendared in print, for part of the period, in *Letters and Papers, Foreign and Domestic, of the Reign of Henry VIII* (1864–1932). Other calendered government archives consulted include the *Calendars of Patent Rolls* and the *Acts of the Privy Council*.

3. THE BUILDINGS OF BURFORD

A note on sources

The buildings themselves have naturally been the main source for this essay, and each one needs to be surveyed with archaeological thoroughness, for adequate plans of houses below manor-house status are rarely, if ever, available. The project has been, and still continues to be, a spare-time one. Apart from the first year, 1957–8, when I had more time, fieldwork has been limited to a fortnight or less spent in Burford each year. So long drawn out a project might seem tedious, but in fact it has provided an insight into the fabric of the town that would otherwise have been impossible, for I have been able to examine the construction of many of the buildings as they came to be restored. To do this while living at a distance requires a knowledgeable local correspondent, and I have had an invaluable ally in Mrs Dorothy Wise. Ultimately, however, everything depends on the co-operation of owners and occupants of houses, which has nearly always been most willingly given.

The topics relating to general building history can be followed up from the references to books and articles given in the text. Detailed references to documents have unfortunately had to be cut out for lack of space. Much material comes from R. H. Gretton, *The Burford Records* (1920), an admirable work for its date, but by modern standards weak on buildings, topography and social and economic history. In many cases I have drawn on Gretton's material while disagreeing with his interpretation, sometimes supplementing it with unpublished material from the town archives in the Tolsey Museum, Burford, and early land-tax returns and ratebooks in the possession of the vicar of Burford. The other major sources have been the wills and inventories in the Bodleian Library; the P.C.C. will registers, the census returns and the various legal proceedings before 1714 in the Public Record Office; and title deeds still in private possession. A surprising number of houses in Burford (over 40 per cent so far) have deeds extending back into the eighteenth century, and occasionally into the seventeenth century. Apart from their value in dating buildings and boundary changes in the eighteenth and nineteenth centuries, they are an essential key to relating earlier documents in record offices to specific buildings, for houses in English towns were rarely numbered before the middle of the nineteenth century and are still not numbered in Burford. I have attempted to organise this mass of material by putting each property reference on to a slip, and it is on these slips that references in the essay to ownership or occupancy of property are based.

4. THE ENGLISH URBAN INN 1560–1760

Secondary works
Typical of the many popular general works on inns are: G. C. Harper, *Historic and Picturesque Inns of Old England* (1906); A. E. Richardson, *Old Inns of England* (1934); A. E. Richardson and H. D. Eberlin, *The English Inn* (1925); H. P. Maskell, *Taverns of Old England* (1927); Thomas Burke, *The English Inn* (1930). More scholarly but brief is R. F. Bretherton, 'Country Inns and Alehouses', in R. Lennard (ed.) *Englishmen at Rest and Play* (1931). Of many local studies, varying greatly in quality, the following may be cited as examples: A. Groom, *Old London Coaching Inns and their Successors* (1928); N. Tiptaft, *Inns of the Midlands* (1951); D. C. Maynard, *Old Inns of Kent* (1925); H. W. Hart, 'Sherman of the Bull and Mouth', *Journal of Transport History*, v (1961–2), 12–21 (one of the chief London coaching inns); Robert Dymond, 'The Old Inns and Taverns of Exeter', *Devonshire Association Transactions*, xii (1880), 387–416; C. J. Billson, *Medieval Leicester* (1920), III 'The Inns' (not confined to medieval period); T. P. Cooper, 'Some Old York Inns', *Associated Architectural Soc., Report and Papers*, xxix (2), 273–318; T. P. Cooper, *Old Inns and Inn Signs of York* (1897); G. Benson, *The Taverns, Hotels, and Inns of York* (1913; privately printed). (Other local studies are listed in W. E. Tate's useful 'Public House Bibliography', in *The Local Historian*, vii, 1968). The best of these, such as the articles by Hart, Dymond and Billson, are works of scholarship. The same certainty cannot be said for most of the effusions in this field, either local or general. For a catalogue of the inns of England, or even of London, there is nothing to compare with Bryant Lilly-white's meticulous and monumental volume on *London Coffee Houses* (1963). The local historian of inns will obviously want to consult any available histories on his area, and also the relevant sections of the *Victoria County History*, some of the more recent volumes of which contain useful information about urban inns.

A great deal has also been written on English roads and coaching bearing on the history of the inn. As a rule, in fact, this is the one aspect in their history that normally receives much attention. Typical of what might most charitably be called the 'romantic school' are G. C. Harper, *Stage Coach and Mail in Days of Yore* (1903); and W. Outram Tristram, *Coaching Days and Coaching Ways* (1906). These are the kind of works that sometimes contain useful facts buried in a farrago of Pickwickian nonsense; the species is not yet extinct. More scholarly and wider in scope are, for example, Joan Parkes, *Travel in England in the Seventeenth Century* (1925) (sometimes gushing but a standard work of its kind and valuable for its references to printed sources); Virginia A. LaMar, *Travel and Roads in England* (1960) (one of the Folger booklets on Tudor and Stuart Civilisation; short but excellent; with a very helpful bibliography); J. Crofts, *Packhorse, Wagon and Post: Land Carriage and Communications*

under the Tudors and Stuarts (1967); John Copeland, *Roads and their Traffic,
1750–1850* (1968); Edmund Vale, *The Mail-Coach Men of the Late Eighteenth
Century* (1960). With the growth in travel from Queen Elizabeth onwards,
'road books' began to appear, many of which give the names of some of the
principal coaching and carrying inns. The standard guide to these is Sir Herbert
Fordham, *The Road Books and Itineraries of Great Britain, 1570 to 1850: A
Catalogue with an Introduction and a Bibliography* (1924).

Of the many well-known travellers who used these roads in the seventeenth
and eighteenth centuries and whose tours, diaries or letters have been published
and shed incidental light on the history of inns, among the most useful (apart
from the obvious Pepys and Evelyn) are: Daniel Defoe, *A Tour through the
Whole Island of Great Britain* (1727) (relates to late seventeenth century and
early eighteenth; many editions); *The Travels through England of Dr
Richard Pococke . . . during 1750, 1751 and Later Years* (Camden Soc., new
series, xlii, xliv, 1888–9); John Byng, Viscount Torrington, *The Torrington
Diaries containing the Tours, through England and Wales . . . between the
years 1781 and 1794* (4 vols, 1934–8). This field is very extensive, however, and
for others the reader must be referred to the standard guide: E. G. Cox, *A
Reference Guide to the Literature of Travel . . .* (University of Washington
Publications in Language and Literature, xii, 1949), iii: *Great Britain* (exhaustive but contains no index of places and subjects).

For some special aspects of the subject the following may be mentioned:
J. Larwood and J. C. Hotten, *History of Sign-Boards from the Earliest Times
to the Present Day* (1867 and subsequent editions, the last in 1951 under the
title *English Inn Signs*) (old-fashioned and out of date, but still a monumental
work); S. and B. Webb, *The History of Liquor Licensing in England* (1903)
(the standard text); W. Branch Johnson, 'The Inn as a Community Centre',
Amateur Historian, ii (1954–6), 134–7 (brief but useful introduction to this
important subject, and helpful on sources). Though outside the period of the
present study, Brian Harrison and Barrie Trinder's 'Drink and Society in an
Early Victorian Country Town: Banbury 1830–1860', *English Historical
Review*, supplement 4 (1969), should be mentioned here as an excellent and
seminal study in this field, one of great importance in the nineteenth century.

On the use of inns as trading centres there is incidental and background
information in several works, in particular R. B. Westerfield, *Middlemen in
English Business, particularly between 1660 and 1760* (Transactions of the
Connecticut Academy of Arts and Sciences, xix, 1915); N. S. B. Gras, *The
Evolution of the English Corn Market . . .* (1926); Peter Mathias, *The Brew-
ing Industry in England 1700–1830* (1959); Alan Everitt, 'The Marketing of
Agricultural Produce', in Joan Thirsk (ed.), *The Agrarian History of England
and Wales*, iv: *1500–1640* (1967).

Primary sources

So far as primary sources for the history of inns are concerned, many will
be apparent from the text of the essay. In the Public Record Office, the 'census
of inns' of 1577 is to be found in SP 12/96; SP 12/116–19; SP 12/122; SP
12/141/55. The returns of 1686 and 1756 relating to beds and stabling are in
the War Office Miscellanea (WO 30/48 and WO 30/49). For James I's reign there
are Victuallers' Recognisances (i.e. licences granted to maintain an inn, etc.) in
E 180/145, 146, 147. Many of the cases in Proceedings in the Court of Requests
and in Chancery Proceedings refer to trading disputes arising in inns, though
the hostelries are usually mentioned only incidentally so that the cases are
tedious to use if one is seeking information about a particular town. The
Requests Proceedings do not, of course, go beyond the 1640s when the court

was abolished. There are said to be many cases of a similar kind in local ecclesiastical courts relating to breach of contract and referring to trading in inns,
though the present writer has rarely utilised these.

In local record offices Innkeepers' Recognisances down to the year 1828 may
be found. There are also the Magistrates' Registers of Licensed Premises
(usually for the nineteenth century). Matters relating to the regulation and
licensing of inns and disputes involving innkeepers frequently came before the
county J.P.s at quarter sessions, or in the boroughs before local corporations,
so that they are recorded in quarter sessions records, Hall Books, Assembly
Books or similar records. (It is a tedious task working through the mass of
other matter to find these, however, unless the records are printed or well
indexed.) For reconstructing the history of innkeeping families, wills, probate
inventories, parish registers and church monuments are obvious sources, together
with miscellaneous facts in such borough records as apprenticeship registers,
freemen's lists and mayors' and chamberlains' accounts. Leases and title deeds
may also obviously yield some precious facts. Inventories will also of course tell
one a good deal about the scale and furnishings of different inns and the wealth
and status of the landlord.

So far as printed sources are concerned, by far the most important is the
newspaper advertisement. These will not of course be found before the
eighteenth century in the provinces, and for many towns not until late in the
century. But there is nothing quite like them for telling one of all the multi-
farious activities that took place in inns and for reconstructing the innkeeping
pattern in any given town. In the Print Room of the British Museum is the
important Heal Collection of contemporary billheads (well indexed). For the
plays put on in assembly rooms attached to inns, the local historian should
consult the Gabrielle Enthoven Collection of Playbills in the Victoria and
Albert Museum.

5. A HANOVERIAN WATERING-PLACE: MARGATE BEFORE THE RAILWAY

Secondary works
The following works represent useful studies on the history of tourism, holidays
and resorts: J. A. R. Pimlott, *The Englishman's Holiday: A Social History*
(1947); A. Hern, *The Seaside Holiday: The History of the English Seaside
Resort* (1967); E. W. Gilbert, *Brighton: Old Ocean's Bauble* (1954); J. A.
Williamson, *The English Channel: A History* (1959); F. A. Bailey, *A History
of Southport* (1955); D. S. Young, *The Story of Bournemouth* (1957); P.
Russell, *A History of Torquay* (1960); C. H. Bishop, *Folkestone: The Story
of a Town* (1973).

Primary sources
Seaside resort towns command an extensive literature in two main sources:
topographical works and newspapers. Some of the local sources used in this
essay have been mentioned either in the text or in the notes.

Local guides vary in quantity and quality, but in the case of seaside resorts
and inland spas, perhaps for more than any other type of town, they occupy a
prominent place among the literature which the historian or geographer can
consult to record the general growth or impressions of a place. The amenities,
as well as the atmosphere and tone, of a resort are often well brought out in
guidebooks, which increase and become particularly abundant throughout the
nineteenth century.

Many sizeable resorts, particularly those which are county boroughs, possess
extensive local history collections in their libraries which are usually sufficient

in themselves to write up most of the local history of the place in question. Towns known to the author with good local collections include Brighton, Folkestone, Ramsgate and Margate. Reference has been made in the essay to Margate Public Library, whose Local Collection in December 1933 comprised 13,867 items, including books, pamphlets and excerpts relating mainly to Margate and Thanet. Since that time this particular collection has benefited from further additions. From the 1760s there is an almost unbroken series of guides relating to Thanet, Margate, Ramsgate and Broadstairs to which reference can be made. For the period 1763–1880, and including all subsequent editions of guides as separate entries, Margate Public Library alone can offer the reader 137 guides on Thanet and Margate. During these 117 years guides were being published at the rate of more than one a year. There are also numerous directories, containing both topographical and commercial information, and excerpts of a topographical nature from various nineteenth-century journals, such as *Chambers's Edinburgh Journal*, the *Illustrated London News*, etc.

As for newspapers and journalism, the press in its entirety represents an abundant source of information on seaside holidays, resorts and excursions. Useful facts and impressions are to be found not only in articles and reports but also in correspondence and advertisements for travelling by railway or steamboat, for property to let or for sale, for lodgings and accommodation, for entertainments, for coastal schools and academies, etc. Newspapers are an inexhaustible mine of information on the history of leisure. The task of consulting them, although rewarding, can be tedious, but *The Times* has the advantage of having been indexed for the nineteenth century.

One further source which, if it survives, is often useful, consists of manuscript or printed letters, diaries and family papers. The upper classes of the eighteenth and early nineteenth centuries were renowned correspondents and diarists, and from this source the historian can draw on the contemporary impressions and reminiscences of real people. Letters and diaries furnish in the broadest sense some idea of the individuals and families who travelled to seaside resorts; their reasons for going, whether for health or pleasure; and their impressions of particular resorts and their amenities. Specific observations are frequently forthcoming on the mode of travel; on the company residing in the selected resort; on lodgings, entertainments, provisions and prices. Some useful examples of letters and diaries are indicated in the notes to this essay, and Pococke, Farington and Catherine Hutton, in particular, went to coastal resorts other than Margate.

6. EARLY VICTORIAN COVENTRY

Much information about urban educational history may be culled from official government publications, particularly those known collectively as Parliamentary Papers. For a detailed survey of these and other useful sources for local educational history, see W. B. Stephens, *Sources for English Local History* 1937), ch. III. See also the list of Parliamentary Papers in VCH *Warwickshire*, vii: *Birmingham*, ed. W. B. Stephens (1964), pp. 546–8, and the official indexes to the Parliamentary Papers. The most important Parliamentary Papers used in the present essay are the *Digest of Returns to the Committee on the Education of the Poor*, Parliamentary Papers (1819), ix (2), and the *Education Enquiry Abstract*, Parliamentary Papers (1835), xiii, vol. III (both providing details topographically arranged of numbers and types of schools), and the much more detailed investigation which formed part of the 1851 census. This last is to be found in *Report of the Commissioners for Taking a*

Census of Great Britain on Education, Parliamentary Papers (1852–3), xc, and in *Day Schools and Sunday Schools in Cities and Municipal Boroughs*, Parliamentary Papers (1852–3), lxxix. For Coventry a very thorough investigation of education in 1838 is to be found in *Reports from Assistant Handloom Weavers' Commissioners*, part iv, Parliamentary Papers (1840), xxiv, and this has been used extensively here. For many areas and large towns specific reports embracing education may be found by searching the indexes to the Parliamentary Papers. Charity Commissioners' reports contain much information on endowed schools, the chief of which were the charity schools and the grammar schools. Those made use of in this essay are the *28th* and *29th Reports of the Commissioners for Charities*, Parliamentary Papers (1834), xxii, and (1835), xxi (2). The *Reports of the Schools Inquiry Commission* (the Taunton Commission), Parliamentary Papers (1867–8), xxviii, provide a great deal of information, much of it retrospective, on endowed grammar and some other schools.

For the cotton and woollen factory districts, evidence on education and child labour may be obtained from the factory inspectors' reports, but Coventry's ribbon industry did not come under the Factory Acts, so that these have not been of use here. The Appendixes to the *2nd Report of the Commissioners on Children's Employment*, Parliamentary Papers (1843), xiv, however, have provided some information, and *Reports and Documents on the State and Progress of Schools of Design*, Parliamentary Papers (1850), xlii, has been used for the Coventry school of design. For other sources on the history of adult education, see T. Kelly, *Select Bibliography of Adult Education in Great Britain* (2nd edn, 1962); J. F. C. Harrison, 'Materials for the Early History of Adult Education', *Adult Education*, xxiii (1950–1).

For all towns and cities the annual *Minutes of the Committee of Council on Education* give much information on education, including inspectors' reports on individual schools. They have been used widely in this essay. G. Porter, *Progress of the Nation* (1851 and other editions), is also a mine of information, some taken from Parliamentary Papers and other reports.

Printed sources for the voluntary (church and chapel) day and Sunday schools used here are: *Reports of the British and Foreign Schools Society* (1815–22, 1830–3, 1838–52); *Reports of the National Society* (1813–32, 1841–58); National Society, *Church Schools Enquiry 1846–7* (copy in library of Department of Education and Science). All these are of equal importance for other cities. National Society, *Annual Reports in the Archdeaconry of Coventry* (1832–3, 1836–7), are of local interest only, but similar reports exist for other areas.

Nineteenth-century directories of Warwickshire, local newspapers (*Coventry Herald*, *Coventry Standard*), and the annual reports of the Coventry Mechanics' Institute have also been used in this essay. All these have counterparts for most other cities.

Unpublished sources here used have been confined to the records of the National Society (which has a file of information for each of the many schools with which it had a connection), and the files in the Public Record Office (class Ed. 7) known as 'preliminary statements of public elementary schools'. These latter give dates of foundation and of buildings, and statements on accommodation, staffing and finances. For many cities, school log-books will also give detailed information, but there are none surviving for this period for Coventry. J. Gutteridge, *Lights and Shadows in the Life of an Artisan* (1893), is an autobiography of a Coventry working man: such works often contain personal reminiscences of schooldays.

Secondary sources used in this study of Coventry are mainly of purely local importance, but others of the same nature are often to be found for other cities. J. W. Docking, *Victorian Schools and Scholars* (Coventry and North Warwickshire History Pamphlets, no. 3, 1967) is based on the author's 'Development of Church of England Schools in Coventry 1811–1944' (Leeds M.Ed. thesis, 1966). For the political and industrial background, see B. Poole, *Coventry: Its History and Antiquities* (1870); J. Prest, *The Industrial Revolution in Coventry* (1960); P. Searby, *Coventry Politics in the Age of the Chartists* (Coventry and North Warwickshire History Pamphlets, no. 1, 1964); VCH *Warwickshire*, viii: *Coventry and Warwick*, ed. W. B. Stephens (1969). The last-named volume includes, apart from general articles, a short section on education and a bibliography of education sources. VCH, *Warwickshire*, ii, ed. W. Page (1908), contains articles on the charity schools and the Grammar School.

To the books and articles of general interest cited in the notes below may be added the publications of the Manchester Statistical Society, and articles in the *Journal of the Royal Statistical Society of London*.

7. THE OLD CENTRE OF CROYDON

How can one best set about studying similar Victorian decay and redevelopment elsewhere? A good starting-point is the 1851 or 1861 census returns. These will make it quite clear which parts of the town centre were in decay at that time. Then one should walk the districts in question looking for evidence of comprehensive late Victorian or Edwardian development. If the buildings themselves are not dated, a quick examination of the local directories will show when demolition and rebuilding was taking place. Next, the files of the local newspapers for that period can be used to provide information about the personalities involved, and the controversial issues and the way they were or were not resolved. For Croydon these comprised the *Croydon Advertiser, Croydon Guardian, Croydon Chronicle* and *Norwood News*.

Thus armed with knowledge of the place, the period, the people and the problems involved in the town's main redevelopment scheme, one can begin the arduous but usually rewarding search for contemporary documents. These will commonly be found, perhaps only after persistent enquiry, in the library or town hall. The likelihood is that they have never been studied before, which makes their examination all the more worthwhile. From that point it is impossible to predict where the search will lead.

The following list of the principal primary sources used in this study gives some idea of the kind of material that may be found for other towns.

Croydon Public Library

1. Croydon Improvement Act, Commissioners' Minute Book (1838).
2. Local Board of Health, Croydon, Minutes, *passim*. Formal manuscript minutes.
3. Local Board of Health, Sanitary Committee minutes, *passim*. Manuscript minutes, more detailed and directly relevant to the present study than the formal minutes listed above.
4. *Croydon Local Board of Health Report 1863–1866*; *Report of the Poor Dwellings Committee*, presented to Croydon Town Council at its meeting, 22 Sep 1884. Both provide background information about the market area.
5. Minutes of the High Street Improvement Scheme; Minutes of the High Street Special Committee. To some extent these overlap. Together they make it possible to trace the details of the newly created corporation's intervention and negotiations in the market area redevelopment scheme.

Public Record Office
   HO 107, 1601; RG 9, 447–51: the 1851 and 1861 census returns, which of course give a complete list of the inhabitants of the market area in those years.

8. TOWN AND COUNTRY IN VICTORIAN LEICESTERSHIRE
For a guide to sources, see pp. 220–1 of Chapter 8.

References and Notes on Text

INTRODUCTION *Alan Everitt*

1. Coalville is, however, a good example of a dreary place whose history, on closer inspection, turns out to be surprisingly interesting: cf. Sarah E. Wise, 'Coalville: The Origins and Growth of a Nineteenth Century Mining Town' (Leicester M.A. thesis, 1968).

2. One excellent study has recently appeared: R. G. Wilson, *Gentlemen Merchants: The Merchant Community in Leeds, 1700–1830* (1971).

3. Anna W. Cooper, 'Newark, 1830–1901' (Leicester M.A. thesis, 1968), pp. 11 *et passim*.

I. LATE MEDIEVAL STAMFORD *Alan Rogers*

1. I am grateful to Prof. G. H. Martin of Leicester University and Mr Alan Cameron of Nottingham University for their comments on this paper.

2. The borough Hall Books commence in 1465; in 1492 a hiatus in the records occurs, only for three years but nevertheless important for this study. Most of the quotations are drawn from this source.

3. Nicholas Byllesdon, First Twelve 1487–94, 1499–1507; there is of course always the possibility that there were two men of the same name, perhaps father and son. The class of burgess with which this paper deals is not always well documented and thus the biographical details are often obscure. Another case occurs where the uncertainty is greater: John Murdoke, First Twelve 1465–9, 1472, 1481–5 (in 1483–4 he was called Thomas Murdoke). There may well have been more than one John Murdoke.
William Bewshire, Second Twelve 1485–7, 1496–8. There were, however, almost certainly two Bewshires in Stamford, one a butcher and taverner, the other a husbandman.

4. First Twelve: twenty-eight members, thirteen died, six resigned, nine unknown (seven probably died). Second Twelve: forty-eight members, eighteen promoted, three died, four retired, twenty-three unknown.

5. William Sutton, the leader from 1465 to 1476, Thomas Holton from 1476 to 1485, and John Wykes, 1485–90, all died in office or retired. Robert Crane, leader 1490–2, was promoted to the First Twelve between 1492 and 1494.

6. R. Butcher, in his *Survey and Antiquity of Stamford* (1646), p. 16, says incorrectly that the charter mentioned both Twelves, and most later writers have followed him.

7. PRO, Ministers' Accounts, SC 6/1115/6, 7, 9.

8. In the seventeenth century the pre-election was on the Thursday after 24 August: Butcher, *Survey*, pp. 37–8.

9. BM, Harl. MS 3658, ff. 48–9, 66.

10. Town Hall Records, Book of Charters, ff. 107–19; Hall Book, i, ff. 11, 24, 49, 65d; PRO, SC 6/913/26; SC 6/914/1–4; E 315/398, 399, 403; Peterborough Abbey Records, Black Book of Peterborough, ff. 167–9.

11. Hall Book, i, f. 25; PRO, SC 2/188/2–3; Prior's Kitchen, Durham, Durham Priory Records, Bailiffs' Accounts of St Leonard's Priory, Stamford.

12. John Kirkby in 1452; perhaps John Basse in 1486, John Goylin in 1495

and George Kyrkham in 1505; no clear mention after 1452. PRO, KB 9/65a; Hall Book i, ff. 40d, 63, 80.

13. Cf. J. Wedgwood, *History of Parliament 1439–1509: Biographies* (1936), p. 297; Hall Book, i, f. 75. He died in 1504.

14. R. F. Hunnisett, *The Medieval Coroner* (1961), p. 140, says there were twelve coroners in Stamford, perhaps a confusion with the lawmen of whom there were once twelve. The Hall Books record only one who held office apparently for five or six years, not for one year only as the charter prescribed.

15. By the seventeenth century the elections were confined to the First Twelve, who chose the members of both themselves and the Second Twelve; but the wording of the Hall Books seems quite clear that this did not happen in the fifteenth century. The election by the commons, however, was not by ballot but *'une voce'*, although there were three candidates.

16. On at least one occasion it was the 'greater part of the community of Stamford' who took part in the election (Hall Book i, f. 65); but later it was more explicit: 'all the burgesses and the commons of the borough' (*ibid.*, f. 74).

17. There was one forfeited property in particular which changed hands rapidly between a number of royal servants: Chevercourt (1453), Murdoke (1456), Hussey (1464), Trunke and Forster, both household servants (1465), among others. Often there was an increment on the farm. In 1481 the forfeiture was granted to the corporation (*Calendar of Fine Rolls, passim*).

18. He was perhaps a partner in the Cely business at Calais, and kept a resident attorney there: *Cely Papers* (Camden Soc., 3rd ser., i, 1900), 105, 134–5, 166.

19. George Chapman, mercer, was involved in a suit in Gloucester in 1493, Robert Hans in Leicester in 1494.

20. PRO, C 219/17/1; interestingly enough, despite the charter, in this case it was the sheriff who acted as returning officer for the borough, not the alderman.

21. This omits Forster, for he served for one year only; the occupations of five councillors are not known, nor those of two aldermen.

22. Only one year (1466, William Browne, alderman) had no admissions; and three years had significantly large numbers (1472, 1489 and 1494), when the aldermen were successively Robert Hans, fishmonger, Thomas Philippe, mercer, and Thomas Edward, pewterer. The high figure for admissions in the last year was the result of three years of non-recording of admissions. In neither of the other two years, 1472 or 1489, did members of the aldermen's respective trades predominate among the admissions.

23. *Associated Architectural Societies' Reports and Papers*, xxxvii (1923–5), 250; Bodleian Library, Rawlinson, MSS, 8 352, f. 41; Stamford Town Hall Records, Book of Charters, ff. 167 et seq.; LAO, Visitation 1473; LAO, Inv., 2/68. The gild feast of Holy Trinity was on Corpus Christi day, which may imply that membership of this gild was incompatible with membership of the Corpus Christi gild.

24. Hykeham is called 'alderman' in the inscription in the chapel; he was alderman of the borough in 1457, 1464 and 1479, but this reference may be to his position in the gild. For its property, see *Associated Architectural Societies' Reports and Papers*, xxxvii (1923–5), 101–2; PRO, SC 6/1115/13; SC 6/914/1; SC 2/188/2; LAO, Wills, Register 26, f. 175; Stamford Town Hall Records, Book of Charters. The gild was used as an executor by several councillors, notably John Dykens, glover, for his chantry and William Radclyffe, gentleman, for his school.

25. A gild book survives in Gonville and Caius Library, Cambridge; cf. also B. L. Deed, *History of Stamford School* (1954), pp. 80–1. The gild ordinances were printed by the Early English Text Society, old series, xl (1870), 187–92.

26. Pishey Thompson, *History of Boston* (1856 edn), pp. 118–21.

27. *Stonor Letters* (Camden Soc., 3rd ser., xxix, 1919), pp. xxxiii–v.

2. YORK UNDER THE TUDORS *D. M. Palliser*

1. D. M. Palliser, 'Some Aspects of the Social and Economic History of York in the Sixteenth Century' (Oxford D.Phil. thesis, 1968), pp. 26–34.

2. B. M. Wilson, 'The Corporation of York, 1580–1660' (York M.Phil. thesis, 1967), p. 6.

3. Historians of other inland towns may not be so unlucky. T. S. Willan's pioneer study of the provincial port books (see the bibliographical note, p. 243 above) indicates that most ports' books did normally record overseas cargoes.

4. York City Archives, c2 and c3.

5. Professor E. M. Carus-Wilson has shown that the accounts of aulnagers, purporting to show the total production of cloths, are unreliable. But it is not therefore essential to question the *ranking* of York, which is given so far above the other towns as to be credited with almost as many cloths as the next two (Ripon and Halifax) together.

6. *York Civic Records*, ed. Angelo Raine, vi (Yorks. Arch. Soc., Record Ser.), 17.

7. *Statutes of the Realm*, iii (1817), 908.

8. V CH, *York*, ed. P. M. Tillott (1961), p. 98.

9. *York Civic Records*, iii, 72.

10. The document, printed in *York Mercers*, pp. 135–6, is there dated tentatively to 1536, but Professor A. G. Dickens has convincingly suggested 1552.

11. York City Archives, B31, f. 246r.

12. BM, Lans. MS 54, f. 141r.

13. York City Archives, B32, ff. 290–9.

14. *Ibid.*, B31, f. 33.

15. York Dean and Chapter Archives, v, box xii.

16. G. Burnet, *History of the Reformation*, ed. E. Nares (n.d.), iv, 458.

17. *York Civil Records*, vi, 135.

18. C. J. D. Ingledew, *The Ballads and Songs of Yorkshire* (1860), p. 116.

19. PRO, SP 12/117, no. 37; T. P. Cooper, *Some Old York Inns* (n.p., n.d.), pp. 20–9, which prints a lost census of innkeepers.

I am grateful to the three main York archive offices – the City, the Dean and Chapter, and the Borthwick Institute – for permission to use material from their archives. I am also indebted to Miss B. M. Wilson for permission to use, and to quote from, her unpublished thesis.

3. THE BUILDINGS OF BURFORD *Michael Laithwaite*

1. W. G. Hoskins, *Provincial England* (1963), pp. 87–8.

2. I. Origo, *The Merchant of Prato* (1957), p. 349.

3. PRO, Chancery Proceedings, c2/James I/s.38/38; Chancery Depositions (Whittington), c22/755/12.

4. Based on PRO, E179/161/172 and 198. I have disregarded Witney, where four-fifths of the subsidy was paid by one man.

5. CSPD, *1635*, p. 475; CSPD, *1637*, p. 511. I have no figure for Witney.

6. R. H. Gretton, *The Burford Records* (1920), pp. 445–62, 624–9. I have identified some of the property-owners in 1652 and 1685 from other sources.

7. National Monuments Record, photograph CC 57/429.

8. Gretton, *Burford Records*, p. 161. An error in transcription led Gretton to confuse this with another Brasenose property at the bottom of the High Street.

9. It needs to be stressed, though, that very little in Burford has been faked.

10. I owe my knowledge of this subject to Mr George Swinford, who has had many years' experience in the local quarries. See also W. J. Arkell, *Oxford Stone* (1947).

11. See, e.g., M. W. Barley, *The English Farmhouse and Cottage* (1961), pp. 35–6. Monmouthshire certainly had a timber-framed tradition replaced in the post-medieval period by stone: see Sir C. Fox and Lord Raglan, *Monmouthshire Houses* (3 vols, 1951–4). I owe much of my understanding of this topic to a lecture given by Dr R. W. Brunskill to the Vernacular Architecture Group in 1967.

12. Fox and Raglan, *Monmouthshire Houses*.

13. It has been suggested that this was the case in Cambridgeshire. See P. Eden, 'Post-Medieval Houses in Eastern England', in L. M. Munby (ed.), *East Anglian Studies* (1968), p. 74.

14. Large areas of carved stonework seem to have been a feature of only the grandest town houses, such as Colston's house at Bristol, or Grevil's house at Chipping Campden.

15. For a definition, see R. A. Cordingley, 'British Historical Roof-Types and their Members: a Classification', *Transactions of the Ancient Monuments Society* (1961).

16. Cf. J. T. Smith, 'Cruck Construction: A Survey of the Problems', *Medieval Archaeology* (1964), pp. 133–4.

17. E. F. Jacob, 'The Building of All Souls College', in J. G. Edwards (ed.), *Essays in Honour of James Tait* (1933).

18. PRO, Chancery Proceedings (Whittington), C 10/25/52.

19. See, e.g., R. B. Wood-Jones, *Traditional Domestic Architecture in the Banbury Region* (1963), p. 12.

20. M. V. J. Seaborne, 'Cob Cottages in Northamptonshire', in *Northamptonshire Past and Present* (1964). In 1547 there was even a mud wall in London (*Cal. Pat. Rolls*, Edw. VI, i, 199).

21. PRO, Chancery Proceedings, C 2/James I/F 1/15.

22. PRO, Inquisitions Post Mortem, C 142/215, n. 249.

23. D. Portman, *Exeter Houses, 1400–1700* (1966).

24. Hoskins, *Provincial England*, ch. 7.

25. This is best illustrated in W. G. Davie and E. G. Dawber, *Old Cottages, Farmhouses, and Other Stone Buildings in the Cotswold District* (1905).

26. Date-plaque shown in Buckler drawing, BM, Add. MS 36,372, rev. f. 181.

27. Gretton, *Burford Records*, pp. 445–53. It is clear from title deeds that some of the properties described on the list as two tenements were originally one.

28. The evidence for the Great House comes from the town records, which received an annual rent from it under a will of 1605; that for the Methodist Chapel mainly from the title deeds of Chapel House adjoining.

29. These are traditional names that are commonly used in the probate inventories, but of course the name and function of a room could vary according to individual taste. The presence of a shop obviously involved change of use. In 1654, for example, one house had a dining-room on the first floor, over the shop, where one would normally expect to find a bedroom (PRO, C 10/25/52).

30. See P. Eden, *Small Houses in England 1520–1820* (1969).

31. V. Parker, *The Making of King's Lynn* (1971).

32. I found a late medieval partition of this type in a house recently demolished at Ashburton, Devon: M. Laithwaite, 'Two Medieval Houses in Ashburton', *Proceedings of the Devon Archaeological Society* (1971).

33. Barley, *English Farmhouse and Cottage*, pp. 18, 19.

34. W. A. Pantin, 'Medieval English Town-House Plans', *Medieval Archaeology* (1962–3), pp. 223–8.

35. W. J. Monk, *History of Burford* (1891), p. 163; BM, Add. MS 36,439, f. 486.

36. The house has been gutted, but see M. S. Gretton, *Burford Past and Present* (1945 ed.), p. 121n.

37. Lecture on Tewkesbury given by Mr S. R. Jones to the Vernacular Architecture Group in 1969; W. A. Pantin, 'The Development of Domestic Architecture in Oxford', *Antiquaries' Journal* (1947).

4. THE ENGLISH URBAN INN 1560–1760   *Alan Everitt*

1. See bibliography for this chapter, pp. 245–6.

2. *The Buildings of England*: John Newman, *North-East and East Kent* (1969), p. 241.

3. The Buildings of England: Nikolaus Pevsner, *South Devon* (1952), p. 162; *Daily Advertiser*, 2 June 1774; *Kentish Gazette*, 17–20 May 1775. I owe the latter references to Mr John Whyman.

4. C. N. Wright, *Commercial and General Directory of Leicester . . .* (1884); *Post Office Telephone Directory*, section 80: *Leicester Area* (1970).

5. PRO, SP12/96; SP12/116–19; SP12/122; SP12/141/55. I owe these references to Professor M. W. Beresford. The 1577 figures for Essex were: 399 alehouses, 77 inns, 17 taverns. According to Dr B. W. Quintrell, 'The Government of the County of Essex 1603–1642' (London Ph.D. thesis, 1965), p. 226, there were said to be at least 800 alehouses in the county in the early Stuart period.

6. *Letters and Papers of Henry VIII*, Add. 1, no. 1192; *ex inf.* Dr D. M. Palliser.

7. N. J. Williams, *Tradesmen in Early-Stuart Wiltshire* (Wilts. Arch. and Nat. Hist. Soc., Records Branch, xv, 1960), pp. xiv, xv; *Derbyshire Archaeological Journal*, xv (1893), 136; G. H. Green and M. W. Green, *Loughborough Markets and Fairs (through 7½ Centuries)* (n.d.), p. 36. The Northampton figure is based on references in the Assembly Books, Apprenticeship Registers, Mayors' Accounts, Chamberlains' Accounts and probate inventories, and on contemporary advertisements in the *Northampton Mercury*.

8. *The Northampton Directory and Almanack* (1845); E. R. Kelly, *The Post Office Directory of Kent* (1870).

9. *The Travels through England of Dr Richard Pococke . . . during 1750, 1751 and Later Years* (Camden Soc., new ser., xlii, xliv, 1888–9), 121, 141, 193 *et passim*.

10. But on occasion greater distances were covered in the seventeenth century, e.g. Northampton to London in one day in 1674, and Oxford to London in one day in 1669: Joan Parkes, *Travel in England in the Seventeenth Century* (1925), p. 86.

11. Cf. CSPD, *1644–5*, p. 170; W. Outram Tristram, *Coaching Days and Coaching Ways* (1906), pp. 344–5.

12. John Morton, *The Natural History of Northamptonshire* (1712), p. 27; *The Buildings of England*: Nikolaus Pevsner, *Northamptonshire* (1961), p. 347. Morton was incorrect in attributing the origin of Foster's Booth to some-one named Foster; but it is interesting that he listed it alongside the market towns of the county though it was never formally a market.

13. Edward Hasted, *The History and Topographical Survey of the County of Kent* (2nd edn, 1797–1801), vi, 151–3; *The Imperial Gazeteer* (1870), *sub* Sittingbourne.

14. Hasted, *History of Kent*, p. 152; visual evidence of surviving buildings; information from the Ministry of Housing and Local Government's duplicated lists of buildings of architectural or historic interest [hereafter MHLG]; NM, advertisements 1720–60.

15. PRO, E134, 18 James I, E1.

16. *Ex inf.* Professor W. G. Hoskins.

17. Tristram, *Coaching Days*, p. 34; Quintrell, 'Government of Essex', p. 227; *The Imperial Gazetteer* (1870), *sub* Moulsham.

18. Cf. Alan Everitt, 'Leicester and its Markets: The Seventeenth Century', in A. E. Brown (ed.), *The Growth of Leicester* (1970), pp. 41, 43–4. This study is based principally on references in the printed volumes of *Records of the Borough of Leicester*, iii–vi; VCH, *Leicestershire*, iv: *The City of Leicester*; C. J. Billson, *Medieval Leicester* (1920), esp. ch. III. I owe the reference to the removal of the town gates in 1774 to Dr Peter Eden.

19. See the communication of Dr R. H. Little in *Country Life*, 20 Feb 1969, p. 419.

20. *History of Northampton Castle Hill Church 1674–1895* (1896), illustra-tion facing p. 61; *The Buildings of England*: Nikolaus Pevsner, *Wiltshire* (1963), pp. 302–3; Tristram, *Coaching Days*, pp. 53–5; MHLG, section on Sittingbourne; Billson, *Medieval Leicester*, p. 35; Northants. Record Office, probate inventories of Northampton innkeepers; Daniel Defoe, *A Tour through the Whole Island of Great Britain*, ed. G. D. H. Cole (1927), ii, 486; HMC, *Reports*, XIII, ii, 289.

21. *The Buildings of England*: Nikolaus Pevsner, *Nottinghamshire* (1951), p. 112; Tristram, *Coaching Days*, pp. 13, 328; Anthony Burgess, *Coaching Days of England* (1966), p. 16.

22. NM, advertisements 1720–60, *passim*; Northants. Record Office, probate inventory of John Bateman, 1682.

23. NM, 11 June 1759; Billson, *Medieval Leicester*, pp. 36, 37–8.

24. Brian Dunning, 'With Garrick at Stratford', *Country Life*, 1 May 1969, p. 1071.

25. HMC, Reports, XIII, ii, 290; Defoe, *Tour*, ii, 588; Tristram, *Coaching Days*, pp. 69–71, quoting Fanny Burney.

26. *York Memorandum Book*, part 1 (Surtees Soc., CXX, 1912), 45, 46; *York Civic Records*, ii, ed. Angelo Raine (Yorks. Arch. Soc., Record Ser., ciii, 1941), 91. I owe these references to Dr D. M. Palliser. For the topic of inns and trading generally, see Alan Everitt, 'The Marketing of Agricultural Produce', in Joan Thirsk (ed.), *The Agrarian History of England*, iv: *1500–1640* (1967), 559–61.

27. Peter Mathias, *The Brewing Industry in England 1700–1830* (1959), pp. 505–6; NM, 28 Nov 1743, 14 Oct 1751.

28. *Ex inf.* Professor F. E. Hyde, from handbill of 1698; NM, 27 May 1745, 4 Feb 1750/1, 10 July 1758.

29. Green, *Loughborough Markets*, p. 36.

30. P. Whittle, *The History of the Borough of Preston . . .* (1837), p. 119; NM, 31 July 1749, 5 Dec 1737; T. M. James, 'The Inns of Croydon, 1640–

1830' (Leicester M.A. thesis, 1969), pp. 40–1; Clarence G. Paget, *By-Ways in the History of Croydon* (1929), p. 13.

31. Everitt, 'Marketing', p. 560 and n.; R. B. Westerfield, *Middlemen in English Business, particularly between 1660 and 1760* (Transactions of the Connecticut Academy of Arts and Sciences, xix, 1915), 318; Paul Mantoux *The Industrial Revolution in the Eighteenth Century* (1961 edn), quoting account of French tour of 1788; NM, 17 Apr 1758.

32. *The Bloody Innkeeper, or Sad and Barbarous News from Gloucestershire* . . . (1675).

33. NM, 30 Apr 1739, 30 June 1740, 5 Aug 1751, 2 Sept 1751, 31 July 1749, 12 Aug 1754; Defoe, *Tour*, ii, 486.

34. NM, 16 Nov 1723, 3 Feb 1723–4, 11 May 1724; VCH, *Northants.*, ii, 313, incorrectly attributes the removal to Peacock to 1726.

35. NM, 1721–60, *passim.*

36. NM, 13 Nov 1758, 6 June 1737, 29 Jan 1759.

37. NM, 19 July 1736.

38. NM, 31 July 1739, 18 Dec 1749, 26 Feb 1738–9.

39. NM, 6 May 1754. The Bull's Head in Sheep Street was a different inn from the Bull's Head in St James's End referred to earlier.

40. Cf. Lawrence Stone, *The Crisis of the Aristocracy, 1558–1641* (1965), pp. 511–13; Everitt, 'Marketing', pp. 559–63.

41. See, for example, E. G. Forrester, *Northamptonshire County Elections and Electioneering 1695–1837* (1941), p. 18, where Thomas Cartwright spent £1,216 on 55 inn and alehouse bills in the election of 1695. G. E. Mingay, *English Landed Society in the Eighteenth Century* (1963), pp. 124, 126, refers to inn bills totalling over £5,000 spent during elections in Denbighshire in 1741.

42. Quintrell, 'Government of Essex', p. 134; R. A. Church, *Economic and Social Change in a Midland Town: Victorian Nottingham 1815–1900* (1966), p. 19; Alan Everitt, *The Community of Kent and the Great Rebellion 1640–60* (1966), pp. 95–6 and n., 131, 313; Robert Dymond, 'The Old Inns and Taverns of Exeter', *Devonshire Association Transactions*, xii (1880), 402–4.

43. CSPD, 1641–3, p. 279; CSPD, 1666–7, p. 555; CSPD, 1680–1, p. 543, 643 *et passim*; *A True Account of the Presentment of the Grand Jury for the last General Assizes held for the County of Northampton* . . . (1683). The last item gives the names of the Northamptonshire 'cabal'.

44. CSPD, 1680–1, p. 535; CSPD, 1683 (Jan–June), p. 86. For the Tories and the Goat Inn, cf. HMC, *Finch* ii, 184, 439, and CSPD, 1680–1, p. 644.

45. HMC, *Finch*, ii, 184, 439; Thomas Arnold and J. J. Cooper, *The History of the Church of Doddridge* (n.d.), pp. 122–3; NM, 10 Sep 1744, 28 Dec 1747.

46. Billson, *Medieval Leicester*, ch. III, 'The Inns'; for the White Lion, see John Nichols, *The History and Antiquities of the County of Leicester*, ii (1795), 60n.

47. NM, advertisements 1720–70, *passim*; R. M. Serjeantson, *A History of the Church of All Saints, Northampton* (1901), p. 115.

48. L. T. C. Rolt, *Thomas Telford* (1958), p. 38, 56; Billson, *Medieval Leicester*, p. 35.

49. Green, *Loughborough Markets*, pp. 38–41.

50. *The Buildings of England*: John Newman, *West Kent and the Weald* (1969), p. 417; John Byng, Viscount Torrington, *The Torrington Diaries*, i (1934), 350; Hasted, *History of Kent*, vii, 201; Richard Church, *Kent* (1948), pp. 270–1.

51. Hasted, *History of Kent*, vii, 534, 539; *The Letters of Mrs Elizabeth Montague* (4 vols, 1809–13), *passim.*

52. Except where other references are given, this and the following paragraphs are based primarily on advertisements in the *Northampton Mercury* between 1720 and 1760.

53. HMC *Reports*, XI, iv, 253 (my italics).

54. *Gentleman's Magazine*, xv (1745), 501.

55. NM, 3 Dec 1753.

56. NM, 11 Dec 1721, 26 Oct 1731.

57. NM, 29 June 1752.

58. NM, 5 Nov 1753.

59. NM, 21 Nov 1737, 4 Dec 1752. After its visit to Northampton, the exhibition moved on to Birmingham, Wolverhampton and Warwick (NM, 11 Dec 1752). I have not been able to identify 'Mr Motet'. It seems very unlikely that the sixteenth-century sculptor of that name can be referred to, who in any case carved in wood, not marble.

60. NM, 6 Jan 1755, 23 June 1755, 16 Oct 1758, 3 Dec 1759, 10 Jan 1723/4, 27 Feb 1723/4.

61. *Gentleman's Magazine*, xvi (1746), 475.

62. Northampton Borough Records, Assembly Book 1627–1744, f.8.

63. *Ibid.*, ff. 67, 82.

64. Except where other references are given, this and the following paragraphs are based primarily on scattered references in the advertisement pages of the *Northampton Mercury*, 1720–60.

65. Defoe, *Tour*, p. 486; NM, 30 Apr 1739.

66. Serjeantson, *All Saints, Northampton*, p. 160; NM, 22 Feb 1741/2, 5 May 1746, 14 Oct 1745; HMC, *Egmont*, Diary, iii, 297.

67. The probate inventories mentioned in this and later paragraphs are in the Northants. County Record Office. The modern estimates suggested, here and elsewhere in this essay, of contemporary values given in the inventories must be regarded only as the roughest of guides: there is no way of arriving at accurate modern equivalents of the value of goods like furniture and kitchenware.

68. Except where other sources are given, this and the following paragraphs in this section are based on miscellaneous references in the Northampton Borough Records (chiefly Mayors' and Chamberlains' Accounts and Assembly Books), in the *Northampton Mercury* advertisements, and on wills and inventories.

69. NM, 28 Dec 1747. 'Mountain' is a Spanish wine from the Malaga area.

70. NM, 6 May 1751.

71. NM, 17 Aug 1752. Another service by berlin started in June 1752 from the Lion and Lamb (NM, 22 June 1752).

72. NM, 9 Apr 1733, 10 Jan 1736/7, 7 Feb 1736/7.

73. Northampton Borough Library, Tobias Coldwell's MS history of Northampton, under the year 1692.

74. NM, advertisements 1720–60, *passim*.

75. The family histories in this section are based on many scattered references in contemporary wills, inventories and related probate records; in the Assembly Books, Apprenticeship Registers, and Mayors' and Chamberlains' Accounts in the Borough Records; in the advertisement pages of the *Northampton Mercury*; in the parliamentary poll-books for Northampton of 1768 and 1784; and on family monuments in Northampton's four ancient churches and in those of some neighbouring villages.

76. Pococke, *Travels* (Camden Soc., new series, xlii, 1888), 167.

77. Cf. NM, 26 Apr 1736, 27 Feb 1748–9, 29 Apr 1745 (General Wade disperses a gang operating in the Whittlewood Forest and Whaddon Chase

areas), 22 Aug 1737 (a lace-dealer is set upon between Northampton and Newport Pagnell).

78. NM, 28 Feb 1731/2, 24 Apr 1731/2.

79. John Conant, *The Life of the Reverend and Venerable John Conant D.D.* . . . (1823), p. 77. The author was Conant's son, who died in 1723. The biography was evidently written after his father's death in 1694. I have not been able to discover the exact date of its composition. The father was vicar of All Saints', Northampton.

5. A HANOVERIAN WATERING-PLACE: MARGATE BEFORE THE RAILWAY *John Whyman*

1. Mrs Pilkington, *Margate!!! or Sketches amply Descriptive of that Celebrated Place of Resort* (1813), p. 93.

2. *The Margate Guide . . . In a Letter to a Friend* (1770), p. 15.

3. Nathaniel Spencer, *The Complete English Traveller* (1772), p. 163.

4. [Daniel Defoe], *A Tour through the Whole Island of Great Britain* (8th edn, 1778), p. 139.

5. E. W. Brayley, *The Beauties of England and Wales; or Delineations Topographical, Historical, and Descriptive*, viii: *Kent* (1808), 956.

6. J. Lewis, *The History and Antiquities Ecclesiastical and Civil of the Isle Tenet* (1723); *The History and Antiquities, as well Ecclesiastical as Civil, of the Isle of Tenet, in Kent* (1736).

7. Lewis Melville, *Brighton: Its History, its Follies, and its Fashions* (1909), p. 10.

8. E. W. Gilbert, *Brighton: Old Ocean's Bauble* (1954), p. 55.

9. *The Travels through England of Dr Richard Pococke . . . during 1750, 1751 and Later Years* (Camden Soc., new ser., xliv, 1889), 86.

10. *The Margate Guide . . . In a Letter to a Friend*, p. 16.

11. James Greig (ed.), *The Farington Diary* (1923), ii, 278–9.

12. *The Kentish Traveller's Companion* (5th edn, 1799), p. 265.

13. *The New Margate, Ramsgate, and Broadstairs Guide* (6th edn, 1816), p. 59.

14. *The Kentish Companion for the Year of Our Lord 1792* (1792), p. 160.

15. *The New Margate and Ramsgate Guide in a Letter to a Friend* (1789), p. 12.

16. Mrs Beale (ed.), *Reminiscences of a Gentlewoman of the Last Century: Letters of Catherine Hutton* (1891), 25.

17. *Picture of Ramsgate* (1833), p. 9.

18. John Poole, 'Margate', *The Amaranth* (1839), p. 69.

19. G. A. Cooke, *A Topographical or Statistical Description of the County of Kent* (1830 edn), p. 1.

20. G. W. Bonner, *The Picturesque Pocket Companion to Margate, Ramsgate, Broadstairs, and the Parts Adjacent* (2nd edn, 1831), pp. 6–7.

21. Lord Herbert (ed.), *Pembroke Papers (1780–1794): Letters and Diaries of Henry, 10th Earl of Pembroke, and his Circle* (1950), 322.

22. Castalia Countess Granville (ed.), *Lord Granville Leveson-Gower, Private Correspondence 1781–1821* (1917), i, 223.

23. Lady Dorchester (ed.), *Recollections of a Long Life by Lord Broughton* (1909), II, 133.

24. George Keate, *Sketches from Nature, Taken and Coloured in a Journey to Margate* (5th edn, 1802), 66.

25. Defoe, *Tour*, p. 139.

26. *Farington Diary*, ii, 277. The Meyers were the wife and daughter of Philip James Meyer, a musician.

27. 'The Isle of Thanet', in *The Land We Live In* (nd. [c. 1840]); 'The Seaside Resorts of the Londoners', *Chambers's Edinburgh Journal*, 12 Nov 1853.

28. PRO, HO 107/468/2–6; J. Whyman, 'Visitors to Margate in the 1841 Census Returns', *Local Population Studies*, No. 8 (1972).

29. F. M. L. Thompson, *English Landed Society in the Nineteenth Century* (1963), p. 1.

30. Anthony Hern, *The Seaside Holiday: The History of the English Seaside Resort* (1967), p. 124.

6. EARLY VICTORIAN COVENTRY *W. B. Stephens*

1. See two articles by M. Sanderson: 'Social Change and Elementary Education in Industrial Lancashire 1780–1840', *Northern History*, iii (1968); 'Education and the Factory in Industrial Lancashire', *Economic History Review*, 2nd ser., xx (1967) Cf. for Halifax, Yorks., L. Stone, 'Literacy and Education in England, 1640–1900', *Past and Present*, xlii (1969), 93.

2. G. Ward, 'The Education of Factory Child Workers', *Economic History*, iii (1937), 123; A. H. Robson, *The Education of Children Engaged in Industry in England 1833–76* (1931), *passim*.

3. *Report from Select Committee on Manchester and Salford Education*, Parliamentary Papers (1852), xi, 413.

4. J. F. C. Harrison, *Learning and Living 1790–1960* (1961), p. 19.

5. Sanderson, 'Education and the Factory', p. 277.

6. For Wilderspin and his methods, see W. A. C. Stewart and W. P. McCann, *The Educational Innovators 1750–1880* (1967), ch. 14.

7. *Report from the Select Committee on the Education of the Poorer Classes*, Parliamentary Papers (1837–8), ii, p. viii.

8. See, e.g., S. J. Curtis, *History of Education in Great Britain* (1957 edn), pp. 187–97; H. C. Barnard, *History of English Education from 1760* (1961 edn), pp. 5–7; M. Sturt, *The Education of the People* (1967), pp. 5–7. The standard work on charity schools (M. Jones, *The Charity School Movement*, [1938]) is confined to the eighteenth century. A newer view is in B. Simon (ed.), *Education in Leicestershire, 1540–1940* (1968), ch. 3; the gloomy picture painted here is not precisely reflected at Coventry.

9. For a comparative analysis of urban church attendance in 1851, see *Journal of Ecclesiastical History*, xi (1960), 81–2.

10. Cf. W. B. Stephens, 'Social History of Coventry from 1700', VCH, *Warwickshire*, viii (1969).

7. THE OLD CENTRE OF CROYDON *R. C. W. Cox*

1. For a general introduction to the history of Croydon in this period, see R. C. W. Cox, 'Some Aspects of the Development of Croydon 1870–1940' (Leicester M.A. thesis, 1966).

2. J. O. Pelton, *Relics of Old Croydon* (1891); C. M. Allan, 'The Genesis of British Urban Development with Special Reference to Glasgow', *Economic History Review*, 2nd ser., xviii (1965), 598 ff.

3. Croydon Public Library: W. Ranger, *Report to the General Board of Health on a Preliminary Inquiry into the Sewerage, Drainage, and Supply of Water, and the Sanitary Condition of the Inhabitants of . . . Croydon . . . 12 April 1849*, p. 5.

4. Croydon Public Library: Croydon Improvement Act, Commissioners' Minute Book, 20 June 1839, 3 July 1839; *Croydon Advertiser*, 27 Jan 1875, p. 3; 31 May 1879, p. 3; *Croydon Chronicle*, 2 June 1888.

5. Croydon Public Library: *Return of Deaths from Fever in . . . Croydon from 7 November 1852 to 2 March 1853, with Results of Inquiry as to Causes in each Case and the General Prevalence of Disease.* . . .

6. *Croydon Chronicle*, 1 Mar 1862.

7. *Croydon Advertiser*, 30 June 1888, p. 8.

8. *Ibid.*, 21 July 1888, p. 8.

9. *Croydon Chronicle*, 2 June 1888.

10. Allan, 'British Urban Development', pp. 598–9.

11. What little is known of this society was discovered only when its one edifice, Shaftesbury Buildings, in Ellis David Road, was demolished in 1962. Various documents were then found buried in the foundations and these are now deposited in Croydon Public Library (*Croydon Times*, 22 June 1962, p. 6).

12. *Croydon Chronicle*, 22 Aug 1868.

13. *Ibid.*, 2 Dec 1876.

14. *Croydon Advertiser*, 13 Feb 1909, p. 7.

15. *Ibid.*, 9 Oct 1886, p. 2.

16. *Ibid.*, 14 Aug 1882, p. 5.

8. TOWN AND COUNTRY IN VICTORIAN LEICESTERSHIRE
Alan Everitt

1. W. H. Hudson, *A Shepherd's Life* (Everyman edn, 1949), pp. 14, 18–19. This book was first published in 1910, but much of it relates to the late nineteenth century.

2. Siegfried Sassoon, *Memoirs of a Fox-Hunting Man* (1928), pp. 112–13.

3. John Watson (ed.), *The Annals of a Quiet Valley* (n.d. [c. 1895]), pp. 195–6.

4. Anna W. Cooper, 'Newark 1830–1901' (Leicester M.A. thesis, 1968), pp. 33, 34, 41.

5. The information on Northamptonshire in this essay is based principally on *Kelly's Directory of Northamptonshire* (1898).

6. *The National Gazetteer of Great Britain and Ireland* (1868), xii, Appendix, p. 4.

Notes on Contributors

R. C. W. COX is one of the growing band of scholarly amateurs in the field of local history. Formerly a schoolmaster, he is now Assistant Education Officer (Building and Development), London Borough of Croydon. For his studies of Victorian Croydon he was awarded M.A. and Ph.D. degrees by Leicester University in 1966 and 1970 respectively, and the university's John Nichols Prize in 1967.

ALAN EVERITT is Hatton Professor of English Local History in the University of Leicester. His publications include: *Suffolk and the Great Rebellion 1640–1660* (1961), *The Community of Kent and the Great Rebellion 1640–60* (1966), *Change in the Provinces: the Seventeenth Century* (1969), *The Pattern of Rural Dissent: the Nineteenth Century* (1972), and sections on 'Marketing of Agricultural Produce' and 'Farm Labourers', in Joan Thirsk (ed.), *The Agrarian History of England*, iv: *1500–1640* (1967).

MICHAEL LAITHWAITE is Senior Research Fellow in the Department of English Local History at Leicester University. He is now engaged on an intensive survey of the buildings and topography of the port of Totnes in Devon. Formerly he worked for some years on the London Survey, and he has also undertaken studies of vernacular architecture in Faversham, Banbury and other provincial towns as well as at Burford.

DAVID PALLISER, a native of York, began his researches into its history as a postgraduate student at Oxford, under Professor W. G. Hoskins. The author of *The Reformation in York 1534–1553*, and of a forthcoming general survey, *Tudor York*, he is now a researcher with the York Archaeological Trust.

ALAN ROGERS is Lecturer in Medieval and Local History in the Department of Adult Education at Nottingham University. In 1965 he edited a volume on *The Making of Stamford* for the quincentenary celebrations of the borough, and in 1970 published *The Medieval Buildings of Stamford*. He is at present working on a history of Stamford in the later Middle Ages. Among his other publications are *A History of Lincolnshire* (1969) and *This Was Their World: Approaches to Local History* (1972). He is chairman of the projected *History of Lincolnshire*, planned to appear in twelve volumes over the next few years.

W. B. STEPHENS is Senior Lecturer in Education in the Department of Education at Leeds University. His researches in urban history have been widely distributed in Devon, Lancashire, Warwickshire and other counties. They have included work on Exeter, Birmingham, Congleton, Warrington and Coventry. He is the author of *Sources for English Local History* (1973).

JOHN WHYMAN is a Lecturer in Economic and Social History at the University of Kent at Canterbury. He has been engaged for some years on a study of the origins and evolution of the Thanet seaside resorts in the eighteenth and nineteenth centuries. He has responsibility at the university for Kentish history and is editor of *Cantium: A Magazine of Kent Local History*.

Index

Village names in chapter 8 have not been included except where they are of special significance.